The Soul of Rumi

THE SOUL OF
RUMI

A NEW COLLECTION OF ECSTATIC POEMS

Translations, Introductions,
and Notes by

COLEMAN BARKS

with John Moyne, Nevit Ergin, A. J. Arberry,

Reynold Nicholson, and M. G. Gupta

HarperSanFrancisco
A Division of HarperCollins*Publishers*

HarperCollins books may be purchased for educational, business, or sales promotional use. For information please write: Special Markets Department, HarperCollins Publishers Inc., 10 East 53rd Street, New York, NY 10022.

HarperCollins Web site: http://www.harpercollins.com

HarperCollins®, 📖®, and HarperSanFrancisco™ are trademarks of HarperCollins Publishers Inc.

FIRST HARPERCOLLINS PAPERBACK EDITION PUBLISHED IN 2002

Designed by C. Linda Dingler

Library of Congress Cataloging-in-Publication Data
Jalal al-Din Rumi, Maulana, 1207–1273
  [Selections. English. 2001]
  The soul of Rumi : a new collection of ecstatic poems / translations, introductions, and notes by Coleman Barks, with John Moyne . . . [et al].— 1st ed.
    p.cm.
  Includes bibliographical references and index.
  ISBN 0–06–060453–0 (cloth : alk. paper)—ISBN 0–06–060452–2 (paper)
    1. Jalâl al-Dân Râmâ, Maulana, 1207–1273—Translations into English. 2. Sufi poetry, Persian—Translations into English. I. Barks, Coleman. II. Title.
PK6480.E5 J35 2001
891'.5511—dc21   2001024621

02 03 04 05 06 RRD(H) 10 9 8 7 6 5 4 3 2 1

for friendship and friends, such blessing

John Ryan Seawright
1956–2001

CONTENTS

Preface

My academic training, at Berkeley and Chapel Hill, was in modern litera-ture. I wrote a dissertation on Conrad and taught twentieth-century American poetry courses and creative writing at the University of Geor-gia in Athens for years. I had never even heard Rumi's name until 1976, when Robert Bly handed me a copy of A. J. Arberry's translations, saying, "These poems need to be released from their cages."

How any translator chooses to work on one poet, and not on others, is a mysterious thing. Some attunement must be there. I felt drawn imme-diately to the spaciousness and longing in Rumi's poetry. I began to explore this new world, rephrasing Arberry's English. I sent some early attempts to a friend, Milner Ball, who was teaching law at Rutgers–Camden. He, inexplicably, read them to his torts class. A young law stu-dent, Jonathan Granoff, came up afterward, asked him for my address, and started writing, urging me to come meet his teacher in Philadelphia.

In September of 1978 when I finally did walk into the room where the Sri Lankan saint Bawa Muhaiyaddeen sat on his bed talking to a small group, I realized that I had met this man in a dream the year before. Here's the dream from May 2, 1977, my holy day: I am sleeping out on the bluff above the Tennessee River where I grew up. I wake *inside the dream*, still asleep, but awake in the sleeping bag I'm in. A ball of light rises from Williams Island and comes over me. I think it's a UFO; then it clarifies from the center out, revealing a man sitting cross-legged with head bowed and eyes closed, a white shawl over the back of his head. He raises his head and opens his eyes. *I love you,* he says. *I love you too,* I answer. The landscape, that beautiful curve of river, feels suddenly drenched with dew, and I know that the wetness is love. I felt the *process* of the dew forming and I knew, somehow, what the *essence* of it was.

When I visited him in Philadelphia, Bawa told me to continue the Rumi work. "It has to be done." But, he cautioned, "If you work on the words of a *gnani,* you must become a *gnani,*" a master. I did not become one of those, but for nine years, for four or five intervals during each year, I was in the presence of one.

Rumi says,

> Mind does its fine-tuning hair-splitting,
> but no craft or art begins
> or can continue without a master
> giving wisdom into it.

I would have little notion what Rumi's poetry is or where it comes from if I were not connected to this Sufi teacher. Though it's not necessary to use the word Sufi. The work Bawa did and does with me is beyond religion. "Love is the religion, and the universe is the book." Working on Rumi's poetry deepens the inner companionship. My apprenticeship continues, and whatever else they are, these versions or translations or renderings or imitations are homage to a teacher. And yet not as a follower, more as a friend. In some way I am very grateful for, these poems feel as if they come as part of a continuing conversation. I once asked Bawa if what I saw in his eyes could someday come up behind my eyes and look out. He began to talk about the subtle relationship between a teacher and the community. "Not until the *I* becomes a *we.*"

There was a childhood joke I did not get until recently. At age six I was a geography freak. I memorized all the capitals of all the countries in the 1943 *Rand McNally Atlas,* which I still have. I grew up on the campus of a boys' school in Chattanooga, Baylor. My father was headmaster, and the teachers there were always testing this odd expertise of mine. "Bulgaria," someone would call out across the quadrangle. "Sophia," I'd answer. I could not be stumped, until the ecstatic trickster James Pennington went down in his basement Latin classroom and came up with a country that had no capital, on his map at least. "Cappadocia," he called. The look on my face, he laughed, what I *didn't* know, named me. From then on I was called "Cappadocia," or "Capp." To be more precise, *Pennington* called me that, but he did it loudly and often.

I almost fell down a few years ago when I remembered the nickname and realized that the central city of that Anatolian area was Iconium, now Konya, where Rumi lived and is buried. *Rumi* means "the one from *Rum,* the part of Anatolia under Roman influence." I don't mean to claim a special relationship with Rumi. Mevlana's poetry has been a large part of my life for twenty-five years. It has brought many friends and wonderful opportunities. The synchronicities that introduced me to Rumi continue to delight and exfoliate in wonderful ways. This work involves an emptying out, a surrender (despite the strut of personal incidents here). That's how the collaboration feels. It's also a form of healing, a way to play and praise, to feel grief and gratitude, and an unfolding friendship with a teacher. Or say these poems are love poems, the intimate conversation of self with deep self, Cappadocia with Bawa, me with you. Rumi's poetry is God's funny family talking on a big open radio line.

Forty Sections of Poetry

with Commentaries

and Book IV of the *Masnavi*

Introduction

RUMI'S LIFE AND TIMES

The thirteenth century in the Near East was a time of tremendous political turmoil and war: the Christian military expeditions called *crusades* continued to set out from the European west across the Anatolian peninsula, and from the east the inexorable Mongol armies rode down from the Asian steppes.

It was also a time of brilliant mystical awareness, when the lives of three of the world's great lovers of God's presence in humanity, and in existence itself, overlapped: Francis of Assisi (c. 1182–1226) at the beginning of the century, Meister Eckhart (c. 1260–1328) at the end, and Jelaluddin Rumi (1207–73) at the center. They were all magnificently surrendered souls, and wonderful creators with language.

Rumi was born near the city of Balkh, in what is now Afghanistan, then the eastern edge of the Persian empire, on September 30, 1207. He was the descendant of a long line of Islamic jurists, theologians, and mystics. His father, Bahauddin Walad, wrote an intimate spiritual diary, the *Ma'arif* ("Love Notes of Self to Soul"), which Rumi treasured.

When Rumi was still a young man, his family fled from Balkh, just ahead of the invading armies of Genghis Khan, who was extending his Mongol empire through Persia and would eventually reach all the way to the Adriatic Sea. Rumi and his family traveled to Damascus and on to Nishapur, where they met the poet and teacher Fariduddin Attar, who recognized the teenaged boy Rumi as a great spirit. He is reported to have said, as he saw Bahauddin walking toward him with the young Rumi a little behind, "Here comes a sea, followed by an ocean!" To honor this insight, Attar gave Rumi his book, the *Ilahinama* ("The Book of God").

3

Rumi's family eventually settled in Konya, in south-central Turkey, where Bahauddin resumed his role as the head of the dervish learning community, or *medrese*. Several years later, when Rumi was still in his twenties, his father died, and Rumi assumed the position, directing the study of theology, poetry, music, and other subjects and practices related to the growth of the soul, including cooking and the husbandry of animals. Rumi gained a wide reputation as a devout scholar, and his school numbered over ten thousand students.

The work of the dervish community was to open the heart, to explore the mystery of union, to fiercely search for and try to say truth, and to celebrate the glory and difficulty of being in a human incarnation. To these ends, they used silence and song, poetry, meditation, stories, discourse, and jokes. They fasted and feasted. They walked together and watched the animals. Animal behavior was a kind of scripture they studied. They cooked, and they worked in the garden. They tended orchards and vineyards.

The great human questions arose. What is the purpose of desire? What is a dream? A song? How do we know the depth of silence in another human being? What is the heart? What is it to be a true human being? What is the source of the universe and how do these individual awarenesses connect to that? They asked the Faustian question in many guises: What is it at bottom that holds the world together? How do we balance surrender and discipline? This high level of continuous question-and-answer permeated the poetry and music, the movement, and each activity of the community. They knew that answers might not come in discursive form, but rather in music, in image, in dream, and in the events of life as they occur.

There was also more practical inquiry. How should I make a living? How do I get my relatives out of my house? Could you help me postpone payment of this loan? The dervishes had jobs in the workday world: mason, weaver, bookbinder, grocer, hatmaker, tailor, carpenter. They were craftsmen and -women, not renunciates of everyday life, but affirmative makers and ecstatics. Some people call them *sufis*, or mystics. I say they're on the way of the heart.

At about this time Burhan Mahaqqiq, a meditator in the remote mountain regions north and east of Konya, returned, not knowing that *his* teacher, Rumi's father, had died. Burhan decided to devote the rest of his life to the training of his teacher's son. For nine years he led Rumi on many, sometimes consecutive, forty-day fasts (*chillas*). Rumi became a

4

deep and radiant adept in the science of that mystical tradition. He taught students to open their hearts, and he wrote poetry that encouraged the process. By "mystical" I do not mean to refer to a secret lineage or to anything esoteric. It is a vague and imprecise word in English, like "spiritual," which I also try to avoid using, unsuccessfully. The area of experience that "mystical" and "spiritual" refer to is often not empirically verifiable; that is, a camera can't photograph it, a scale can't weigh it, nor can words do much to describe it. It is not exclusively physical, emotional, or mental, though it may partake of those three areas. Like the depths of our loving, mystical experience can be neither proven, *nor denied.* It does happen, and it is the region of human existence Rumi's poems inhabit.

Rumi married twice (his first wife died), and he raised four children. We do have some sense of Rumi's daily life at this time, because his oldest son, Sultan Velad, saved 147 of Rumi's personal letters.[1] In them we learn how closely he was involved in the community's life. In one letter he begs a man to put off collecting money owed to another man for fifteen days. He asks a wealthy nobleman to help out a student with a small loan. Someone's relatives have moved into the hut of a devout old woman; he asks if the situation can be remedied. Sudden lines of poetry are scattered throughout the letters. Rumi was a practical worker in the world as well as an ecstatic.

In late October 1244 the meeting with Shams of Tabriz occurred. It was to become the central event in Rumi's life and the one that galvanized him into becoming perhaps the planet's greatest mystical poet. Shams was a fierce God-man, man-God. He wore an old black cloak. Sufi stories tell of his wandering in search of a friend, someone who could endure the rigors and depth of his presence. Shams would alternate between periods of ecstatic soul trance and days of physical labor as a mason. Whenever students would gather around him, as they inevitably did, he would wrap his black robe around his shoulders, excuse himself, and be gone.

Shams had one continuous internal question, "Is there no friend for me?"

Finally a voice came, "What will you give?"

"My head."

"Your friend is Jelaluddin of Konya."

There are several versions of their initial meeting. In one, Rumi was

5

teaching by a fountain in a small square in Konya, reading from his father's *Ma'arif*. Shams cut through the crowd and pushed that book and others off the ledge into the water.

"Who are you, and what are you doing?" Rumi asked.

"You must now live what you've been reading about."

Rumi turned to the volumes on the bottom. "We can retrieve them," said Shams. "They'll be as dry as they were."

Shams lifted one of them out to show him. Dry.

"Leave them," said Rumi.

With that relinquishment Rumi's deep life began, and the poetry. He said, "What I had thought of before as God I met today in a human being." His time as a theological scholar ended too. He and Shams spent months together in retreat. Their mystical conversation (*sohbet*) and the mysterious Friendship unfolded.

Some people in the community, though, were jealous. They distrusted Shams and resented his diverting their teacher from his teaching. They forced Shams away to Damascus, but Rumi called him back. Finally, it seems, some of Rumi's students—probably including one of his sons, Allaedin—killed Shams and hid the body. In his grief Rumi began circling a pole in his garden and speaking the poetry that has come to be regarded as the most intimate record we have of the search for divine companionship. His turning is, of course, the origin of the moving meditation of the Mevlevi dervishes. It is an emblem, simultaneously, of discipline and the abandon of surrender. It is a dance in concert with the galaxies, the molecules, and the spiraling form that is the source and essence of the cosmos. But it is good to remember that Rumi's ecstasy began in grief.

He spoke his poems. They were written down by scribes, and later revisions were made by Rumi on the page, but for the most part his poetry can be considered spontaneous improvisation. All of the poems in his *Divan-i Shams-i Tabrizi* ("The Works of Shams of Tabriz") can be heard as the inner conversation of their Friendship. Rumi wandered for a time in search of Shams, until he realized, in Damascus one day, that he need not search any longer. He felt, and knew, that Shams existed in the Friendship, and that he (Rumi) *was* that. The poetry comes from there.

The poems in the *Divan* are *ghazals* (often translated "odes" in English), which are composed of a series of independent couplets and sometimes run as short as eight lines, sometimes much longer. The form makes irrational, intuitive leaps from image to image and thought to thought. This agility makes it an appropriate vehicle for Rumi's passionate longing. Rumi and Shams met in the heart, and their Friendship widens in the poetry beyond all categories of gender and age, beyond romance, beyond any ideas of mentoring and discipleship. The poems open to include "sunlight" and "what anyone says." Their Friendship is a universe they inhabit. Instead of being connected by a love, they are the living atmosphere of love itself. Rumi's poetry breathes that air. The poems feel fresh and new, like something we have not absorbed yet, or understood, here seven hundred years later.

For the last twelve years of his life Rumi wrote one long continuous poem, the *Masnavi*, sixty-four thousand lines of poetry divided into six books. It has no parallel in world literature. It surges like an ocean (his image) around many subjects. It is self-interrupting, visionary, sometimes humorous commentary on the health of the soul and on Qur'anic passages; it is full of folktales, jokes, and remarks to people physically present as the poems were being composed. Rumi dictated this sublime jazz to his scribe, Husam Chelebi, as they walked around Konya, through the nearby vineyards of Meram, during teaching sessions, and in the streets and public baths. Husam was a student of Shams, so this long poem can be considered an extension of Rumi's conversation with the Friend. The best metaphor for its strange unified diversity is the way Rumi was with the community around him: sometimes he attended to the growth of the group as a whole, sometimes he addressed the needs of individuals. Readers of the *Masnavi* may dive in anywhere and swim around. It is a flow whose refrain is the ecstatic exclamation, "This has no end!" or "This cannot be said. I am drowning in this!" One complete book (IV) of the *Masnavi's* six is included in this collection.

Rumi died at sunset on December 17, 1273. His tomb in Konya is still visited by thousands each month. It is said that representatives from all major religions attended his funeral. They saw Rumi and his poetry as a way of deepening their own faith. He is often called Mevlana, or Maulana, meaning "master" or "lord." Every year on December 17, the anniversary of his death is celebrated the world over as the night of his union with the divine. It is called his *urs*, or wedding night. Rumi felt this union was something as natural as breathing. He knew it as the core inside each impulse to praise, and he acknowledged it as the presence he calls "beloved" or "Friend." Rather than be exclusively part of an organized religion or cultural system, he claimed to belong to that companion who transpires through and animates the whole universe.

> I belong to the beloved, have seen the two
> worlds as one and that one call to and know,
>
> first, last, outer, inner, only that
> breath breathing human being.

SOME CLAIMS ABOUT POETRY
AND CONSCIOUSNESS

Fana *and* Baqa: *Two Streamings Across the Doorsill of Rumi's Poetry*

No one can say what the inner life is, but poetry tries to, and no one can say what poetry is, but let's be bold and claim that there are two major *streamings* in consciousness, particularly in the ecstatic life, and in Rumi's poetry: call them *fana* and *baqa*, Arabic words that refer to the play and intersection of human with divine.

Rumi's poetry occurs in that opening,[2] a dervish doorway these energies move through in either direction. A movement out, a movement in. *Fana* is the streaming that moves from the human out into mystery—the annihilation, the orgasmic expansion, the dissolving swoon into the all. The gnat becomes buttermilk; a chickpea disappears into the flavor of the soup; a dead mule decays into salt flat; the infant turns to the breast. These wild and boundaryless absorptions are the images and the kind of poem Rumi is most well known for, a drunken clairvoyant tavern voice that announces, "Whoever brought me here will have to take me home."

"What was in that candle's light that opened and consumed me so quickly!" That is the moth's question after *fana*, after it becomes flame. The king's falcon circles in the empty sky. There is an extravagance in the magnificent disintegration of *fana*. In one wheat grain a thousand sheaf stacks. Which is literally true: a single wheat seed can, after a few years, become thousands of stacks of sheaves. But it's that special praise for the

8

natural abundance of existence that identifies this state. Three hundred billion galaxies might seem a bit gaudy to some, but not to this awareness; in *fana* what is here can never be said extravagantly enough.

Fana is what opens our wings, what makes boredom and hurt disappear. We break to pieces inside it, dancing and perfectly free. We are the dreamer streaming into the loving nowhere of night. Rapt, we are the devouring worm who, through grace, becomes an entire orchard, the wholeness of the trunks, the leaves, the fruit, and the growing. *Fana* is that dissolution just before our commotion and mad night prayers become silence. Rumi often associates surrender with the joy of falling into the freedom of sleep. It's human-becoming-God, the *Ana'l-Haqq* ("I am the truth") of Al-Hallaj Mansour. The arms open outward. This is the ocean with no shore into which the dewdrop falls.

My friend, the poet Daniel Abdal-Hayy Moore, scolds me for not saying outright that *fana* is *annihilation in Allah.* I avoid God-words, not altogether, but wherever I can, because they seem to take away the freshness of experience and put it inside a specific system. Rumi's poetry belongs to everyone, and his impulse was toward experience rather than any language or doctrine about it: our lives as text, rather than any book, be it Qur'an, Gospel, upanishad, or sutra.

There is a fierce desolation in *fana*, though, that I may not be communicating. Abdal-Hayy is right. The absence experienced in *fana* is complete. There is no soft focus around anything. It's the hard-edged *jelal* ("majesty") desert sword of Shams. I have much to learn in these matters.

Baqa goes the other way across the doorsill. The Arabic word means "a living within": it is the walk back down Qaf Mountain, where the vision came; life lived with clarity and reason; the turning again toward what somehow always was. The concentration of a night of stars into one needle's eye. A refinement, companionship, two people walking along some *particular* county road. The absorbing work of *this* day. The precise painting of a piece of trim. The arms folding inward across the chest and the bow to one another. Courtesy and craftsmanship. God-becoming-human. The qualities associated with this motion are honesty, sobriety, carefulness, a clarity Rumi sometimes calls "reason," compassion, and work within a community. *Baqa* is also a return from expansion into each's unique individuation work, into pain and effort, confusion and dark comedy: the end of a frayed rope, the deep knowing of absence.

9

Baqa is where animal and angel meet in an awkward but truly human dance. It's a breathtaking birth, the dying and then being born again that all religions know is the essence of soul growth. It can be overheard in the poetry as a conversation between Jelaluddin and the mystery.

Baqa might say:

> Friend, our closeness is this:
> Anywhere you put your foot feel me
> in the firmness under you.

while *fana* asks, in the same quatrain:

> How is it with this love,
> I see your world, but not you?

Baqa is felt in Rumi's spring-morning poems, very present, green and alive with the camaraderie of a picnic by the water.

> Stay together, friends.
> Don't scatter and sleep.
>
> Our friendship is made
> of being awake.
>
> The waterwheel accepts water
> and turns and gives it away, weeping.
>
> That way it stays in the garden. . . .
> Stay here, quivering with each moment
> like a drop of mercury.

You feel a tremulous intensity *within limits*. Bodhisattval service walking to the well. The common joy of ducks riding a flooded river. Kindness and acts of anonymous helping. *Baqa* brings the next stage in the process of prayer: there's the opening into annihilation, then the coming back to tend specific people. A melody, the little German band coming up through Beethoven's *Ninth*. This is the ocean come to court the drop! A fall to the knees, the frustrating satisfaction of the spoken word.

By letting these two conditions, *fana* and *baqa*, flow and exist simultaneously in his poetry, Rumi is saying that they are one thing, the core of a true human being, which he was and out of which these poems are spoken. This is how alive his model of the human psyche is, where the secular and the sacred are always mingling, the mythic and the ordinary, dream vision and street life.

The Question of the Personal

Rumi's poems are not personal in the way we've come to expect in the Western tradition of poetry and poetry readings. We do not learn who Rumi was *as a personality* from his poems. They are not subjective, but rather objective, or *iconic*. They conduct and transform energies. They do the work of icons: they connect us more deeply with our souls. When we look at an image of Christ or Dionysos, we feel the core of grief and compassion there. When we see the archaic torso of Apollo in the Vatican, we take in some of its graceful balance and power, and we *do* change out lives. The form of Kali transmits the force of making a clean cut with the past, the edge of focused rage. And try someday to walk into the Kwan Yin room of the Nelson-Atkins Museum in Kansas City. Take in her high humor and grounded acceptance.

Neither of the conditions, *fana* or *baqa*, involves the false self of a personal ego. Rather, they are motions of the essence of a human-divine encounter. Rumi's poetry means to take us beyond the personal into the mystery that is here, the source of dream vision, the spring of longing, into a presence that asks the question, "Who am I?" Ramana Maharshi and Rumi would agree: the joy of being human is in uncovering the core we already are, the treasure buried in the ruin.

I am told that at the end of a Mevlevi initiation, which consists of various kinds of physical work, *zikr* ("remembering God"), fasting, abstinence, and long retreats, a condition of entrancement called *hulul* is reached. Rumi's poetry gives a taste of that trance, as well as other stations. All of his poetry continues the work of transformation he experienced with Shams-i Tabriz; it has to, because it comes out of that Friendship.

I have never gone through the Mevlevi initiation, and I do not live in the states of *fana* and *baqa* that Rumi speaks from. No doubt I oversimplify or misrepresent what they are. My own experience of these states, if I can be allowed any claim, comes from remembering my teacher, Bawa Muhaiyaddeen, who told me to do this Rumi work. He lived in both worlds. Also, I get some taste when I move from a wild perception of the vast beauty in and around us to the equally enjoyed attention to my nine-year-old grandaughter's latest written song, which happens to be about the sun.

I feel the source of the power of Rumi's spontaneous poetic derives from his continual balance of surrender and discipline, his visionary radiance held in the level calm of ordinary sight. Splendor and practice, meditation and chore—somewhere in the dynamic of those lies the vitality and validity, the knack of Mevlana.

> The universe and the light of the stars come through me.
>
> *(fana)*

> I am the crescent moon put up over the gate to the festival.
>
> *(baqa)*

The "cresent moon" is undoubtedly some plywood device nailed over the fairground entrance. *Baqa* often includes a little joke about the grandeur.

A NOTE ABOUT THIS BOOK

This collection plots a variable surfline between the personal statements in the paraphernalia (the introductions and notes) and Rumi's enlightened-master poetry. If there's drift between them, I hope it's attuned with his making.

You might say that personality molds its hearth-god images, the family totems, while the Rumi-Shams poetic impulse disintegrates those and blows their dust away as it comes through. If the personal persists then, it's like the cheap Philco within which we hear Mozart's amazing joy.

Or you could say that soul is what makes beauty from the dance of the personal with the great mystery, and that we're still working with Rumi's question, "What *is* the soul?"

Entitling this collection *The Soul of Rumi* then may seem a bold move, *soul* being the mystery that cannot be said. Here are some quotations that may help:

> The soul is undiscovered
> though explored forever
> to a depth beyond report.[3]
>
> Heraclitus

Self-knowledge reveals to the soul that its natural motion is not, if uninterrupted, in a straight line, but circular, as around some inner object, about a center, the point to which it owes its origin.[4]

Plotinus

The Self is a circle, whose center is everywhere and whose circumference is nowhere.[5]

Carl G. Jung

There is a *with-ness* in Rumi's sense of soul, a friendship, as in a spiraling cone the periphery stays *with* the center it began from.

The titles given to the poems in the first section of the book have been added as part of the process of translation. Rumi's *ghazals* (odes) have no individual titles in Persian.

This time with the *Masnavi* I have changed the free-verse lineations to a fluctuating-length, line–half-line, more visually formal arrangement. It mimics, sort of, the middle-of-the-line rhymes in Persian, and I like the delicacy of random breakings, the surflike look on the page, the C. K. Williams ramble for the ear.

Despite what Archie Bunker said, Edith was never a dingbat. *Dingbat* is a printer's term for a device that divides text, recognizing some pause deeper than the space between paragraphs, but less profound than the full stop at the end of a chapter. Dingbats dance in the gap. Dingbats come out in the indecisive twilight. I made the dingbats used on the following pages with a monster Magic Marker on blank postcards bought at the Tru-Valu Hardware in Provincetown, Massachusetts. They are greatly reduced from the postcards, and some of them have migrated to the margins of Book IV to relieve the monumental daunt of a long poem. I don't guess they're technically dingbats there. Swimmers.

Dingbats are helpful when you're not making sustained, connected sense. Just put in a dingbat, and there's oneiric coherence. Dingbats let possibly awkward transitions move in graceful ellipsis. They should become part of freshman composition, and children could make them new as they learn penmanship.

There will be a pause now in my work with Jelaluddin Rumi,[6] whatever you call what I do with his poetry: collaborative translation, interpretation, the making of versions or imitations, that work is done for a time, after twenty-five years. I will continue the morning sessions—turning at random to a scholarly translation of a *ghazal* or a page of the *Masnavi* and putting it into free verse lines appealing to my ear—but I'll wait a while to publish those. I'll send out my own poetry, such as it is.

I have allowed myself to put a lot of personal material in the introductory sections and in the notes, a practice not tolerated in scholarly work. This is not scholarship. This is the fumbling conversation of my personal self with the deep being I've *met*, and not become. So I'll stand by the decision to put the journal-like bits, paragraphs, in here, ephemera of my days. They ground me. For the time being, it feels more honest to have them. I hope they don't distract from the poetry. It may be that, in time, the personal parts will seem indulgent and silly, or worse, charming. It won't be the first time. What I deeply want, though, despite the gab, is for Rumi to become vitally present for readers, part of what John Keats called our *soul-making*: that process that is both collective and uniquely individual, that happens outside time and space and inside, that is the ocean we all inhabit and each singular droplet-self. No image can hold the mystery of its continuous revision.

1. A Green Shawl: Solomon's Far Mosque

In the early 1990s—it was December—I was sitting in meditation under the green dome that houses Rumi's tomb in Konya. Someone came up and gave me a green shawl. As you might imagine, I treasure it still and use it in my meditation. I love the wrapped, rapt feeling.

Going in, feeling the limpid contentment in being oneself and the endless discovery there: the green shawl is that, reminiscent of a child's tent-making delight, the rainy-day times when you spread a sheet over a card table and a chair, anchored it with safety pins, and crept under the shelter where imagination could flower. How we forget this *tent making* for such long spans is a mystery in itself.

Rumi tells of Solomon's practice of building each dawn a place made of intention and compassion and *sohbet* (mystical conversation). He calls it the "far mosque." Solomon goes there to listen to the plants, the new ones that come up each morning. They tell him of their medicinal qualities, their potential for health, and also the dangers of poisoning.

I suggest we all get green shawls. "Remember, the entrance door to the sanctuary is *inside* you" ("Entrance Door"). Mary's hiding place and the great warehouse ("What Was Told, *That*") are other images of the listening tent, where conversation thrives and love deepens.

Rumi often hears it as the birdlike song-talk that begins at dawn under the dome of meditation. Build a far mosque where you can read your soul-book and listen to the dreams that grew in the night. Attar says,

> Let love lead your soul.
> Make it a place to retire to,
> a kind of cave, a retreat
> for the deep core of being.

ENTRANCE DOOR

How lover and beloved touch is
familiar and courteous, but there

is a strange impulse in that to
create a form that will dissolve

all other shapes. Remember, the
entrance door to the sanctuary is

inside you. We watch a sunlight
dust dance, and we try to be that

lively, but nobody knows what music
those particles hear. Each of us

has a secret companion musician to
dance to. Unique rhythmic play, a

motion in the street we alone know
and hear. Shams is a king of kings

like Mahmud, but there's not another
pearl-crushing dervish Ayaz like me.

WHAT WAS TOLD, *THAT*

What was said to the rose that made it open was said
to me here in my chest.

What was told the cypress that made it strong
and straight, what was

whispered the jasmine so it is what it is, whatever made
sugarcane sweet, whatever

was said to the inhabitants of the town of Chigil in
Turkestan that makes them

so handsome, whatever lets the pomegranate flower blush
like a human face, that is

being said to me now. I blush. Whatever put eloquence in
language, that's happening here.

The great warehouse doors open; I fill with gratitude,
chewing a piece of sugarcane,

in love with the one to whom every *that* belongs!

MARY'S HIDING

Before these possessions you love slip away, say what
Mary said when she was

surprised by Gabriel, *I'll hide inside God.* Naked in
her room she saw a form

of beauty that could give her new life. Like the sun
coming up, or a rose as it

opens. She leaped, as her habit was, out of herself
into the divine presence.

There was fire in the channel of her breath. Light and
majesty came. I am smoke

from that fire and proof of its existence, more than
any external form.

I want to be where
your bare foot walks,

because maybe before you step,
you'll look at the ground.
I want that blessing.

Would you like to have revealed to you
the truth of the Friend?

Leave the rind,
and descend into the pith.

Fold within fold, the beloved
drowns in its own being. This world
is drenched with that drowning.

⌒

Imagining is like feeling around
in a dark lane, or washing
your eyes with blood.

You *are* the truth
from foot to brow. Now,
what else would you like to know?

THE HUSK AND CORE OF MASCULINITY

Masculinity has a core of clarity, which does not act
from anger or greed or

sensuality, and a husk, which does. The virile center
that listens within takes

pleasure in obeying that truth. Nobility of spirit,
the true spontaneous energy

of your life, comes as you abandon other motives and move
only when you feel the majesty

that commands and is the delight of the self. Remember
Ayaz crushing the king's pearl!

2. Initiation: The Necessary Pain of Changing

This initiation Rumi speaks of is not the crossover a young person makes from adolescence to mature membership in a community, nor is it the passage an adult may make to the level of elder or shaman, though these transitions may be involved as well.

"It's time for that merging in me now!" the young man calls out when he hears the death cry in the mosque. He wants immediate transformation, and he's willing to risk everything for it ("A Surprise of Roses").

The moment of initiation is actual, and it may come at almost any point in your life. Rumi says it's more important than how you decide to make your livelihood. This is your work in the invisible, the connection to God! Rumi suggests that you bear down there at least as diligently as you do in daily work.

Whatever mystery this changing is, it may be reached through a living teacher, through the doorway of humbling human experiences, or through an invisible presence, a *companion* known only to you. There are as many ways through the opening of this transformation as there are human beings.

There's a push and another push, from what Rumi calls the first soul to your second soul, and so on, the *necessary dyings*, the ground crumbling that lets wildflowers come up ("A Necessary Autumn Inside Each").

This may sound like poetic talk, and it is. But it does happen. And something like friendship seems to be involved. There's help with the passages. Identity has layers of inner vastness that nourish each other, as, for example, when attendance at dawn nourishes a friendship where the star-candles of the mind go out.

WORK IN THE INVISIBLE

The prophets have wondered to themselves, "How *long*
should we keep pounding

this cold iron? How *long* do we have to whisper into an
empty cage?" Every motion

of created beings comes from the creator. The first soul
pushes, and your second

soul responds, beginning, so don't stay timid. Load the ship
and set out. No one knows

for certain whether the vessel will sink or reach the harbor.
Cautious people say, "I'll

do nothing until I can be sure." Merchants know better.
If you do nothing, you lose.

Don't be one of those merchants who won't risk the ocean!
This is much more important

than losing or making money. This is your connection to God!
You must set fire to have

light. Trust means you're ready to risk what you currently
have. Think of your fear and

hope about your livelihood. They make you go to work
diligently every day. Now

consider what the prophets have done. Abraham wore fire
for an anklet. Moses spoke

to the sea. David molded iron. Solomon rode the wind.
Work in the invisible world

at least as hard as you do in the visible. Be companions
with the prophets even though

no one here will know that you are, not even the helpers of
the *qutb*, the *abdals*. You

can't imagine what *profit* will come! When one of those
generous ones invites you

into his fire, go quickly! Don't say, "But will it burn
me? Will it hurt?"

A NECESSARY AUTUMN INSIDE EACH

You and I have spoken all these words, but as for the way
we have to go, words

are no preparation. There is no getting ready, other than
grace. My faults

have stayed hidden. One might call that a preparation!
I have one small drop

of knowing in my soul. Let it dissolve in your ocean.
There are so many threats to it.

Inside each of us, there's continual autumn. Our leaves
fall and are blown out

over the water. A crow sits in the blackened limbs and talks
about what's gone. Then

your generosity returns: spring, moisture, intelligence, the
scent of hyacinth and rose

and cypress. Joseph is back! And if you don't feel in
yourself the freshness of

Joseph, be Jacob! Weep and then smile. Don't pretend to know
something you haven't experienced.

There's a necessary dying, and then Jesus is breathing again.
Very little grows on jagged

rock. Be ground. Be crumbled, so wildflowers will come up
where you are. You've been

stony for too many years. Try something different. Surrender.

PAIN

Pain comes from seeing how arrogant you've been, and
pain brings you out of this

conceit. A child cannot be born until the mother has pain.
You are pregnant with real

trust. The words of the prophets and saints are midwives
that help, but first you must feel

pain. To be without pain is to use the first person wrongly.
"I" am this. "I" am that.

"I" am God, like al-Hallaj, who waited till that was true to
say it. "I" at the wrong

time brings a curse. "I" at the right time gives a blessing.
If a rooster crows early,

when it's still dark, he must have his head cut off. What is
this beheading? As one might

extract a scorpion's sting to save it, or a snake's venom to
keep it from being stoned,

headlessness comes from your cleansing connection to
a teacher. Hold to

a true sheikh. Strength will come. Your strength is his
gathering you closer. Soul

of the soul of the soul, moment to moment, hope to draw breath
from that one. No matter

how long you've been apart. That presence has no separation
in it. Do you want to understand

more about this friendship? Read the sura called *Daybreak*.

A SURPRISE OF ROSES

A long cry at midnight near the mosque, a dying cry.
The young man sitting there

hears and thinks, "That sound doesn't make me afraid.
Why should it?

It's the drumbeat announcing a celebration! It means
we should start cooking

the joy soup!" He hears beyond his death fear to the
union. "It's time

for that merging in me *now*." He jumps up and shouts to
God, "If you can be human, come

inside me now!" The signal of the death yell splits him
open. The mystery pours from all

directions, gold coins, liquid gold, gold cloth, gold bars.
They pile up blocking

the doors to the mosque. The young man works all night
carrying the gold away in sacks,

burying it, and coming back for more. The timid congregation
sleeps through it all.

If you think I'm talking about actual gold, you're like those
children who pretend

that pieces of broken dishes are money, so that anytime they
see pottery shards they think

of money, as when you hear the word *gold* and wish for it. This
is the other gold,

that glows in your chest when you love. The enchanted mosque
is in there too, where

the pointed cry is a candle flame on the altar. The young man
becomes a moth who gambles himself

and wins. A true human being is not human! This candle does
not burn. It illuminates.

Some candles burn themselves and one another up. Others
taste like a surprise of

roses in a room, and you just a stranger who wandered in.

MORE RANGE

We're friends with one who kills us,
who gives us to the ocean waves. We

love this death. Only ignorance says,
Put it off a while, day after tomorrow.

Don't avoid the knife. This friend
only seems fierce, bringing your soul

more range, perching your falcon on a
cliff of the wind. Jesus on his cross,

Hallaj on his—those absurd killings
hold a secret. Cautious cynics *know*

what they're doing every moment and why.
Submit to love without thinking, as

the sun this morning rose recklessly
extinguishing our star-candle minds.

CHOOSE A SUFFERING

Yesterday in the assembly I saw my
soul inside the jar of the one who

pours. "Don't forget your job," I
said. He came with his lighted

face, kissed the full glass, and as
he handed it to me, it became a

red-gold oven taking me in, a ruby
mine, a greening garden. Everyone

chooses a suffering that will change
him or her to a well-baked loaf.

Abu Lahab, biting his hand, chose
doubt. Abu Huraya, his love for

cats! One searches a confused mind
for evidence. The other has a

leather sack full of what he needs.
If we could be silent now, the

master would tell us some stories
they hear in the high council.

Grief settles thick in the throat
and lungs: thousands of sorrows

being suffered, clouds of cruelty,
all somehow from love. Wail and be

thirsty for your own blood. Climb
to the execution place. It is time.

The Nile flows red: the Nile flows
pure. Dry thorns and aloe wood are

the same until fire touches. A
warrior and a mean coward stand here

similar until arrows rain. Warriors
love battle. A subtle lion with

strategy gets the prey to run *toward*
him, saying *Kill me again.* Dead

eyes look into living eyes. *Don't
try to figure this out.* Love's work

looks absurd, but trying to find a
meaning will hide it more. Silence.

WATCH A ONE-YEAR-OLD

Anger rises when you're proud
of yourself. Humble that. Use

the contempt of others, and your
own self-regarding, to change, like

the cloud in folklore that became
three snake shapes. Or if you like

the dog-barking lion wrath, enjoy
the hurt longer. Watch a one-year-

old, how it walks, the slow wisdom
there. Sometimes a sweet taste

makes you sour and mean. Listen
to the voice that says, *It was for*

you I created the universe. Then
kill and be killed in love. You've

been two dogs dozing long enough!

3. Baqa: *Inside This Ordinary Daylight*

Rumi adores this stubborn, horny, mean, radiant, arrogant, hilarious planet we inhabit. He looks at it; he holds up to the light anything human beings do, and uses each action as a lens to examine the growth of the soul.

The most amazing quality of his poetry is that it can also give a sense of the presence our lives occur within. That most elusive mystery that enters every gesture of the hunt—bow, release, the deer's blood, the hunter's eye—each careful stitch of tapestry becomes the ground felt under the poetry.

Rumi caresses the exactness, the distinct shape of the human story, even as he conveys the oceanic intelligence that surges through. This is *baqa:* coming back from annihilation with cleansed enthusiasm for particulars. In the state of *baqa* one reenters the moment fully, doing small quiet work, sewing the robe of absence.

The poet Hayden Carruth survived a suicide attempt and came back from it with a renewed sense of the sheer good luck of being alive. "My happiness was not a state of doing but of being. . . . Is this what St. Theresa felt? I suspect that in its sensational manifestation my happiness is indeed close to religious ecstasy." He wouldn't, but I'd say he was experiencing *baqa*.

Rumi loves animals. Surely one of the oldest joys of human beings is watching them. The cave walls celebrate the animal grace of sentience. Rumi's poetry loves the mixture of animal, human, and spirit, which is the elaborate dance of true human beings.

With dreams, the *baqa* state comes in as one makes some *practical application* of the wisdom given in them.

WALKINGSTICK DRAGON

I want to dance *here* in *this* music,
not in spirit where there is no time.

I circle the sun like shadow. My
head becomes my feet. Covered with

existence, Pharaoh; annihilated, I
am Moses. A pen between God-fingers,

a walkingstick dragon, my blind mind
taps along its cane of thought. Love

does no thinking. It waits with soul,
with me, weeping in this corner. We're

strangers here where we never hear
yes. We must be from some other town.

THE OPENER

Hangovers come with love, yet
love's the cure for hangovers!

A shrill pipe, and the battalion
scatters. *Ya Fattah* is here!

Bitter goes sweet in the mouth.
Lightning burns through cloud

cover. A water carrier's call
becomes thunder on the desert

road. We're told to deepen.
As the storm of Shams Tabriz

moves across the sky, ocean
waves lift and scour the shore.

SOUL LIGHT AND SUN THE SAME

If a lover isn't continually burning,
he should sit and crack his knuckles

with the old men. A lover doesn't fit
in groups very well, or with himself.

He rides quickly away from doubt and
appearances. A spring, a green branch,

every day new, the first time you feel
held, curved like a lute playing grief

music. Gazelle and lioness walking
together, soul light and sun, the same.

THE PATTERN IMPROVES

When love itself comes to kiss you,
don't hold back! When the king

goes hunting, the forest smiles.
Now the king has become the place

and all the players, prey, bystander,
bow, arrow, hand and release. How

does that feel? Last night's dream
enters these open eyes. When we die

and turn to dust, each particle will
be the whole. You hear a mote whirl

taking form? My music. Love, calm,
patient. The Friend has waded down

into existence, gotten stuck, and
will not be seen again outside of

this. We sometimes make spiderwebs
of smoke and saliva, fragile thought-

packets. Leave thinking to the one
who gave intelligence. In silence

there is eloquence. Stop weaving,
and watch how the pattern improves.

~

You're from a country beyond this universe,
yet your best guess is
you're made of earth and ashes.

You engrave this physical image everywhere
as a sign that you've forgotten
where you're from!

~

Essence is emptiness.
Everything else, accidental.

Emptiness brings peace to your loving.
Everything else, disease.

In this world of trickery emptiness
is what your soul wants.

~

We're not afraid of God's blade,
or of being chained up, or
of having our heads severed.

We're burning up quickly, tasting
a little hellfire as we go.

You cannot imagine
how little it matters to us
what people say.

Come to this street with
only your sweet fragrance.

Don't walk into *this* river
wearing a robe!

Paths go from here to there,
but don't arrive from somewhere!
It's time now to live naked.

Spring overall. But inside us
there's another unity.

Behind each eye here,
one glowing water.

Every forest branch moves differently
in the breeze, but as they sway,
they connect at the roots.

This is how I would die
into the love I have for you:

as pieces of cloud
dissolve in sunlight.

How will you know the difficulties
of being human, if you're always
flying off to blue perfection?

Where will you plant your grief seeds?
Workers need ground to scrape and hoe,
not the sky of unspecified desire.

Love is the way messengers
from the mystery tell us things.

Love is the mother.
We are her children.

She shines inside us,
visible-invisible, as we trust
or lose trust, or feel it start to grow again.

BEGIN

This is now. Now is. Don't
postpone till then. Spend

the spark of iron on stone.
Sit at the head of the table;

dip your spoon in the bowl.
Seat yourself next your joy

and have your awakened soul
pour wine. Branches in the

spring wind, easy dance of
jasmine and cypress. Cloth

for green robes has been cut
from pure absence. You're

the tailor, settled among his
shop goods, quietly sewing.

The ocean can do without fish. My soul,
let me tell you a secret: it's rare to

meet a fish like the ocean! Seawater is
the nursing mother. Fish, the crying

babies. But sometimes the ocean comes
looking for a particular fish to hear

what it wants. The ocean will not act
before it knows. That fish is an

emperor then; the ocean its minister.
But don't call such a fish a *fish!* How

long will I keep talking in riddles?
Shams is the master who turns the earth

fragrant. When plants feel him near,
they open out. I would not have a soul,

if after tasting the taste of Shams,
I could go back to being who I was.

THREE TRAVELERS TELL THEIR DREAMS

Three devout men of different religions fall in together
by chance traveling. They stop

at a caravanserai where the host brings as a gift a sweet
dessert, some taste of God's

nearness. This is how people out in the country serve
strangers. The Jew and

the Christian are full, but the Muslim has been fasting all
day. The two say, "Let's

save it for tomorrow." The one, "No. Let's save self-denial
for tomorrow!" "You want it

all for yourself!" "Divide it into three parts, and each can
do as he wants." "Ah,

but Muhammad said not to share." "That was about dividing
yourself between sensuality

and soul. You must belong to one or the other." But finally,
for some reason, he gives in,

"I'll do it your way." They refrain from tasting. They sleep,
and then wake and dress themselves

to begin morning devotions. Christian, Jew, Muslim, shaman,
Zoroastrian, stone, ground,

mountain, river, each has a secret way of being with the
mystery, unique and not to be

judged. This subject never ends! Three friends in a grand
morning mood. "Let us tell

what dreams we had last night; whoever has had the deepest
dream gets the halvah."

Agreed. The Jewish man begins the wanderings of his soul.
"Moses met me on the road;

I followed him to Sinai: an opening door, light within
light. Mt. Sinai and Moses and

I merged in an exploding splendor, the unity of the prophets."
This is a true dream. Many

Jews have such. Then the Christian sighs, "Christ took me
in his arms to the fourth

heaven, a pure vast region . . . I cannot say . . ." His is also
deep. The Muslim, "Muhammad came

and told me where you two had gone. 'You wretch,' he said,
'you've been left behind! You

35

may as well get up and eat something.'" "No!" laugh the Christian and the Jew. "How

could I disobey such glory? Would you not do as Moses and Jesus suggest?" "You're right,"

they say. "Yours is the truest dream, because it had immediate effect in your waking life."

What matters is how *quickly* you do what your soul directs.

4. This Speech: The Source of Dream Vision

I do not know the *source* of dream visions, of course, but I have always been amazed by the *art* of dreaming, its living, organic fit with our growing consciousness, and the pure play of it. Surely some of the most astonishing *making* that occurs in the cosmos is the imagery that comes in dream, and the voices there.

Rumi says wherever the soul goes at night, *that* is our true home! ("A Trace"). So remembering dreams is particularly important. He often refers to the biblical figure of Joseph, whose ability to interpret dreams saved Egypt from famine. It was Joseph's service, his work, his way out of prison, and eventually his restored connection to that further freedom, Canaan.

Rumi says that lovers read another book with another eye. Dreamers and lovers have similar knowing, and hearing. There is a continuous speech moving through form; like the presence and absence of the sun it is sometimes palpable, sometimes not, but it is always there generating the juice of life.

I love the story of Omar and the old poet in this section. Not much happens; it's barely a story at all. There's an old poet, a harp player past his prime. He wants something, perhaps what every artist wants, new harp strings: something that will turn his making fresh again, taut with resonance and energy. He prays for this renewal and goes to sleep, using the harp for a headrest. This falling asleep gives Rumi a chance to celebrate the vast release that comes with dreaming. He rarely misses an opportunity to do that.

The caliph Omar is napping nearby. The poem goes into Omar's sleep, where a voice tells him how to answer the old poet's prayer. Omar gives the harper enough to buy new harp strings, and the rest of the story is simply the poet's response to that generosity, the grace that has come. In his gratitude he breaks free of the personal, from wishing and wanting, from regret and repentence, into the God-annihilated state of *fana*. As Rumi describes them, the states of sleep and surrender are very close to being one thing. The conditions of dreaming and *fana* mix, and for that there are no images or language. We are left with an oceanic feeling, a disappearing into sunlight that is both empty and full, and the core of ecstatic vision.

LOOKING INTO THE CREEK

The way the soul is with the senses and the intellect is
like a creek. When desire weeds

grow thick, intelligence can't flow, and soul creatures
stay hidden. But sometimes

the reasonable clarity runs so strong it sweeps the clogged
stream open. No longer weeping

and frustrated, your being grows as powerful as your wantings
were before, more so. Laughing

and satisfied, the masterful flow lets creations of
the soul appear. You look

down, and it's lucid dreaming. The gates made of light
swing open. You see in.

FORTH

You that pour the pourers day
and night, so that in sleep we

keep tasting, no head, turban,
the soul's heart sliced to bits,

Egyptian women out of hand,
waterbag full of wind, this is

how love catches up and wants
to be our friend, as we hold

each other, and the good secret
inside slides forth continuous.

HOMETOWN STREETS

Sleep dissolves your mind, but how
do the insane sleep? What do the

love-crazed know of night-and-day
differences? God-lovers, mostly in

another world, read another book
with another eye. Try changing to

a bird or a fish. Be lost on some
road inside the beloved. You will

not know what a *matzoob* feels until
you're one of them. Shams sets

these new lights adrift through our
hometown streets, the universe.

A TRACE

You that give new life to this planet,
you that transcend logic, come. I am

only an arrow. Fill your bow with me
and let fly. Because of this love for

you, my bowl has fallen from the roof.
Put down a ladder and collect the pieces,

please! People ask, "But which roof is
your roof?" I answer, "Wherever the

soul goes at night, my roof is in that
direction! From wherever spring arrives

to heal the ground, wherever searching
rises from in a human being." Remember,

the looking itself is a trace of what
we're looking for, but we've been more

like the man who sat on his donkey and
asked the donkey where to go! Be quiet

now and wait. It may be that the ocean
one we desire so to move into and become

desires us out on land a little longer,
going our sundry roads to the shore.

CREATOR OF ABSENCE AND PRESENCE

Mevlana was asked about a passage from the *Masnavi*:
Brother, you *are* that thought. Your bones and
nerves are something else.

(II, 277)

He said, "Consider this. The word *thought* must be expanded to mean *essence*, or it doesn't apply to what I'm saying there. Everything that gets exchanged between people, whether it's spoken or not, is a form of such *thought*. Human beings are discourse. The rest is blood and bone and nerves. Call it speech, that flowing between us. Compare it to the sun, which is always warming us, even when we can't see it. This speech-sun is invisible, except when it takes form in language. God is extremely subtle, until these gross bodies make *that* apparent. There was a certain man who said that the word 'God' meant nothing to him. Then someone began pointing to the *actions* of God, and he saw. There are people who can't eat honey unless it's mixed with rice and turmeric.

"This speech I'm describing is continuous, like the sun's light and heat. Usually we require a medium to enjoy it, but there are ways of understanding without forms, an ocean of subtlety full of miraculous beings and new colors. This speech moves through you whether you say anything or not. Philosophers claim, 'Man is the speaking animal.' And just as your animality is always there with you, so the speaking is constantly there.

"Human beings live in three spiritual states. In the first we pay no attention to God. We notice only the stones and the dirt of the world, the wealth, the children, the men and women. In the second we do nothing but worship God. In the third, the most advanced state, we become silent.

We don't say, 'I serve God' or 'I don't serve.' We know that God is beyond being present or absent. The creator of absence and presence! And other than both.

"These opposites that generate each other are not qualities of God. There are no likenesses. God did not create God. When you reach this point, stop! At the edge of the ocean footprints disappear. Language, science, and all human skills derive their relish from this speech. This flowing exchange gives flavor to every event.

"Like the man courting the wealthy woman who owns large flocks of sheep and many horses and great orchards. He tends them. He waters the fruit trees and looks after the horses, but all the while he's thinking of the woman. If she were suddenly not there, his work would be distasteful and boring. Like that, everything that happens is filled with pleasure and warmth because of the delight of the discourse always going on, and if it weren't moving there, nothing would have any meaning."

A SHIP GLIDING OVER NOTHING

Only union with you gives joy. The rest is
tearing down one building to put up another.

But don't break with forms! Boats cannot
move without water. We are misquoted texts,

made right when you say us. We are sheep in
a tightening wolf circle. You come like a

shepherd and ask, "So how are you?" I start
crying. This means something to anyone in a

body, but what means something to you? You
can't be spoken, though you listen to all

sound. You can't be written, yet you read
everything. You don't sleep, but you're the

source of dream vision, a ship gliding over
nothing, deep silence, praise for one who

told Moses on Sinai, *You shall not see me.*

The poet has grown old. His voice is choked sounding
and harsh, and some of his

harp strings are broken. Poetry that once refreshed
the soul now is no use to

anyone, the sound adored by Venus become a faint braying
from an old donkey. What found

the falcon's prey now catches gnats. All fair things decay.
What roof has not fallen

to be this where we walk? Only the inward voice heard in
the chest does not fade. Only

that amber continually draws to it with steady strength all
thought and every art. So

this poet has grown feeble and also poor because no one wants
to hear him anymore. He goes

to the graveyard at Medina and prays, "Lord, you always accept
counterfeit coins from me! Take

these prayers again and give me enough to buy new silk strings
for my harp." He speaks

a few lines with the strings remaining, "For seventy years
I've been forgetful, but

not for a moment has this flowing toward me slowed or stopped.
I deserve nothing. I am

the guest the mystics talk about. I play this living music for
my host. Everything today is

for the host." Then he puts the instrument down for a pillow
and goes to sleep. The bird

of his soul escapes! Free of the body and the grieving, flying
in a vast simple region that is

itself, where it can sing its truth. "I love this having no
head, this tasting without

mouth, this memory without regret, how without hands I gather
rose and basil on an infinitely

stretching-out plain that is my joy." So this waterbird
plunges in its ocean, Job's

fountain where Job is healed of all affliction, the pure
sunrise. If this *Masnavi*

were suddenly sky, it could not hold half the mystery this
poet enjoys in sleep.

If there were a clear way into that, no one would stay here!
Meanwhile, to the Caliph Omar,

napping nearby, a voice comes, "Give seven hundred gold dinars
to the man sleeping in the

cemetery." Everyone understands this voice when it arrives.
It speaks with the same

authority to Turk and Kurd, Persian, Arab, Ethiopian, one
language! Omar runs

to the graveyard to do as the voice says, but no one's there
except the old man asleep.

"Surely not God's favorite!" Omar prowls the place like a lion
after prey, finding nothing.

It must be the ragged vagrant. "This hidden heart is a mystery!"
Omar sits down beside him and

sneezes. The wanderer jumps up thinking the great man is there
to accuse him. "No. Sit here.

I have a secret to tell you. There is gold enough in this sack
to buy new silk strings for

your harp. Take it, buy them, and come back here." The
old poet hears and feels

the generosity that has now become visible. He weeps in his
life, then throws

the harp on the ground and breaks it. No one knows the
value of any particular day!

"These songs, breath by breath, have kept me minding the
musical modes of Iraq and the

rhythms of Persia. The minor *zirafgand*, the liquid freshness
of the twenty-four modes, these

have distracted me while caravan after caravan was leaving.
My poems have kept me in

my self, which was your greatest gift to me, that now I
surrender back!" When someone

is counting out gold for you, don't look at your hands, or
the gold. Look at the giver!

"But even this wailing self-recrimination," says Omar,
"is just another shape for

enclosure, another joint on the reed. Remembering the
past and anticipating the

future puts you in a cylinder segment of time. Pierce the
segments and be hollow, with

perforated walls, so flute music can happen. Let God's
breathing flow in and

through. Don't be a searcher wrapped in the importance
of his quest. Repent of

your repenting!" The man's heart wakes, no longer in love
with treble and bass. Without

weeping or laughter, his animal soul drains away; this
other soul begins to live.

In a true bewilderment he goes out beyond any seeking,
beyond words and telling,

drowned in the beauty, drowned beyond deliverance. Waves
cover the old man. Nothing

more can be said of him. He has shaken out his robe, and there's nothing in it

anymore. There is a chase where a falcon dives into the forest and doesn't come

back up. Every moment the sunlight is totally empty and totally full. The world, like

an old poet, gets freshened with soul water and light rising new with the sun, this

variegated, diffuse, and musical weather no one could imagine, except in sleep.

5. One Altar: The Inner Meaning of Religions

All acts of praise, contrition, and forgiveness join with the living core at the center of all religions.

His friendship with Shams Tabriz, that ineffable and yet particular connection, consumed the structure of religion for Rumi. The friendship became his worship, absorbing Islam, Muhammad, Jesus, and all doctrines in the ocean of its reality, the heart. After his meeting and *sohbet* with Shams, theological discussion was no longer relevant. As he says, Shams's face is what every religion tries to remember ("Your Face").

The *way* that Rumi and Shams clarified for the world of mystical experience is their continuously unfolding friendship. The source of that friendship—sunlight, everything the sun lights, and the mystery of the inner sun—is what he worships. This is a difficulty some traditional believers have with Rumi: he does not stress the *distance* between human beings and Allah, the absolute, but rather a *remembered intimacy*, the original agreement in which friend and friendship become one sea-changing union. He does not stress prayer so much as continuous conversation. If our real consciousness is beyond time and space, the core of worship must be beyond any cultural or religious system.

I don't mean to be dogmatic about this, or even argumentative. There is a Rumi loved by Muslims whose almost every poem is read as a commentary on the Qur'an. This is a true Rumi too, along with my gnostic, without-religious-form one. The man is a grace, a *baraka*, a powerful blessing. We can meet and talk and proclaim our takes on his poetry, but all within the embrace of his presence, surely. Kabir Helminski recently published a book of traditional Mevlevi prayers. In it a prayer by the 1910 Mevlevi Sheikh recognizes "Our Mevlana and the Mevlana of the gnostics." I take consolation in that phrase. Evidently there have been others down the line who have also heard Rumi's poems outside of any system, in the shared heart, part of no religion and all.

ONE SONG

What is praised is one, so the praise is one too,
many jugs being poured

into a huge basin. All religions, all this singing,
one song.

The differences are just illusion and vanity. Sunlight
looks slightly different

on this wall than it does on that wall and a lot different
on this other one, but

it is still one light. We have borrowed these clothes, these
time-and-space personalities,

from a light, and when we praise, we pour them back in.

THE INDIAN TREE

A learned man once said, for the sake of saying *something*,
"There is a tree

in India. If you eat the fruit of that tree, you'll never grow
old and never die."

Stories about "the tree" were passed around, and finally
a king sent his envoy

to India to look for it. People laughed at the man. They
slapped him on the back

and called out, "Sir, I know where your tree is, but it's far
in the jungle and you'll need

a ladder!" He kept traveling, following such directions and
feeling foolish, for years.

He was about to return to the king when he met a wise man.
"Great teacher, show me

some kindness in this search for the tree." "My son, this is
not an actual tree,

though it's been called that. Sometimes it's called a *sun*,
sometimes an *ocean*, or

a *cloud*. These words point to the wisdom that comes through
a true human being, which

may have many effects, the least of which is eternal life!
In the same way one

person can be a father to you and a son to someone else,
uncle to another and nephew

to yet another, so what you are looking for has many names,
and one existence. Don't

search for one of the names. Move beyond any attachment
to names." Every war

and every conflict between human beings has happened because
of some disagreement about

names. It's such an unnecessary foolishness, because just
beyond the arguing there's a long

table of companionship, set and waiting for us to sit down.

YOUR FACE

You may be planning departure, as a
human soul leaves the world taking

almost all its sweetness with it.
You saddle your horse. You must be

going. Remember you have friends
here as faithful as grass and sky.

Have I failed you? Possibly you're
angry. But remember our nights of

conversation, the well work, yellow
roses by the ocean, the longing, the

archangel Gabriel saying *So be it.*
Shams-i Tabriz, *your face,* is what

every religion tries to remember.

LET THE WAY ITSELF ARRIVE

Desires come, my wishes and longing.
I am tied up, knot on top of knot.

Then you that untie me come. Enough
talk of being on the "path"! Let

the *way* itself arrive. You picked up
a handful of earth; I was in that

handful. I can say the difference
between good and bad, but not how I

know your beauty. Mind refuses to
burn with love. Saladin is central,

yet hidden. The *qutb,* the pole of
love, reaches here to this ground.

There are those who accept the law of Moses and not the
grace and love of Jesus,

like the Jewish king who killed Christians. This is not
seeing right. Moses is

inside the soul of Jesus as Jesus is in the soul of Moses.
One era belonged to one;

then it was the other's turn, but they are one being. A
teacher said to a slightly

cross-eyed student, "Hand me the glass bottle there." "Which
one?" "There are not two."

"Don't scold me, teacher, but I see two." "Smash one of
them." Of course, both

were broken. This is how it is when we see through the
double vision of lust,

anger, or some religious self-interest. A bribed judge
cannot distinguish the one

who's been cruel from the victim. A good prayer is, *Lord,
help us see both worlds as one.*

DEAR SOUL

Dear soul, when the condition comes that we call being
a lover, there's no patience,

and no repenting. Both become huge absurdities. See
regret as a worm and love

as a dragon. Shame, changeable weather. Love, a quality
that wants nothing. For this

kind of lover love of anything or anyone is unreal. Here,
the source and object are one.

FOUR WORDS FOR WHAT WE WANT

A man gives one coin to be spent among four people.
The Persian says, "I want

angur." The Arab says, "*Inab,* you rascal." The Turk,
"*Uzum!*" The Greek,

"Shut up all of you. We'll have *istafil.*" They begin
pushing each other, then

hitting with fists, no stopping it. If a many-languaged
master had been there,

he could have made peace and told them, *I can give each of
you the grapes you want*

*with this one coin. Trust me. Keep quiet, and you four
enemies will agree.*

*I also know a silent inner meaning that makes of your
four words one wine.*

FOUR INTERRUPTED PRAYERS

Four Indians enter a mosque and begin the prostrations.
Deep, sincere praying.

But a priest walks by, and one of the Indians, without
thinking, says, "Oh,

are you going to give the call to prayer now? Is it time?"
The second Indian, under

his breath, "You spoke. Now your prayers are invalid."
The third, "Uncle, don't scold him!

You did the same thing. Correct yourself." The fourth,
"Praise to God, I

have not made the mistake of these three." So all four
prayers are interrupted, with

the three faultfinders being more at fault than the
original speaker. Blessed

is one who sees his weakness, and blessed is one who, when
he sees a flaw in someone

else, takes responsibility for it. *Because,* half of any person
is wrong and weak and off

the path. Half! The other half is dancing and swimming and
flying in the invisible joy. You

have ten open sores on your head. Put what salve you have
on yourself. And point out

to everyone the dis-ease you are. That's part of getting
well! When you lance yourself

that way, you become more merciful and wiser. Even if you
don't have a particular

fault at the moment, you may soon be the one who makes some
act notorious. Don't feel

self-satisfied. Lucifer lived eons as a noble angel. Think
what his name means now.

Don't try to be famous until your face is completely washed
of any fear. If your beard

hasn't grown out, don't joke about someone's smooth chin.
Consider how Satan swallowed

soul poison, and be grateful that you taste only the
sweetness of being warned.

SPIRITUAL WINDOWSHOPPERS

These spiritual windowshoppers, who idly ask, *How much
is that? Oh, I'm just*

looking. They handle a hundred items and put them down,
shadows with no capital.

What is spent is love and two eyes wet with weeping. But
these walk into a shop,

and their whole lives pass suddenly in that moment, in
that shop. Where did you

go? *Nowhere.* What did you have to eat? *Nothing much.*
Even if you don't know what

you want, buy *something* to be part of the general exchange.
Start a huge, foolish project,

like Noah. It makes absolutely no difference what
people think of you.

———————

The clear bead at the center
changes everything. There are

no edges to my loving now.
You've heard it said there's

a window that opens from one
mind to another, but if there's

no wall, there's no need for
fitting the window, or the latch.

6. A Small Dog Trying to Get You to Play: The Lighthearted Path

The clumps go marching two by two, taroo, taroo. This is what I say when I hear my lover coming down the hall, rising, roaming, from her writing desk, to make tea, maybe to entice me to throw the racquetball with her. We have one handy in the pencil glass. Maybe Ping-Pong. The clumps go marching two by two, taroo. Where did *taroo* come from? Some forgotten Irish ballad? A trumpet note? Horns of elfland faintly blowing. It's an apricot picked along the lighthearted way.

One needs a ball to throw. A shawl and a ball. Watch dogs and learn to be ready for the next ploy. In Rumi's view the self is divided into two main parts, the small I (personality) and a vast being (the soul). Their interaction is like when a small dog (the personal self) tries to get you (the eternal soul) to play with it.

Sufis say that love is God's sweetest secret. Gratitude and laughter are key attributes of the love state Rumi celebrates. It is love that hatches out new human awareness, for which everything, each experience, is a street dervish begging a generous response. How would it be to give that to *that?* To meet each moment as though it were prophetic, as though it were Rabia, Shams, or Rinzai. Basho coming along Broad Street on a fall night in Athens, or Rumi. There's the feel of a town in this lovingness, the myriad amble and good humor.

Remember Dante's tremendously poignant placing in limbo of Paolo and Francesca, the lovers who choose the heartbreaking romance of their love over a wider love of life itself. They get their finite choice infinitely extended. That is not the love Rumi says is God's sweetest secret, though it connects to it. All love and desire come from one drawing. You might say that Rumi's love poems from the *Divan* draw us into a morphic field of intention (and attention), where we're held in the annihilation (*fana*) and reabsorption (*baqa*). Science now is beginning to discover the powerful morphic fields that young animals share with ones they imprint upon. We may grow more ready to accept that artists and saints draw us into perception-changing regions and that those regions guide our evolving consciousness.

PICTURES OF THE SOUL

My soul, there is an image of you on
each side of the six-sided mirror cube

we call the universe, but mirrors can
only reveal according to their capacity.

They cannot picture the stages of the
soul's growing. The sun asks the inner

sun, "How can I see you?" *When you set,
I rise,* comes the answer. Intellect

wants to restrain the soul like a camel
with its feet tied, and love longs to

hold the soul's seven levels, but neither
intention is possible. Sometimes in a

harvest circle a single piece of grain
in the cloud of chaff and stems seems

to have legs and wings. That's the size
and effect of mind in the region of soul.

In the ocean once you saw what the soul
is. Since then awe has flooded you.

When soul asks questions, the pleasure
of gold earrings comes to everyone's

ears. Personality is a small dog trying
to get the soul to play. I hear you

call and I'm out walking the road without
legs or feet. What could we do that

might resemble what you do? Days, nights?
We are shade under your tree. Adam left

the spirit world because you are here.
You called. Love is an ocean storm

moving for your touch. To have your
words in this I must stop speaking.

SOUL AND THE OLD WOMAN

What is the soul? Consciousness. The more awareness, the
deeper the soul, and when

such essence overflows, you feel a sacredness around. It's
so simple to tell one who

puts on a robe and pretends to be a dervish from the real
thing. We know the taste

of pure water. Words can sound like a poem but not have
any juice, no flavor to

relish. How long do you look at pictures on a bathhouse
wall? Soul is what draws

you away from those pictures to talk with the old woman
who sits outside by the door

in the sun. She's half blind, but she has what soul loves
to flow into. She's kind; she weeps.

She makes quick personal decisions, and laughs so easily.

THE CORE

Whoever planted this apple orchard hid it in a mist of
language, though some

fragrance comes through. Keep your nose subtle and clear
for that. Coarse companions

can clog you with mucus, so that you forget what's
concealed in word-fog.

Husamuddin's sunlight helps, that which burns in this
book. There is a being

named Quzuh, familiar of cloud and rainbow, snow-moon
and frozen grave mounds.

Leave Quzuh those coverings. Pierce to the core that the
seven blue spheres revolve

around. Venus touches her lute strings to lure out
essence from this poem.

Jupiter lays down money. Saturn, even he, bends to kiss
the hand, "I'm not worthy."

Mars cuts himself sharpening his sword. Astrologers
study the stars as they

die out. Philosophers talk about "thought," but what
does that mean? Mystical

poets make metaphors. Sensualists order dessert. Bread
dissolves in the

belly. Every face lifts toward light. As minerals move
in plants, as animals drink

from the wet grass, Khidr leans to the wisdom spring;
another being sets down his

load lightheartedly with the Friend; life never ends.

Who is Joseph? Your heart that's seeking truth, your
heart now tied up in prison.

They bring you straw off the floor to eat, when you
want nothing but a face-

to-face meeting. Some invitations to leave home are
dangerous. Joseph

left the protection of his father. "It will be exciting,"
said his brothers. Never

leave the Friend for amusement, or money. The treasurer
himself offers to increase

your investment a hundred times, but it involves leaving
a friend of God. *Don't*

do it. Once in a famine year, a few companions of Muhammad
left his side when they

heard a caravan was coming. They wanted to get provisions
before theirs depleted. Never

leave a prophet to buy bread! They were running toward
wheat, away from the giver

of wheat! Trust the friendship more than wealth, or any
satisfaction. One day a

falcon invited a duck to leave the lake and see the high
plateau. The wise duck

said, "Water is my source and fortress, my peace and
joy. Don't tempt me with

where *you* love to be. You have soaring gifts. I love
this low marsh." The duck

stayed in the stronghold where it felt complete. And
you, be patient

where you sit in the dark. The dawn is coming.

PEBBLE *ZIKR*

Abu Jahl has some pebbles in his hand. "Muhammad!
Quick, tell me what I

have hidden in my fist. You say that you're the
messenger of God, who

knows all mysteries. Solve this!" "How do you want
me to do it? By saying

what they are? Or shall they say what I am?" Abu Jahl
is puzzled. "The latter

sounds more interesting." Immediately, from inside the
fist come the voices

of the round stones chanting the *zikr*. *La'illaha il'*
Allah. There is no

reality but God; there is only God. *La'illaha il'Allah*.
Every pebble threads

the pearl. Abu Jahl, the skeptic, throws them down.

FEET BECOMING HEAD

The sun came up differently today.
Souls move in the changing light.

Jupiter, the moon, the good luck
house we inhabit, the Friend, all

one presence today, this grand
health where we're servants to

each other. One who pours wine
and makes toasts arrives at the

banquet just as it's over: the
perfect beginning for ending, as

feet become head in this new way.

7. Thirst: Water's Voice

In the necessity and delight of companionship there's a hint of nearness.

Talking may help with this longing for the Friend. Rumi feels the futility of speech (as a dog howls at the moon, I talk), yet he says that the *Masnavi* is a sublime conversation. In it you can get a taste of a being within that wants to drink the entire Oxus River!

WHAT WE HEAR IN A FRIEND'S VOICE

If you are my soul's friend, what I say won't be just an
assertion. You may hear me

at midnight, *Come out in the dark, and don't be afraid.*
"Nearness" and "kinship" are

assertions, but the sound of a voice is not. The delight a
friend feels when he hears

a friend's voice brings all that matters. There are those
who hear within a voice

the essence being said, and there are those who can't. When
one who grew up speaking

Arabic says in Arabic, "Arabic is my mother tongue," you
know it's true. Or

someone writes in beautiful calligraphy, "I can read and
write." The accomplished

script *is* that. A sufi might say, "Last night you saw me
carrying my prayer rug

on my shoulder. I explained something then about clairvoyance.
Let that guide you." Your

dreaming soul says, "Yes!" Such confirmation is like
your lost camel. You

listen with interest when someone says he saw it, but you feel
differently if it's there

in front of you. To a man dying of thirst you hand a cup of
spring water. Will he demand

a certificate saying, "This liquid is of the aqueous variety"?
Does an infant ask his mother

to validate the breast? When a true human being appears
in a community thirsty for

the taste of soul, they immediately hear in the voice
the meaning of *I am near.*

TALKING AND GOD'S LOVE OF VARIETY

Noah talked for nine hundred years trying to help people
change. They stayed cynical,

but he never quit talking; he never crept into a cave of
silence. He said to himself,

"Does a caravan stop when dogs bark? Everyone has something
to do from his or her

essential nature. The moon crosses the sky, and the dog
howls. I talk."

The motto of this market is, "Everyone sells something
different, because God enjoys

the variety." Fire eats thorns for dessert. Hogs think dung
a delicious sweetbread. Snakes

spew their venom here, while deep on the mountainside the
beehive sweetens. Motes fly

left, right, up and down in the air, part of one natural
movement of the sun. The sap

of a tree branches many directions. It's true what the
Qur'an says, *We are returning.*

Numbers scuffle and fight, though they all derive from zero.
We cannot say what great peace

rains on the wild river. Still we talk, Husam and I. No one
can drink the entire Oxus, but

a taste from the six books of this *Masnavi* may slake
your thirst for a moment.

AMAZED MOUTH

The soul: a wide listening sky
with thousands of candles: when

anything is sold, soul gets given
in the cash: people waiting at a

door, a ladder leaning on a roof,
someone climbing down, the market

square bright with understanding.
Listening opens its amazed mouth.

———

No longer a stranger, you listen
all day to these crazy love words.

Like a bee you fill hundreds of homes with
honey, though yours is a long way from here.

8. The King's Falcon on a Kitchen Shelf: How It Feels to Live Apart from Majesty

There is a state of awareness Rumi calls splendor, or majesty. In that, the connection between creation and creator is wild, fragrant, fresh, and passionately alive in the moment. What life looks like outside of that is felt in the dull satiety of the city of Saba. The lack of energy and the boredom with prophecy are indications that the connection has been severed. Even more poignant is the hunting falcon's absurdly pampered, cramped position in the old woman's kitchen.

THE CITY OF SABA

There is a glut of wealth in the city of Saba. Everyone
has more than enough. Even

the bath stokers wear gold belts. Huge grape clusters hang
down on every street and

brush the faces of the citizens. No one has to do
anything. You can balance

a basket on your head and walk through an orchard, and it
will fill by itself with

overripe fruit dropping into it. Stray dogs stray in
lanes full of thrown-out

scraps with barely a notice. The lean desert wolf gets
indigestion from the rich

food. Everyone is fat and satiated with all the
extra. There are no

robbers. There is no energy for crime, or for gratitude,
and no one wonders about

the unseen world. The people of Saba feel bored with
just the mention of prophecy.

They have no desire of any kind. Maybe some idle curiosity
about miracles, but that's

it. This overrichness is a subtle disease. Those
who have it are blind

to what's wrong and deaf to anyone who points it out.
The city of Saba cannot be

understood from within itself! But there is a cure, an
individual medicine, not

a social remedy: sit quietly, and listen for a voice
within that will say, *Be*

more silent. As that happens, your soul starts to revive.
Give up talking and

your positions of power. Give up the excessive money.
Turn toward teachers and

prophets who don't live in Saba. They can help you
grow sweet again and fragrant

and wild and fresh and thankful for any small event.

THE THIEF

A man hears footsteps in his house during the night. He
reaches for a flint

to spark and make light. But the thief comes and sits behind
him. Whenever the tinder

starts to catch, the thief snuffs it. The man thinks it's
dying by itself. "It must

be moist." Sometimes we do not see what extinguishes our
light, our love.

Something in the dark does it. You may as well say that day
flares and goes out and night

comes on with nothing moving in those changes. Whatever
happens or doesn't, a presence is helping.

THE KING'S FALCON

The king had a noble falcon who wandered away one day,
and into the tent of an

old woman, who was making dumpling stew for her children.
"Who's been taking care

of you?" she asked, quickly tying the falcon's foot. She
clipped his wings and cut

his fierce talons and fed him straw. "Someone who doesn't
know how to treat falcons,"

she answered herself, "but your mother knows!" Friend,
this kind of talk is a prison.

Don't listen. The king spent all day looking for his
falcon, and came at sunset to

that tent and saw his fine raptor standing on a shelf in
the smoky steam of the old

woman's cooking. "You left me for this?" The falcon
rubbed his wings against

the king's hand, feeling wordlessly what was almost lost.
The falcon is like one who,

through grace, gets to sit close to the king, and so thinks
he's on the same level as

the king. Then he turns his head for a moment and he's in
the old woman's tent. Don't

feel *special* in the king's presence. Be mannerly and
thankful and very humble. A

falcon is an image of that part of you that belongs to the
king. Once there was a blind

falcon who fell in with owls in a wilderness. They thought
he wanted to take over the ruin

they were living in. They tore his feathers. "Wait! I
have no interest in this

place. My home is the forearm of the king." The owls
thought this was some kind

of bragging trick to distract them. "No! I don't claim
to be *like* the king. I am

a ragged, blind falcon. All I can do is listen for
the king's drum and

fly to the sound when I hear it. I am not of
the king's species or genus,

but I have taken in some of the king's light, the way
air is swept up into a fire,

the way water becomes plant. My ego has died into
the king's being. I roll in

the dust at the feet of his horse. Don't let this
blind-falcon form fool you.

I am really a delicious dessert that you should taste
now, you owls, before

I hear the drum again, because then I'll be gone."

THE GROUND'S GENEROSITY

Remember: prayer gets accepted no matter how
impure: like that of

a woman in excessive menstruation, her asking dense
with blood, so your praise

is full of blood ties, full of how attached you are.
That tangle of limited

surrender is the human mire. We're sodden in bodiness,
where the clearest sign of

grace is that from dung come flowers, from the bulbous
sludge, buds and then sweet

pears. The ground's generosity takes in our compost
and grows beauty! Try to

be more like the ground. Give back better, as a rough
clod returns an ear of

corn, a tassel, a barley awn, this sleek handful of oats.

SICK OF SCRIPTURE

My head turns around my feet, one
of which is fixed to the ground

like a compass, the other, mad
with the wandering moon and slow-

burning with Mars. Bored, ashamed,
floating in a gold sky, in deep

ecstasy, all secrets told, the son
of a lion is out looking for heart-

blood to drink. You think I'm sick,
so you read the first sura, but

scripture is what I'm sick of.
When Hallaj spoke his truth, they

crucified him for the words. If
Hallaj were here, he'd point them to

me. Unlike this teacher here who
will not bow, I don't wash corpses

or carve markings on stone. The
universe itself recognizes Shams

Tabriz, but not you. I am tired
of being around such blindness.

Thirteen prophets come as a group to the city of Saba,
which has been so blessed

with material wealth. "Where is your gratitude for this?
The one who gives you

your head wants only *one bow*." The Sabaens answer,
"There is no thanksgiving

in us, only weariness with receiving gifts. We're
tired of wonder, tired

of rest, tired of excitement. No more orchards, please,
no more beauty. The gift

of being does not delight us anymore." "But this is the
soul sickness we

cure," say the prophets. "Your death-in-life makes sweet
things bitter and those

who poison you seem like noble friends. Your perception
is jaded. You hear

fresh phrasing that carries truth and you say, 'Clichés.
I've heard all that

before.' When we make you well, you'll hear new
implications in every old

story. Ordinary doctors check the heart by finding a pulse.
We listen without intermediary.

We see from the high belvedere of clairvoyance. Physicians
tend the health of animal

energies, whereas the ray of divine majesty moves through
us with right language and

action. We know what keeps you on the way and what
distracts. Physicians look

at urine samples. We wait for inspiration and ask no
fee, the feel of sacred

ambiance being enough. So bring your malaise, your dullness, your callous

ingratitude. As we meet you, the coming together itself will be medicine. *We*

are the cure, the look that opens your looking."

9. Witness: Stay at the Flame's Core

The manifest world moves by, held in the witness, stars reflecting in the night creek. There is a natural motion to the way of love, as well as the passionate still points. The mystery of the witness is that there's no *experience* involved, nor anything one does or feels, just the background of a quiet, interstellar absence.

THE CREEK AND THE STARS

Spirit is so mixed with the visible world that giver,
gift, and beneficiary are

one thing. You *are* the grace raining down; the grace
is you. Creation is

a clear, flat, fast-moving creek, where qualities reflect.
Generations rush by, while

the stars stay still without a splash. When you lose your
appetite for food, you'll

be given other nourishment. There's well-being that is not
bodily and beings

that live on fragrance. Don't worry about losing animal
energy. Go the way of love

and ask provisions. Love more the star region reflected,
less the moving medium.

NIGHT THIEVES

There was a king roaming his country at night. He met
up with a band of thieves.

"Who are you?" they asked. "I am one of you." So they
walked together, and each

spoke of the special skill that suited him for this
night work. One said,

"My genius is in my ears. I can understand what a dog
says when it barks." The

others laughed, "Not much value in that!" Another thief
said, "My specialty is in

my eyes. Whatever I see by night, I can recognize in
daylight." Another,

"My strength is in my arm. I can tunnel through any wall!"
Another, "My nose. I sniff

the ground to find where treasure is hidden." And the last
thief revealed, "It's my hand.

I can throw a lasso around anything." Then they asked the
king-in-disguise what his

contribution was. "It's this beard. Whenever I turn it
toward criminals, they are freed."

"Oh-ho! You *are* a good one to have with us." So they
continued on, as it

happened, toward the palace. A watchdog barked, and the
listener thief interpreted,

"He's saying, *The king is with us!*" The sniffer thief
smelled the ground. "This is

prime land." The lassoer quickly threw a rope over the
wall. The tunneler tunneled

into the treasury, and they loaded up with gold embroidery
and huge pearls. The king

watched, and slipped quietly away. The next day the robbery
was discovered; the king sent

his guards to make arrests. As the thieves were brought in,
the one who could recognize

night things by day said, "This is the friend who
went with us last night,

the beard man!" That night-and-day man was a mystic.
He understood what

had happened. "This king embodies the text that says,
And He is with you.

He knows our secrets. He played our game with us.
The king is the witness;

in his clear truthfulness is the grace we need."

INSHALLAH

Some people work and become wealthy. Others do the same and
remain poor. Marriage

fills one with energy. Another it drains. Don't trust ways.
They change. A means

flails about like a donkey's tail. Always add the gratitude
clause, *if God wills.* Then

proceed. You may be leading a donkey, no, a goat, no, who can
tell? We sit in a dark pit

and think we're home. We pass around delicacies. Poisoned
bait. You think this

is preachy double-talk? Those who do not breathe the *God
willing* phrase live in a

collective blindness. Rubbing their eyes in the dark,
they ask, "Who's there?"

THINKING AND THE HEART'S MYSTICAL WAY

A peaceful face twists with the poisonous nail of thinking.
A golden spade sinks into

a pile of dung. Suppose you loosen an intellectual knot.
The sack is empty. You've grown

old trying to untie such tightenings, so loosen a few more,
why knot! There is a big one

fastened at your throat, the problem of whether you're in
harmony with that which has

no definition. Solve that! You examine substance and
accidents. You waste

your life making subject and verb agree. You edit hearsay.
You study artifacts and think

you know the maker, so proud of having figured the derivation.
Like a scientist you collect

data and put facts together to come to some conclusion.
Mystics arrive at what they

know differently: they lay a head upon a person's chest
and drift into the answer.

Thinking gives off smoke to prove the existence of fire. A
mystic sits inside the burning.

There are wonderful shapes in rising smoke that imagination
loves to watch. But it's

a mistake to leave the fire for that filmy sight. Stay
here at the flame's core.

PARADOX

Paradoxes: best wakefulness in sleep, wealth in having
nothing, a pearl necklace

fastened around an iron collar. Fire contained in boiling
water. Revenues growing from

funds flowing *out*. Giving is gainful employment. It brings in
money. Taking time for

ritual prayer and meditation saves time. Sweet fruit hide in
leaves. Dung becomes food

for the ground and generative power in trees. Nonexistence
contains existence. Love

encloses beauty. Brown flint and gray steel have orange
candlelight in them. Inside

fear, safety. In the black pupil of the eye, many
brilliancies. Inside

the body-cow, a handsome prince.

EMPTY BOAT

Some huge work goes on growing. How
could one person's words matter? Where

you walk heads pop from the ground. What
is one seed head compared to you? On

my death day I'll know the answer. I have
cleared this house, so that your work can,

when it comes, fill every room. I slide
like an empty boat pulled over the water.

WHEREABOUTS UNKNOWN

Every moment a taste of that beauty
in our mouths, another stashed in

a pocket. Impossible to say what:
no cypress so handsome, no sunlight,

a lonely hiddenness. Other pleasure
gathers a crowd, starts a fight, lots

of noise there. But soul beauty
stays quiet: Shams and his amazing

whereabouts unknown inside my heart.

THE LEVEL OF WORDS

God has said, "The images that come with human language
do not correspond to me,

but those who love words must use them to come near."
Just remember, it's

like saying of the king, "He is not a weaver." Is that
praise? Whatever such

a statement is, words are on *that* level of God-knowing.

TO THE EXTENT THEY CAN DIE

A Chinese mirror shows all sides
of a human being. That's for you.

Someone born deaf has no more use
for high notes than newborn babies

for a fine merlot. What would a
land bird be doing out over open

sea? We are rinds thrown out by
the tavern of absolute absence,

unconcerned about profits or dowry,
or what to wear. We are a hundred

thousand years beyond insanity.
Plato does not speak of this.

The physical beauty of men and
women is not an image here. Lovers

are alive to the extent they can
die. A great soul approaches

Shams. *What are you doing here?*
Answer: *What is there to do?*

10. *Soul Joy: You Feel a River Moving in You*

"Everything is soul and flowering" ("Roses Underfoot"). This is the ease of living one's truth. Here it finds the image of a river constantly regenerating the landscape it moves through with new stories and poems, the movements of a human life enjoying the soul: living pieces as they fit together.

Movement unlocks new blessings, a forty-five-minute walk, the lovely errands of the day, to the post office, deli, gas station, grandchildren, grave. Some see a mysterious pattern emerging. I feel it more than see it.

MOVING WATER

When you do things from your soul, you feel a river
moving in you, a joy.

When actions come from another section, the feeling
disappears. Don't let

others lead you. They may be blind or, worse, vultures.
Reach for the rope

of God. And what is that? Putting aside self-will.
Because of willfulness

people sit in jail, the trapped bird's wings are tied,
fish sizzle in the skillet.

The anger of police is willfulness. You've seen a magistrate
inflict visible punishment. Now

see the invisible. If you could leave your selfishness, you
would see how you've

been torturing your soul. We are born and live inside
black water in a well.

How could we know what an open field of sunlight is? Don't
insist on going where

you think you want to go. *Ask* the way to the spring. Your
living pieces will form

a harmony. There is a moving palace that floats in the air
with balconies and clear

water flowing through, infinity everywhere, yet contained
under a single tent.

UNCLE OF THE JAR

Some talk of cup and jar and river,
and how they depend on each other.

What flows in the river fills the jar,
but only a potter knows the state

of the cup. One drinks from the
other. We know what was in what by

the residue. Some naive people
haven't gotten close enough to smell

the musk, so they cannot judge. But
still they do, and others repeat the

their lack of knowledge. What shall
we call that? Another time fragrance

from a jar drives thousands of Turks
mad, and Hindus too, or a witch rides

the jar town to town witch-laughing
at the jarless witches! It's best

to follow some fragrance you catch
on your own, alone. Let that take

you to the face of someone who's
escaped from jars and cups. You've

heard the old saying among drunks,
"I'm the uncle of the jar." Find one

like that and sit down beside him.
There'll be no inexperienced gossip,

no words at all maybe. A silence
resides in an empty jar, as fragrance,

as a river in spring flood. That's
the jar you've been looking for.

WHEN WORDS ARE TINGED WITH LYING

Muhammad gave this indication of how to know what's
real. "When you feel

a peaceful joy, you're near the truth. Unquiet and
off center, jealous or

greedy, what you do seems pretentious and those around
you insincere. Speak

the clearest truth you know, and let the dis-ease heal."
If words are tinged with

lying, they're like water dripping into an oil lamp. The
wick won't light, and

the pleasure and rest of your love room will diminish.

———

Joy moves always to new locations,
the ease of its flow never freezing.

A long winter's tale is over. Now
with each spring day a new story.

THE SOURCE OF JOY

No one knows what makes the soul wake
up so happy! Maybe a dawn breeze has

blown the veil from the face of God.
A thousand new moons appear. Roses

open laughing. Hearts become perfect
rubies like those from Badakshan. The

body turns entirely spirit. Leaves
become branches in this wind. Why is

it now so easy to surrender, even for
those already surrendered? There's no

answer to any of this. No one knows
the source of joy. A poet breathes

into a reed flute, and the tip of
every hair makes music. Shams sails

down clods of dirt from the roof, and
we take jobs as doorkeepers for him.

———

A road might end at a single house,
but it's not love's road.

Love is a river.
Drink from it.

———

Rise. Move around the center
as pilgrims wind the Kaaba.

Being still is how one clay clod
sticks to another in sleep,

while movement wakes us up
and unlocks new blessings.

A STORY THEY KNOW

It's time for us to join the line of your
madmen all chained together. Time to be

totally free, and estranged. Time to give
up our souls, to set fire to structures and

run out in the street. Time to ferment. How
else can we leave the world-vat and go to

the lip? We must die to become true human
beings. We must turn completely upside down

like a comb in the top of a beautiful woman's
hair. Spread out your wings as a tree lifts

in the orchard. As seed scattered on the
road, as a stone melts to wax, as a candle

becomes the moth. On a chessboard the king
is blessed again with his queen. With our

faces so close to the love mirror, we must
not breathe, but change to a cleared place

where a building was and feel the treasure
hiding inside us. With no beginning or end we

live in lovers as a story they know. If you
will be the key, we'll be tumblers in the lock.

ROSES UNDERFOOT

The sound of salaams rising as
waves diminish down in prayer,

hoping for some trace of the one
whose trace does not appear. If

anyone asks you to say who you
are, say without hesitation,

soul within soul within soul.
There's a pearl diver who does

not know how to swim! No matter.
Pearls are handed him on the

beach. We lovers laugh to hear,
"This should be more that and

that more this," coming from
people sitting in a wagon tilted

in a ditch. Going in search of
the heart, I found a huge rose

under my feet, and roses under
all our feet! How to say this

to someone who denies it? The
robe we wear is the sky's cloth.

Everything is soul and flowering.

———

I open and fill with love and
other objects evaporate. All

the learning in books stays put
on the shelf. Poetry, the dear

words and images of song, comes
down over me like mountain water.

———

Any cup I hold fills with wine
that lovers drink. Every word

I say opens into mystery. Any
way I turn I see brilliance.

11. *Turning the Refuse of Damascus:*
Work with the One Who Keeps Time

Self-forgiveness finds in these poems a superb working image: turning garbage over in the streets of Damascus, letting the wet underlife open to the sun. That turning over the shadow side to light and air starts new processes going. Make a mistake, look up, *checkmate:* accepting the troubles we've been given brings fortunate consequences.

Rumi loves to see the personal self in ruins; the absence of air that allows pickax work to be done. The treasure of deep being is buried under the rubble of personality. I think of Wordsworth walking through the remains of Tintern Abbey, though he had little to say of the scraps of stonework and no digging was done. He felt a *motion* rolling through. I like to walk the ruins of old mills near where I live along the Oconee River. They date from before the turn of the last century. Big trees grow in the millrace and in the roofless mill buildings. One could say mystical poetry walks the ruins of its dervishes looking for likely spots to dig.

Something in the psyche loves the wreckage of human effort and how the natural world cleans up the fire damage and redecorates. The brick cistern that served as a water tank is now dry above the Princeton mill. I climb down in it, and would make a writing studio of it if I could. Ideas for poems come thick to my spiral notebook there. That's the Wordsworthian motion I worship, listening for the spirit's telling.

It's beyond judgment, beyond betrayal and trust, the truth Rumi can only *live,* and not say.

MASHALLAH

There's someone swaying by your
side, lips that say, *Mashallah*,

Mashallah. Wonderful, God inside
attraction; a spring no one knew

of wells up on the valley floor.
Lights inside a tent lovers move

toward. The refuse of Damascus
gets turned over in the sun: be

like that yourself. Say *mercy*,
mercy to the one who guides your

soul, who keeps time. Move, make
a mistake, look up. *Checkmate*.

CLEANSING CONFLICT

What is a saint? One whose wine has turned to vinegar.
If you're still wine-drunkenly

brave, don't step forward. When your sheep becomes a lion,
then come. It is said

of hypocrites, "They have considerable valor among themselves!"
But they scatter when

a real enemy appears. Muhammad told his young soldiers, "There
is no courage *before*

an engagement." A drunk foams at the mouth *talking* about what
he will do when he gets his sword

drawn, but the chance arrives, and he remains sheathed as
an onion. Premeditating,

he's eager for wounds. Then his bag gets touched by a needle,
and he deflates. What sort of

person says that he or she wants to be *polished* and *pure*,
then complains about being

handled roughly? Love is a lawsuit where harsh evidence *must*
be brought in. To settle

the case, the judge must *see* evidence. You've heard that every
buried treasure has a snake

guarding it. Kiss the snake to discover the treasure! The
severe treatment is not toward

you, but the qualities that block your growth. A rug beater
doesn't beat the rug, but

rather the dirt. A horse trainer switches not the horse, but
the going wrong. Imprison

your mash in a dark vat, so it can become wine. Someone
asks, "Don't you worry

about God's wrath when you spank your child?" "I'm not
spanking my child, but the demon

in him." When a mother screams, "Get out of here!" she means
the *mean* part of the child.

Don't run from those who scold, and don't turn away from
cleansing conflict, or you will

remain weak. Also, don't listen to bragging. If you go along
with self-importance, the work

collapses. Better a small *modest* team. Sift almonds. Discard
the bitter. Sour and sweet

sound alike when you pour them out on the rattling tray, but
inside they're very different.

SHADOW AND LIGHT SOURCE BOTH

How does a part of the world leave the world?
How does wetness leave water? Don't try to

put out a fire by throwing on more fire! Don't
wash a wound with blood. No matter how fast

you run, your shadow keeps up. Sometimes it's
in front! Only full overhead sun diminishes

your shadow. But that shadow has been serving
you. What hurts you, blesses you. Darkness is

your candle. Your boundaries are your quest.
I could explain this, but it will break the

glass cover on your heart, and there's no
fixing that. You must have shadow and light

source both. Listen, and lay your head under
the tree of awe. When from that tree feathers

and wings sprout on you, be quieter than
a dove. Don't open your mouth for even a *coo*.

WEALTH WITHOUT WORKING

In the time of David there was a man who used to pray
out loud, "Lord, give me

wealth without working! You created me lazy and slow, so
let me have my daily bread

by being just that. Pay me for sleeping in the shade!
It's your shade. Give

me sudden riches with no fatigue on my part. Let this
prayer be all that I do."

He prayed this way before a wise teacher, or in front
of the town simpleton.

It made no difference who was listening. He prayed day
and night, every day.

People laughed at him, of course. "This weak-bearded
idiot!" "Did someone

give him hashish?" "Livelihood comes with effort, but
this guy says, 'I will

climb up into the sky without a ladder.'" "Oh, please
sit. The messenger has

come with the news you've been waiting for." "Could
I have a little part of

what you get from this prayer?" So it went. But nothing
made him stop. He became

famous for being the one who keeps looking for cheese in
an empty food pouch. He was

a living proverb on foolishness. Then one morning, suddenly,
a large cow walked into his

house. With her horns she broke the lock and butted the
bolt back and came in!

The man quit praying. He bound the cow's legs, cut her
throat, and ran to get

the butcher. There was enough food and leather for a long
time! Do that for me,

you who make demands like an embryo growing inside. Help
me with this long poem! You

ask for gold. First, give me gold in secret. All these
images and words have to come

from you. Everyone and everything, every action glorifies
you, but sometimes the way

one does it is not recognized by another. Human beings
rarely understand how inanimate

objects are praising, the walls and the doors and the rocks,
those masters of

glorification! We squabble over the doctrines of the Sunnis
and the Jabris, their

seventy-two interpretations. It never ends. But we don't
hear the inanimate ones

speaking to each other, and to us! How do we listen to
what doesn't speak? Only

with the help of one whose love opens into the mystery of
the spirit's telling.

LOVE FOR CERTAIN WORK

Traveling is as refreshing for some as staying at home
is for others. Solitude

in a mountain place fills with companionship for this
one, dead-weariness

for that one. This person loves being in charge of the
working of a community. This

one loves the ways that heated iron can be shaped with
a hammer. Each has been

given a strong desire for certain work, *love* for those
motions, and all motion

is love. The way sticks and pieces of dead grass and
leaves shift about in

the wind and with the directions of rain and puddle water
on the ground, those

motions are following the love they've been given.

THE HOOPOE'S TALENT

Whenever a pavilion is pitched in the countryside for
Solomon, the birds come

to pay respects and talk with him. Solomon understands
bird language.

There is no confused twittering in his presence. Each
species speaks its call

distinctly. Being understood is such a joy! When a
person is with people

he or she cannot confide in, it's like being tied up.
And I don't mean a cultural

kinship. There are Indians and Turks who speak the same
language, and there are Turks

who do not understand each other. I'm talking of those
who are inside the one love

together. So, the birds are asking Solomon questions and
telling him their special

talents. They all hope that they will be asked to stay in
Solomon's presence. It comes

the turn of the hoopoe. "My king, I have only one talent,
but I hope it will be useful

to you." "Say it." "When I fly to the highest point of
my ability and look down,

I can see through the earth to the water table. I can see
whether it's muddy with clay,

or clear, running through stone. I can see where the springs
are, and where good wells

may be dug." Solomon replies, "You will make a fine companion
for my expeditions into

the wilderness!" The jealous crow cannot stand it. He
yells out, "If hoopoe

has such keen eyesight, why didn't she see the snare that
caught her once?" "Good

question," says Solomon. "What about this, hoopoe?" "My
water-seeing talent is a

true one. And it's also true that I have been blind to
things that have trapped

me. There is a will beyond my knowing that causes both
my blindness and my

clairvoyance. Crow doesn't acknowledge that."

When school and mosque and minaret
get torn down, then dervishes can

begin their community. Not until
faithfulness turns to betrayal and

betrayal into trust can any human
being become part of the truth.

Not until a person dissolves, can
he or she know what union is.

There is a descent into emptiness.
A lie will not change to truth

with just talking about it.

While you are still yourself,
you're blind to both worlds.

That ego-drunkenness will not
let you see. Only when you are

cleansed of both, will you cut
the deep roots of fear and anger.

12. Grief Song, Praise Song:
Peacefulness with Death

We are here to be a forgiveness door through which freedom comes. I weep when I ask that the door not be shut. Forgiveness loves to flow. Songs that come in grief release a great praising through the chest. An arrow flies from the bow; the bow trembles and sobs.

ON THE DAY I DIE

On the day I die, when I'm being carried
toward the grave, don't weep. Don't say,

He's gone! He's gone. Death has nothing
to do with going away. The sun sets and

the moon sets, but they're not gone.
Death is a coming together. The tomb

looks like a prison, but it's really
release into union. The human seed goes

down in the ground like a bucket into
the well where Joseph is. It grows and

comes up full of some unimagined beauty.
Your mouth closes here and immediately

opens with a shout of joy there.

One who does what the Friend wants done
will never need a friend.

There's a bankruptcy that's pure gain.
The moon stays bright when it
doesn't avoid the night.

A rose's rarest essence
lives in the thorn.

Childhood, youth, and maturity,
and now old age.

Every guest agrees to stay
three days, no more.

Master, you told me to
remind you. Time to go.

The angel of death arrives,
and I spring joyfully up.

No one knows what comes over me
when I and that messenger speak!

When you come back inside my chest,
no matter how far I've wandered off,
I look around and see the way.

At the end of my life, with just one breath
left, if you come then, I'll sit up and sing.

○

Last night things flowed between us
that cannot now be said or written.

Only as I'm being carried out
and down the road, as the folds
of my shroud open in the wind,

will anyone be able to read, as on
the petal-pages of a turning bud,
what passed through us last night.

○

I placed one foot on the wide plain
of death, and some grand
immensity sounded on the emptiness.

I have felt nothing ever
like the wild wonder of that moment.

○

Longing is the core of mystery.
Longing itself brings the cure.
The only rule is, *Suffer the pain.*

Your desire must be disciplined,
and what you want to happen
in time, sacrificed.

TIME TO SACRIFICE TAURUS

This is the night of union when the stars
scatter their rice over us. The sky is

excited! Venus cannot stop singing the
little songs she's making up, like birds

in the first warm spring weather. The
North Star can't quit looking over at Leo.

Pisces is stirring milky dust from the
ocean floor. Jupiter rides his horse near

Saturn, "Old man, jump up behind me! The
juice is coming back! Think of something

happy to shout as we go." Mars washes
his bloody sword, puts it up, and begins

building things. The Aquarian water jar
fills, and the Virgin pours it generously.

The Pleiades and Libra and Aries have no
trembling in them anymore. Scorpio walks

out looking for a lover, and so does
Sagittarius! This is not crooked walking

like the Crab. This is a holiday we've
been waiting for. It is finally time to

sacrifice Taurus and learn how the sky is
a lens to look through. Listen to what's

inside what I say. Shams will appear at
dawn; then even night will change from

its beloved animated darkness to a day
within this ordinary sweet daylight.

A great sheikh has lost two sons, yet he is not
weeping. His family

and his wife wonder at this lack of grief. "Do not
think that I am cold

and uncompassionate. I don't weep because for me
they are not gone. The eye

of my heart sees them distinctly. They're outside of
time but very close by here

playing and coming to hug me. As people sometimes see dead
relatives in dream, I see

my sons constantly in this waking state. I am even more
deeply with them when I hide

for a moment from the world, when I let the sense-perception
leaves drop from the tree

of my being. I weep for those who have ungrateful souls.
I weep when boys throw stones

at dogs. I weep for dogs who bite for no reason. Forgive
the harm that anyone does.

We are here to be a forgiveness door through which freedom
comes. I weep when I ask

that the door not be shut." Some attend to individual
mercies and some to universal

grace. Try to let them merge. Pond water eventually arrives
at the ocean. One saint works

and lingers in the lakes of personal life. Another plays
without limits in the sea.

WHAT'S INSIDE THE GROUND

Whatever gives pleasure is the fragrance
of the Friend. Whatever makes us wonder

comes from that light. What's inside the
ground begins to sprout because you spilled

wine there. What dies in autumn comes up
in spring because this way of saying *no*

becomes in spring your praise song *yes*.

A BRIGHTENING FLOOR

There is a soul spring that adds to
everyone's awareness. A Friend who

brings peace and healing silence to
death. I work for the kindness that

touches stone and pearl the same,
that sees a garden peacock equal with

the road raven. Form dissolves, but
wisdom remains. Your soul and your

loving mix with the mud of your body,
but they have their pleasures apart.

Shams steps into the room bringing
blessings—a brightening floor

and a star decorating the roof.

THE DEATH OF SALADIN

You left ground and sky weeping, mind
and soul full of grief. No one can

take your place in existence or in
absence. Both mourn, the angels, the

prophets, and this sadness I feel has
taken from me the taste of language,

so that I can't say the flavor of my
being apart. The roof of the *kingdom*

within has collapsed! When I say the
word *you*, I mean a hundred universes.

Pouring grief water, or secret dripping
in the heart, eyes in the head or eyes

of the soul, I saw yesterday that all
these flow out to find you when you're

not here. That bright fire bird Saladin
went like an arrow, and now the bow

trembles and sobs. If you know how to
weep for human beings, weep for Saladin.

13. At the Outermost Extension of Empire: Diving into Qualities

Where is it one lives when form is not primary? Not in the boat, but in waves against the boat. Not in gold, but in the refining fire. Alexander gets to the end of his outer ambition, India, the edge of empire, and turns back inside to friendship with the naked, utterly relaxed philosopher Diogenes.

The refuge given by the wind is the helplessness at the core of prayer. Such surrender does not mean giving away one's power.

In these introductions I try to listen to what Rumi says in the poems and paraphrase the wisdom. The spiritual information being transmitted, though, can only filter through my own experience. No doubt I miss a lot. It's good to have many translators wandering the mountain range of Rumi's poetry, the ocean floor.

QUALITIES

There is a sun-star rising outside form.
I am lost in that other. It's sweet not

to look at two worlds, to melt in meaning
as honey melts in milk. No one tires of

following the soul. I don't recall now what
happens on the manifest plane. I stroll

with those I have always wanted to know,
fresh and graceful as a water lily, or a rose.

The body is a boat; I am waves swaying against
it. Whenever it anchors somewhere, I smash

it loose, or smash it to pieces. If I get
lazy and cold, flames come from my ocean and

surround me. I laugh inside them like gold
purifying itself. A certain melody makes

the snake put his head down on a line in
the dirt. . . . *Here is my head, brother: What*

next! Weary of form, I come into qualities.
Each says, "I am a blue-green sea. Dive

into me!" I am Alexander at the outermost
extension of empire, turning all my armies

in toward the meaning of armies, Shams.

WOODEN CAGES

I may be clapping my hands, but I don't
belong to a crowd of clappers. Neither

this nor that, I'm not part of a group
that loves flute music or one that loves

gambling or drinking wine. Those who
live in time, descended from Adam, made

of earth and water, I'm not part of that.
Don't listen to what I say, as though

these words came from an inside and went
to an outside. Your faces are very

beautiful, but they are wooden cages.
You had better run from me. My words

are fire. I have nothing to do with
being famous, or making grand judgments,

or feeling full of shame. I borrow
nothing. I don't want anything from

anybody. I flow through human beings.
Love is my only companion. When union

happens, my speech goes inside toward
Shams. At that meeting all the secrets

of language will no longer be secret.

PRAYER IS AN EGG

On Resurrection Day God will say, "What did you do with
the strength and energy

your food gave you on earth? How did you use your eyes?
What did you make with

your five senses while they were dimming and playing out?
I gave you hands and feet

as tools for preparing the ground for planting. Did you,
in the health I gave,

do the plowing?" You will not be able to stand when you
hear those questions. You

will bend double, and finally acknowledge the glory. God
will say, "Lift

your head and answer the questions." Your head will rise
a little, then slump

again. "Look at me! Tell what you've done." You try,
but you fall back flat

as a snake. "I want every detail. Say!" Eventually you
will be able to get to

a sitting position. "Be plain and clear. I have given you
such gifts. What did

you do with them?" You turn to the right looking to the
prophets for help, as

though to say, *I am stuck in the mud of my life. Help me
out of this!* They

will answer, those kings, "The time for helping is past.
The plow stands there in

the field. You should have used it." Then you turn to
the left, where your family

is, and they will say, "Don't look at us! This conversation
is between you and your

creator." Then you pray the prayer that is the essence
of every ritual: *God,*

I have no hope. I am torn to shreds. You are my first and
last and only refuge.

Don't do daily prayers like a bird pecking, moving its head
up and down. Prayer is an egg.

Hatch out the total helplessness inside.

14. Mutakallim: *Speaking with a Group*

There's an incident told in Rumi's *Discourses* at the beginning of #10 that I keep returning to for what it's trying to show. A government official, the Amir, comes to visit Rumi's father, Bahauddin. Bahauddin tells him he should not have gone to such trouble. "I am subject to various states," he continues. "In one state I can speak and in another I do not speak. In one state I can listen to the stories of other lives and respond to them. In another I withdraw to my room and see no one. In yet another I am utterly distraught, absorbed in God, unable to communicate at all. It's too risky for you to come here on the chance I might be amiable and able to have conversation."

I love the assumption that Bahauddin is not in control of those *states*. They wash over like weather. In his surrendered life, if the inner weather is right, he can come out and give counsel, attend to questions, and do some good for his friends. Otherwise, it's close the door. He's on retreat with his outrageously imperious soul. This has seemed to me justified behavior in a soul-making artist. Picasso, Georgia O'Keefe, Coleridge, van Gogh, Beethoven. Don't interrupt their inspired solitudes.

> Beware! beware!
> His flashing eyes, his floating hair!
> Weave a circle round him thrice.
>
> Samuel Taylor Coleridge, "Kubla Khan"

And should this not also be true for ordinary mystics? No more scheduled *on* times, no office hours. Let students come if and when and however. The improvisational pianist Keith Jarrett, no ordinary mystic, once, after a few tentative noodlings, stood up from the piano, walked to the front of the stage, and said, "Sometimes these events just don't work out."

Anyone who has taught classes knows that one of the most vital *gestures* in the universe is how energy (Rumi calls it the *presence*) circulates, palpitates, evaporates, and reconstitutes, moving through a class on a certain day, around the edges of a group, in the memory. There is no describing these prolonged and intricate motions (that's why class evaluations are so absurd), but Rumi finds many images for the dynamic. He calls it an

electrical, thunderstorming, conductoring *presence*. He says it looks some-
times like a picture-making quill tip, a candle lighting a face; other times,
a flute note, a book opening or being shut, a catch, a blink.

Mutakallim is thought of as one of the names of God. It means "What
speaks through us."

EVIDENCE

Evidence of the presence: eight
times we feel it going out from

behind the veil, catching outsiders,
then back within, confusing even

those with no mind: open book,
awareness dispersed, shut: shiver

of change: picture-making quill
tip, a note from an empty flute,

face that lights a candle. Some
sleep; others lie awake. The

Friend gets up in the early dawn
and goes outdoors. The light-form

of our teacher leaves, but the
glisten of his courage remains.

TWO DONKEYS

Friend, there's a sweetness to the moon's
one pearl, but consider the ocean it

grew in, and the soul's great turning
wheel. Grafitti people on bathhouse walls

have intelligent origins, but think who
drew the mind! It takes know-how to make

oil from suet. These suet-jelly eyes we
see with were also skillfully devised.

It's dawn, and yet this community still sits
amazed with the night. There's a donkey

who likes to be fed barley with other
donkeys, and there's a donkey who loves

the changes that happen in the soul. Now
silence lets the one behind your eyes talk.

THE INDIAN PARROT

A merchant setting out for India asks each servant what
he or she wants to be brought

as a gift. Each says a different exotic object: a piece
of silk, a brass figurine, a

pearl necklace. Then he asks his beautiful caged parrot,
the one with such a lovely

voice. She says, "When you see the Indian parrots, describe
my cage. Say that I need

guidance here in my separation from them. Ask how our
friendship can continue with

me so confined and them flying freely in the meadow mist.
Tell them I remember our

mornings moving together from tree to tree. Tell them to
drink one cup of ecstatic

wine in honor of me here in the dregs of my life. Tell them
that the sound of their

quarreling high in the trees would be sweeter to hear than any
music." This parrot is

the soul-bird in all of us, the part that wants to return to
freedom, and *is* the freedom.

What she wants to be brought from India is herself! So this
parrot gives her message to

the merchant, and when he reaches India, he sees a field full
of parrots. He stops and

calls out what she told him. One of the nearest birds
shivers and stiffens and falls

down dead. The merchant says, "This one is surely kin to my
parrot. I shouldn't have spoken."

He finishes his trading and returns home with the presents
for his workers. When he

gets to the parrot, she demands her gift. "What happened when
you told my story to the Indian

parrots?" "I'm afraid to say." "Master, you must!" "When I
spoke your complaint to

the field of parrots, it broke one of their hearts. She must
have been a close companion,

or a relative, for when she heard about you, she grew quiet
and trembled, and died." As

the caged parrot hears this, she herself quivers and sinks to
the cage floor. The merchant

is a good man. He grieves deeply for his parrot, murmuring
distracted phrases, contradictory—

cold, then loving—clear, then murky with symbolism. A
drowning man reaches for

anything. The Friend loves this flailing about better than
any lying still. The one

who lives inside existence stays constantly in motion, and
whatever you do, that

king watches through the window. When the merchant throws
the dead parrot out of the cage,

it spreads its wings and glides to a nearby tree! The merchant
suddenly understands the mystery.

"Sweet singer, my message taught you this trick!" "She told me
that it was the charm of

my voice that kept me caged. *Give it up and be released!"*
The parrot taught the merchant

one or two more spiritual truths, then a tender good-bye.
"God protect you," says the merchant,

"as you go on your new way. I hope to follow you."

15. Living as Evidence: The Way from Wanting to Longing

There are border stations on the journey from desire to love and compassion. There is a wind that quickens fire, then blows it out. Wanting is the fire. Learn to be wind instead. All day the sun creates shadow as it moves.

I PASS BY THE DOOR

My face and hair age and gray
with being apart from the one

who whispers in my ear, *Don't
listen.* To my eyes, *Don't look.*

With our grief shoes tied by
happy hands, we keep reaching

for big rocks to save us from
sinking! I pass by the door

where the source of my loving
lives and see how it is: face

wild, shirt torn, no sense of
right or left. *How can I help?*

Then begins a moaning for the
one already there in the room!

BORDER STATIONS

We make heads into feet, we enter
and cross the river, we sic armies

into a fight, then jump out of the
world: we sit on love's horse and

fly, we break through form, human
definitions scattered behind us on

the road: the first stage, a blood
swamp, our red feet slogging, then

the border station where Majnun and
Layla live. Horses nervous. Then

the self with its legendary wealth.
That left, we're walking a beach

crunching pearls with every step.
Now soul is flying straight like a

moth to the candle flame of Shams-i
Tabriz. We were always heading here.

WIND THAT MIXES IN YOUR FIRE

I see myself as a thorn: I move near
the rose. As vineyard, I remember the

vintner's skill. As a cup of poison,
I long to be the antidote. I am a

glass of wine with dark sediment: I
pour it all in the river. I'm sick:

I reach for Jesus' hand. Immature, I
look for one who knows. Out of the

ground a poem grows eye medicine. Now
love says to me, "Good, but you can't

see *your own* beauty. I am the wind
that mixes in your fire, who stirs and

brightens, then makes you gutter out."

THE DIFFERENT MOON SHAPES

In this river the soul is a waterwheel
that no matter how it's facing, water

pours through, turning, returning to
the river. Even if you put your side

or your back to the river, water still
comes through. A shadow cannot ignore

the sun that all day creates and moves
it! The soul lives like a mercury drop

in the palm of a palsied man. Or say
the soul is the moon that every thirty

nights has two so empty, in union, that
it disappears. The other twenty-eight

it endures separation, wretched but
laughing. Laughter is the lovers'

way. They live and die tickled, and
always fresh-faced, knowing the return

that's coming. Don't question this!
The answers and then more questions in

response will cause your eyes to see
wrongly. Live the laughing silence.

HUSAM

There is a way of passing away from the personal, a dying
that makes one plural. A

gnat lights in buttermilk to become nourishment for many.
Your soul is like that, Husam.

Hundreds of thousands of impressions from the invisible
world are eagerly wanting

to come through you! I get dizzy with the abundance. When
life is this dear, it

means the source is pulling us. Freshness comes from there.
We're given the gift of

continuously dying and being resurrected, ocean within ocean.
The body's death now to me

is like going to sleep. No fear of drowning, I'm in another
water. Stones don't dissolve

in rain. This is the end of the fifth book of the *Masnavi*.
With constellations in the night sky,

some look up and point. Others can be guided by the
arrangements: the Sagittarian

bow piercing enemies, the Water Jar soaking fruit trees, the
Bull plowing and sowing its

truth, the Lion tearing darkness open to red satin. Use
these words to change. Be kind

and honest, and harmful poisons will turn sweet inside you.

16. Garnet Red: In the Madhouse Gnawing on Chains

I am grateful that I never taught Rumi's poetry in a university classroom. I am retired now from the making of stand-up sense. If I had ever taught Rumi to classes, I might have felt compelled to place his poems in rational categories! Before trying that, one might as well drive down to the Milledgeville asylum and check in. The groupings inevitably run together. Say what color cloth you want, and let the boy Jesus pull it out of the big dark dyeing vat.

There is a passionate confusion at the edge, and beyond the edge, of surrender. Rumi records it as inexplicable wandering, non sequitur questions, sudden fallings-off, a near explosive feel. What is passion? Where is the beauty? I asked my son Benjamin once, "What is all this longing?" He left me a note on the phone table the next morning. "Maybe it's because nobody has any brakes. We can't stop. Whoooooooooeeeeeeeeee!"

EVENING SKY GARNET RED

Morning opens a door with help for
those who don't ask for any. Love

tears its shirt. Mind begins the
sewing repair. You come and both

run off. I burn like aloe wood to
touch the one who set this. Dressed

sometimes like disaster, sometimes
like a guide, the ox of the self

sweetens his mouth in a pasture. A
parrot falls in love with an Arabian

colt. Fish want linen shirts. The
drunken lions hunt drunken gazelles.

It cannot be said how you take form.
One man asks for spoiled cheese.

The prayer rugs all point different
ways. If you would soak again the

evening sky your garnet red, the
qibla tips would turn that way.

THE SWEET BLADE OF YOUR ANGER

What's the use of going to see a mountain
cliff if your face isn't there? Why hear

the secret of secrets if you're not mentioned?
If Adam and Eve and their family knew nothing

of you, whom should I ask? What if I get
prosperity and honors and all satisfactions

anyone could want, and never meet you? What
use is understanding if I don't see the blade

of your anger with honey curling around it?
What use is water, wedding gifts, Joseph's

soul, sparks igniting, hair? The hundreds of
lies that compose one truth? The two worlds

calling each other? I praise stray dogs on
the street, lions wandering wilderness, and

Shams Tabriz. It does not matter what I say.

What if I broke off a whole branch
of roses? What if I lost myself in

the Friend? How would it be to have
no faith? What if I picked a pick-

pocket's pocket? Does it mean any-
thing when a single basket is lost

in Baghdad, when one wheat grain is
missing from the barn? How long will

this illusion last? What remains
when a lover sits quietly with the

beloved *for one second*? Will it
involve you at all if I say some

unsayable things? Will my heart feel
relieved doing that? Something has

passed between lover and beloved.
Are you part of these goings-on?

What does the soul feel when Jesus
heals the body? This is the night

when life decrees can change. If
the moon came to visit me, would

that affect other people? Shams
Tabriz, if I gave workers a holiday

and if I turned the marketplace
upside down, would that be a kind of

image for how you love the world?

ASYLUM

You that pour, ease up. Our
minds have moved to the asylum.

The jar's rim, dark red; the
town burning. This comb has

no handle, all teeth. Each
candle-moment there's a new

moth! Some people, when they
hear how the mind goes crazy

in love, close down. Their
hearts contract. There's a

confusion in surrender that the
intellect so hates, it devises

a key made of fire to destroy
the lock, the door, and the

whole house, but love's madness
has gone before, and there is

nothing left, no rooms, no door,
no lock, just this airy falling

asylum of friends we call Shams.

What's the lover to do
but humiliate himself,
and wander your rooms?

If he kisses your hair,
don't wonder why.

Sometimes in the madhouse
they gnaw on their chains.

Someone who does not run
toward the allure of love
walks a road where nothing

lives. But this dove here
senses the love hawk floating
above, and waits, and will not

be driven or scared to safety.

This mud body
is clear epiphany.

Angels wish they
could move as I move.

Purity? Cherubim babies
long for my innocence.

Courage? Armies of demons
flee my uplifted hand.

There's no light like yours, no breeze
quick enough to carry your fragrance.

When intelligence leaves its castle
and walks through your forest lane,

it doesn't know where or who it is;
it sits on the ground and babbles.

THE SILENT ARTICULATION OF A FACE

Love comes with a knife, not some shy question,
and not with fears for its reputation! I say

these things disinterestedly. Accept them in
kind. Love is a madman, working his wild schemes,

tearing off his clothes, running through the
mountains, drinking poison, and now quietly

choosing annihilation. A tiny spider tries to
wrap an enormous wasp. Think of the spiderweb

woven across the cave where Muhammad slept!
There are love stories, and there is obliteration

into love. You've been walking the ocean's edge,
holding up your robes to keep them dry. You

must dive naked under and deeper under, a thousand
times deeper! Love flows down. The ground

submits to the sky and suffers what comes. Tell
me, is the earth worse for giving in like that?

Don't put blankets over the drum! Open completely.
Let your spirit ear listen to the green dome's

passionate murmur. Let the cords of your robe
be untied. Shiver in this new love beyond all

above and below. The sun rises, but which way
does night go? I have no more words. Let the

soul speak with the silent articulation of a face.

A SMALL GREEN ISLAND

There is a small green island where one white cow lives
alone, a meadow of an island.

The cow grazes till nightfall, full and fat, but during the
night she panics and grows

thin as a single hair. "What shall I eat tomorrow? There's
nothing left!" By dawn,

the grass has grown up again, waist-high. The cow starts
eating and by dark the

meadow is clipped short. She's full of strength and energy,
but she panics in the dark

as before, and grows abnormally thin overnight. The cow
does this over and over,

and this is all she does. She never thinks, "This meadow has
never failed to grow back.

Why should I be afraid every night that it won't?" The cow
is the bodily soul. The

island field is this world where that grows lean with fear and
fat with blessing, lean

and fat. White cow, don't make yourself miserable with what's
to come, or not to come.

Your eyes, when they really see
a rose or an anemone, flood the
wheeling universe with tears.

Wine that stands a thousand years
in a jar tastes less mad
than love only one year old.

BOTH WINGS BROKEN

Love draws a dagger and pulls me close.
Lock and key. Bird with both wings

broken. The love religion is all that's
written here. Who else would say this?

You open me wide open. Or you tie me
tighter. The ball waits on the field

to be hit again. You push me into fire
like Abraham. You pull me out like

Muhammad. "Which do you like better?"
you ask. All the same, if it's your hand,

troubles or peace. Friends become enemies,
faithful faithless. Some knots tighten;

some loosen. Unruly tangle of caution and
rebellion, ropes and uncombed hair, no one

can tell. Then comes the sure attention
of a mother's hand for her hurt child.

17. Extravagance: Exuberance That Informs and Streams Beyond

The *most* extravagant statement is the *zikr* itself, *There is no reality but God; there is only God!* Every anger, every love, every kindness, every fear and greed, every accident, cruelty, and terror, every gentleness. There You are, and we are That.

THERE YOU ARE

You're inside every kindness. When
a sick person feels better, you're

that, and the onset of disease too.
You're sudden, terrible screaming.

Some problems require we go for help:
when we knock on a stranger's door,

you sent us. Nobody answers: it's
you! When work feels necessary, you

are the way workers move in rhythm.
You are what is: the field, the players,

the ball, those watching. Someone
claims to have evidence that you do

not exist. You're the one who brings
the evidence in, and the evidence

itself. You are inside the soul's
great fear, every natural pleasure,

every vicious cruelty. You are in
every difference and irritation.

Someone loves something; someone else
hates the same. There you are.

Whatever eyes see, what anyone wants
or not: political power, injustice,

material possessions, those are your
script, the handwriting we study.

Body, soul, shadow. Whether reckless
or careful, you *are* what we do. It's

absurd to ask your pardon. You're
inside repentance, and sin! The wonder

of various jewels, agate, emerald.
How we are during a day, then at night,

you are those moods and qualities.
The pure compassion we feel for each

other. Every encampment has a tent
where the leader is and also the wide

truth of your imperial tent overall.

COME HORSEBACK

Come horseback through the spiderwebs
of twilight, as fifteen evenings of full

moon, as the sun on holiday. The stars
performing every small zodiac wish wheel

into the presence of these lovers where
you remember me, look around, drawing

the blade of your question, "Where is
the one whose candle burns in the dawn?

Where is the handful of dirt that somehow
joins with the light of the Pleiades?"

You keep resurrecting like St. George.
Again, "Where is the friend who calls

presence out of absence and cuts the
umbilical by mentioning Shams-i Tabriz?"

WILDER THAN WE EVER

The one who pours is wilder than we
ever become drinking, wilder than

wine, the one who fills to the rim
and leaves to live in absence with

a toast: *Go home. There's nothing
for you here.* A pearl in the shell

does not touch the ocean. Be a pearl
without a shell, a mindful flooding,

candle turned moth, head become empty
jar, bird settling nest, love lived.

18. Night: Darkness, Living Water

Night has ways to heal the soul. Star, cloud, and wandering moon; soul water washes over lovers who stay up. Doubt dissolves, and night thieves draw new marginal swirls, glyphs, insignia. A 1930s van delivering laundry with its ancient, amused driver stops to give me a lift.

Last night, the Friend
came to visit.

I asked night
to keep the secret.

"But look!" said night.
"Behind you the sun is rising.

How could I show anyone anything?"

Flowers open every night
across the sky as the peace

of keeping a vigil
kindles the emptiness.

You that prefer, as crows do,
winter's chill and the empty limbs,

notice now this that fills
with new leaves and roses opening
and the night bird's song.

Let your love dissolve also
into *this* season's moment,

or when it's over, you'll buy
lamp after lamp to find it!

Don't sleep now. Let the turning
night wheel through this circle.

Your brow, the moon, this
lantern we sit with.

Stay awake with these
lights. Don't sleep.

WHAT HURTS THE SOUL?

We tremble, thinking we're about to dissolve into
nonexistence, but non-

existence fears even more that it might be given human
form! Loving God is

the only pleasure. Other delights turn bitter. What hurts
the soul? To live

without tasting the water of its own essence. People
focus on death and this

material earth. They have doubts about soul water.
Those doubts can be

reduced! Use night to wake your clarity. Darkness
and the living water are

lovers. Let them stay up together. When merchants eat
their big meals and sleep

their dead sleep, we night thieves go to work.

Midnight, but your forehead
shines with dawn. You dance as

you come to me and curl by curl
undo the dark. Let jealousy end.

SOME KISS WE WANT

There is some kiss we want with
our whole lives, the touch of

spirit on the body. Seawater
begs the pearl to break its shell.

And the lily, how passionately
it needs some wild darling! At

night, I open the window and ask
the moon to come and press its

face against mine. *Breathe into
me.* Close the language-door and

open the love-window. The moon
won't use the door, only the window.

19. Dawn: Spring Morning Listening

There is a sweet knowing in the air of early dawn that Rumi continuously reminds us to breathe: a time when we feel our lineage with wet earth and sun. Breezes then are pregnant with love, and *that* love is pregnant with God.

Some withinness about to be born is the generative power he wakes to praise: when the body begins new ways of knowing: a dropping away of mind that brings the sudden tap of the skimming spoon he calls *true hospitality*. That poem ("Drawn by Soup") makes me want some thick broth for breakfast, as well as the whack that startles one back to the true self, the heart-center.

Rumi praises the strength and tenderness a man feels in the presence of a woman, because that gentle, invigorating feminine *creates* the dawn-light red! ("She Is the Creator").

THE GENERATIONS I PRAISE

Yesterday the beauty of early dawn
came over me, and I wondered who

my heart would reach toward. Then
this morning again, and you. Who

am I? Wind and fire and watery
ground move me mightily because

they're pregnant with love, love
pregnant with God. These are the

early morning generations I praise.

HUNT MUSIC

Musk and amber remind us of the air
of sunrise, when any small motion

seems part of one elaborate making.
The body's harp gets handed to the

soul to play. The strings: rage,
love, jealousy, all the wantings mix

their energy-music. Who *tuned* this
instrument where wind is a string,

and Shams's eyes, in which a gazelle
turns to stalk the hunting lioness?

KNOWLEDGE BEYOND LOVE

Shams has knowledge beyond love, an
emptiness like air. This saddens and

confuses me. Wandering bits of wood
in ocean water. There is a change

that lets Jesus be born every breath.
Mention Shams and your talking and

writing will be lit from within. You
believe this that I say and write is

blood and must not be spilled, a lonely
circulation. My intellect lies in the

hallway listening to language as if it
were band music playing outside. I

don't say my mind ignores my soul, but
this was their conversation yesterday:

Mind: *What will happen?* Soul: *You*
must completely forget me. What I feel

does not occur in time. Fires have
been set on the mountain to help us

in the night passage. Mind dissolves.
You see Joseph everywhere. The tide

comes in. Sometimes the sea becomes
one drop! If Moses, we learn about

the Kabbalah. If Jesus, the Christian
sacrament. If soul, we turn vast

and airy. If earth, we're grounded
and dancing and hungry. We expand like

bread from within. Ego doesn't forgive.
It stands and shouts coarse commands.

But the morning breeze and one handful
of earth from somewhere near Tabriz

will heal my eyes and show what to do.

SOUL, HEART, AND BODY ONE MORNING

There's a morning when presence comes
over your soul. You sing like a rooster

in your earth-colored shape. Your heart
hears and, no longer frantic, begins

to dance. At that moment, soul reaches
total emptiness. Your heart becomes Mary,

miraculously pregnant, and body like a
two-day-old Jesus says wisdom words. Now

the heart, which is the source of your
loving, turns to universal light, and the

body picks up the tempo and elegance of
its motion. Where Shams-i Tabriz walks

the footprints become notations of music
and holes you fall through into space.

DRAWN BY SOUP

I try to imagine the most sumptuous
meal: Bugra Khan, general of the

armies east of here, has an autumn
night banquet celebrating himself!

The archangel Gabriel arrives as
Abraham's guest, fatted calf roasting.

Then the perfect setting, unimaginary:
your voice at dawn and the fragrance

of soup. I follow the simmering that
pulls me into a light-filled kitchen.

I ask the cook for a taste. "This is
not for human beings." *Please.* You

strike my head with a skimming spoon;
mind drops away: *true hospitality.*

SHE IS THE CREATOR

There's a tradition that Muhammad said, "A wise man
will listen and be led by

a woman, while an ignorant man will not." Someone too
fiercely drawn by animal

urges lacks kindness and the gentle affections
that keep men human.

Anger and sharp desiring are animal qualities. A
loving tenderness toward

women shows someone no longer pulled along by wanting.
The core of the feminine

comes directly as a ray of the sun. Not the earthy
figure you hear about in

love songs; there's more to her mystery than that. You
might say she's not from

the manifest world at all, but the *creator* of it.

20. *The Banquet:* This Is Enough *Was Always True*

Rumi doesn't say it this way, but in the transformation Shams brought him he found himself walking inside a great poem, breathing music, feeling the hilarious vibrancy of layers of ocean-awareness that nourish each other.

It's as if he hears the big bang as everything flies into space, and at the same moment he is a solitary child who takes a burning stick from the campfire and writes fading infinity signs in the night air with sparks. Sideways figure-eight, his wondering laugh.

We die with wealth all round. I have a practice with my lover called *Where were we?* We lie in bed in the dark and go over the sequence of the day we've had together. She says some; I pick it up; memory show-offs, the antiphony of moments and how it felt inside them, the tinier the better.

THIS IS ENOUGH

Sugar merchants, I have news: Joseph
has arrived from Egypt with the essence

of sweetness: a fruit cobbler that can
save your soul! Spirit wine. And if

there is something else you want, that
came too. Khidr through an open window.

Aphrodite singing *ghazals*. A sky with
gold streaks across. A stick that finds

water in a stone. Jesus sitting quietly
near the animals. Night so peaceful.

This is enough was always true. We
just haven't seen it: the hoopoe already

wears a tufted crown. Each ant is given
its elegant belt at birth. This love

we feel pours through us like giveaway
song. The source of *now* is here!

THE MUSIC WE ARE

Did you hear that winter's over? The basil
and the carnations cannot control their

laughter. The nightingale, back from his
wandering, has been made singing master

over the birds. The trees reach out their
congratulations. The soul goes dancing

through the king's doorway. Anemones blush
because they have seen the rose naked.

Spring, the only fair judge, walks in the
courtroom, and several December thieves steal

away. Last year's miracles will soon be
forgotten. New creatures whirl in from non-

existence, galaxies scattered around their
feet. Have you met them? Do you hear the

bud of Jesus crooning in the cradle? A single
narcissus flower has been appointed *Inspector*

of Kingdoms. A feast is set. Listen: the
wind is pouring wine! Love used to hide

inside images: no more! The orchard hangs
out its lanterns. The dead come stumbling by

in shrouds. Nothing can stay bound or be
imprisoned. You say, "End this poem here,

and wait for what's next." I will. Poems
are rough notations for the music we *are*.

JOSEPH

Joseph has come, the handsome one of this age,
a victory banner floating over spring flowers.

Those of you whose work it is to wake the dead,
get up! This is a work day. The lion that

hunts lions charges into a meadow. Yesterday
and the day before are gone. The coin of *now*

slaps down in your hand with the streets and
buildings of this city all saying, *The prince*

is coming! A drumbeat starts. What we hear
about the Friend is true. The beauty of that

peacefuless makes the whole world restless.
Spread your robe out to catch what sifts down

from the ninth level. You strange exiled
bird with clipped wings, now you have four

full-feathered pinions. You heart closed up
in a chest, open; the Friend is entering you.

You feet, it's time to dance! Don't talk
about the old man. He's young again. And

don't mention the past. Do you understand?
The beloved is *here!* You mumble, "But what

excuse can I give the king?" When the king is
making excuses to you! You say, "How can I

escape his hand?" When *that hand* is trying
to help you. You saw fire, and light came.

You expected blood; wine is being poured.
Don't run from your tremendous good fortune.

Be silent and don't try to add up what's been
given. An uncountable grace has come to you.

Flow inside me, source of the
source of joy, life essence,

wine of peace moving in my hand,
then out, around, . . . you know

the rest. Wound that opens in
the ground, perfect shot, wing

shadow, face of a strong worker,
still delicate, candle, a secret

completely obvious, you bring in
the gift, you hand us each moment.

You are the value rivering along
in any belonging, lock of hair;

you're the human center. The
ocean of meanings gets a puzzled

look when it sees this hilarious
presence moving through, *yhuuu*.

THE MOMENT

In every instant there's dying and coming back around.
Muhammad said, *This world*

is a moment, a pouring that refreshes and renews itself so
rapidly it seems continuous,

as a burning stick taken from the fire looks like a golden
wire when you swirl

it in the air, so we feel duration as a string of sparks.

21. Poetry: The Song of Being Empty

Cups love to be poured out; poems want silence. The glory of what cannot be said gets celebrated in Rumi's poetry.

These are mystical love poems. Their motive is to draw us out of the personal into the annihilation of *fana* and the resurrection of *baqa*, the two motions of mystical life.

Soul lions hide in the dry language grasses. Speaking this poetry aloud sets fire to the thicket and starts those lions *toward* us.

Then there's the streaming of emotion, a ripped-open robe in tatters. Wrap it around yourself with no hesitation. Claim nothing. Be embers wind ignites.

This poetry is written in the country idiom of longing spoken by iris, oak, jasmine, night bird, rising sun, raucous parrots, and children. What I say makes me drunk.

CUP

The cup wants to be lifted and
used, not broken, but carried

carefully to the next. The cup
knows there's a state for you

beyond this, one that comes with
more vast awareness. The cup

looks still, but it acts in secret
to help. Sometimes you pour cup

to cup: nothing happens. Pour
instead into your deep ocean-self

without calculation. If eyesight
blurs, find a railing to follow.

Spring is how the soul renews and refreshes
itself, fields damp and sprouting. Roses

glowing, birds learning to talk. Morning
wind animating everything: cypress to iris,

Tell me dear . . . Iris to tulip, *Show me how
you're faithful.* Plane trees play their

tambourines. Pine trees clap hands. Doves
do their one-note question, *coo-where,* which

means, *Be here with us.* A pink rose stands
straight. Violets kneel. Grape leaves do

full prostration. A new kind of poetry is
coming. *Glory* makes promises again to

Mutabilis. Thunder says, *Wash your face in
this, and your hands and feet.* Narcissus

blinks and comes near the nightingale to say,
We need a new song. Reply: *This is for*

love's emptiness. Now the green ones dress
like Khidr: *It is time to hear the secrets*

the dervishes know. No, agree the *Penelope*
and jasmine, *Silence is the best alchemy.*

ALL WE SELL

If you love love, look for yourself. If you're a pigeon who
has landed on *this* roof,

nothing can drive you away for long. Husamuddin is throwing
out grain and seed again!

I may fly off for a while, but then the pain hurts *here*.
I come quickly back like

Gabriel to the lotus tree. Waves of pearl break over us,
asking, *How are you today?*

When you're caught by Husam, even if everything is going wrong,
still wisdom comes. This

Masnavi is his music. As for what he doesn't say, God help us!
Husam and I have two mouths,

like the reed flute, one hidden in his lips and mine
wailing out here in the open.

But anyone with *insight* knows what comes out here begins there.
If this flute were not

in secret conversation with his mouth, the world would not
be washed in such sound. If you

have a sharp edge, cut off your head! Then everything you do,
it's not you that does it,

so you're safe. No one can blame you. It's not your
responsibility. Every stall

has different merchandise. Shoemakers carry only leather. If
wood is there, it's to make

a shoe mold. Drapers have undyed silk and other cloth. If
there's iron around, it's for

measuring. This poem is a shop for emptiness. *Fana* and *baqa*,
all we sell. Anything else

you see here is just a come-on, a trick to bring you in.

I don't want anyone to be distressed because of me. During the meditation people came closer, and some of my friends fended them away. This is not what I want. It has been my custom never to turn away those who come. Don't scold anyone on my account.

I love these friends, all of them, so much so that for their entertainment I speak poetry! Why else would I do that? There's nothing worse than that stuff! But it's expected of me.

As when a cook who doesn't like tripe plunges his hands into intestines and washes and prepares those parts, because a guest he has invited loves tripe. A man must consider what people want and stock up on those things, even though he has no interest and he knows the quality of the food is inferior.

To keep you from getting bored, I make up poems. I'm from a long line of scholars and deep mystical souls who passed on to me rare and subtle points. God has indicated that I should carry on that work, and if I were in the country of my birth, I would, but *here*, what to do?

In Balkh it was shameful to be a poet! If I could have remained there speaking and writing as my father did, I would have continued his lineage of study and practice.

IS THIS A PLACE WHERE STORIES ARE ACTED OUT?

Ask someone whose house this is where music
continues to flow out. Is this the Kaaba or

a temple of light? Is something here that
the universe cannot hold? Or is this a place

where stories are acted out? Don't tear it
down! And don't try to talk to the owner.

He's asleep. Make perfume of the dust and
thrown-away matters here, where the framing

is poetry and the kitchen talk pure praise!
Whoever enters this room becomes wise. This

is the house of love, where no one can
distinguish leaf from blossom or trap from

bait. Everything mirrors everything. The
hair tip sinks through the comb. No one knows

anyone's name. Don't wait on the doorsill!
Walk this forest full of lions and don't

consider the danger. No need to set fires
everywhere you go. The lions' thicket is

silence; anything you say will be flame
enough to draw them from where they rest.

A SONG OF BEING EMPTY

A certain sufi tore his robe in grief, and the tearing
brought such relief he gave

the robe the name *faraji*, which means "ripped open," or
"happiness," or "one who brings

the joy of being opened." It comes from the stem *faraj*,
which also refers to

the genitals, male and female. His teacher understood
the purity of the action,

while others just saw the ragged appearance. If you want
peace and purity, tear

away your coverings. This is the purpose of emotion, to
let a streaming beauty

flow through you. Call it spirit, elixir, or the original
agreement between yourself

and God. Opening into that gives peace, a song of being
empty, pure silence.

A SALVE MADE WITH DIRT

I was a thorn rushing to be with a rose,
vinegar blending with honey, a pot of

poison turning to healing salve, pasty
wine dregs thrown in the millrace. I was

a diseased eye reaching for Jesus' robe,
raw meat cooking in the fire. Then I found

some dirt to make an ointment that would
honor my soul, and in mixing that, I found

poetry. Love says, "You are right, but
don't claim those changes. Remember, I

am wind. You are an ember I ignite."

WHAT I SAY MAKES ME DRUNK

The beloved grumbles at me, *Come
on! Come on.* But which way do

I go to that one? Torches at
the door. Who's there? I am!

The one asking from inside and
the one walking up to the door,

who steals the doorknob! Oil
and water together, how can I

be whole? I'm like this hair,
all strands and hiding places,

yet out in the wide-open too like
the moon. I look around the house

for the one who stole my clothing,
with the garment thief's head

laughing through the open window.
I try every possible way out, when

I've been free of this cage now,
since . . . ah . . . eternity. What I say

makes me drunk. Nightingale, iris,
parrot, jasmine: I speak those

languages, along with the idiom
of my longing for Shams-i Tabriz.

22. Pilgrim Notes: Chance Meetings, Dignity, and Purpose

Rumi recommends we each become a threshing floor, a clean sandy spot that gives wheat to the barn for free. Being swept clean for work to come across involves heating up and crying out from our grief and disappointment. Those laments empty us and let the presence come that is a healing calm for others.

The tone of poems in this section is often severe. Rumi says he likes to put a little vinegar with his honey, some scolding with the love to make the ecstasy more familiar. It sounds like the Alabama tonic my father took every morning before breakfast: a fold of honey on the teaspoon, then vinegar.

Also there's the work he calls broom work, a sweeping that raises dust and keeps a brilliance covered that might confuse us. What is that? Using language, I guess. It's not clear. Some work that raises bits of sentimentality?

NOT HERE

There's courage involved if you want
to become truth. There is a broken-

open place in a lover. Where are
those qualities of bravery and sharp

compassion in this group? What's the
use of old and frozen thought? I want

a howling hurt. This is not a treasury
where gold is stored; this is for copper.

We alchemists look for talent that
can heat up and change. Lukewarm

won't do. Halfhearted holding back,
well-enough getting by? Not here.

CRY OUT YOUR GRIEF

Cry out all your grief, your
disappointments! Say them in

Farsi, then Greek. It doesn't
matter whether you're from Rum

or Arabia. Praise the beauty
and kindness praised by every

living being. You hurt and have
sharp desire, yet your presence

is a healing calm. Sun, moon,
bonfire, candle, which? Someone

says your flame is about to be
dowsed, but you're not smoke or

fire. You're infinitely more
alive. Say how that is! This

fluttering love will not stay
much longer in my chest. Soon it

will fly like a falcon to its
master, like an owl saying *HU*.

BROOM WORK

If every heart had such a private
road into the Friend as this, there

would be a garden bench on the tip
of every thorn. Every grief, an

exuberance. Flame-colored souls
enjoy each other. Lightning stands

doorkeeper for the full moon. If it
didn't, the sky's shifting would

start to occur on the ground. If
legs and feet and wings took us to

the beloved, every atom would become
such transportation. If everyone

could see what love is, each would
set up a tent pole in the ocean: the

world's population pitched and living
easily within the sea. What if inside

every lover's tear you saw the face
of the Friend, Muhammad, Jesus, Buddha,

the impossible-possible philosopher,
the glass diamond one, Shams Tabriz?

A friendship fire dissolves divisions:
yesterday becomes tomorrow. Stay low

and lower under the green roof. Keep
sweeping the floor. That broom work

keeps a brilliance covered that would
confuse us more than we can stand.

A CLEAN SANDY SPOT

You blame and give advice, and
recommend medicinal spells. You

make detailed analyses and loud
public conclusions about this

company of lovers. Do you really
consider yourself a lover? A flat,

clean, sandy spot gives wheat to
the barn for nothing! No particle

can grow to seedling from anything
but the whole. You know this. Why

this continuous personal critique?
Love's fire puts a sad smile on.

Advice rarely brings the coolness
of peace. The moon's ashy light

covers this world as love waits
quietly for a bird in the branches

of some town, say Tabriz, to begin.

TWO SACKS

A certain bedouin loads two big sacks on his camel. One is
filled with grain. A smooth-talking

desert philosopher comes up and makes conversation about where
the man is from and many other

things, which he fits together as gracefully as beads on
a string. Finally he says,

"These two sacks, tell me about them." "One is full of wheat.
The other is a sack of sand,

for balance." "Wouldn't it be wiser to pour out the sand sack and put half the wheat on one

side and half on the other? That way the sacks will be lightened and the camel as well."

The Arab is impressed. "Such a subtle thinker, and you in this sorry condition, tired and on foot,

in worn-out clothes. Please, ride on my camel." He helps the philosopher up and continues

his wondering. "Tell me how it goes with you and your ingenuity." "I'm not very

smart or talented, really." "How many camels do you own? How many oxen?" "Don't be

ridiculous! I don't own anything." "You keep shop then. What do you sell?" "I have no

shop. I don't even have a place to live." "You must have money somewhere. Are you a wandering

alchemical advisor whose counsel is much prized?" "Listen. I don't have enough for supper

tonight. As you see, I have no shoes. If someone offers me a loaf of bread, that's where

I go next. My clever mind has gotten me only headaches and fantastic imaginings." The

Arab concludes then, "Your knowledge is unlucky. I don't want to travel with you. It may

rub off. Get down and whichever way you go, I'll take the opposite direction. A sack of

wheat and a sack of sand are my kind of foolishness. At least, my soul is devout and open to grace."

Banish as a traveling companion the figuring, human intellect. Cunning rascals think the old

ones know nothing because they're old. They dismiss patience
and sacrifice and generosity,

and the simplicity that does not calculate. That plain
nomadic man opens a way

for majesty, and majesty walks there.

ANY CHANCE MEETING

In every gathering, in any chance
meeting on the street, there is a

shine, an elegance rising up. Today
I recognized that that jewel-like

beauty is the presence, our loving
confusion, the glow in which watery

clay gets brighter than fire, the
one we call the Friend. I begged,

"Is there a way into you, a ladder?"
"Your head is the ladder. Bring

it down under your feet." The mind,
this globe of awareness, is a starry

universe that when you push off from
it with your foot, a thousand new

roads come clear, as you yourself do
at dawn, sailing through the light.

There is one thing in this world you must never forget to do. If you forget everything else and not this, there's nothing to worry about, but if you remember everything else and forget this, then you will have done nothing in your life.

It's as if a king has sent you to some country to do a task, and you perform a hundred other services, but not the one he sent you to do. So human beings come to this world to do *particular work*. That work is the purpose, and each is specific to the person. If you don't do it, it's as though a priceless Indian sword were used to slice rotten meat. It's a golden bowl being used to cook turnips, when one filing from the bowl could buy a hundred suitable pots. It's like a knife of the finest tempering nailed into a wall to hang things on.

You say, "But look, I'm using the dagger. It's not lying idle." Do you hear how ludicrous that sounds? For a penny an iron nail could be bought to serve for that. You say, "But I spend my energies on lofty enterprises. I study jurisprudence and philosophy and logic and astronomy and medicine and the rest." But consider why you do those things. They are all branches of yourself.

Remember the deep root of your being, the presence of your lord. Give yourself to the one who already owns your breath and your moments. If you don't, you will be like the man who takes a precious dagger and hammers it into his kitchen wall for a peg to hold his dipper gourd. You'll be wasting valuable keenness and forgetting your dignity and purpose.

23. Apple Orchards in Mist: Being in Between Language and the Soul's Truth

Ram Dass once said he heard in Sufi poetry a love for living on the verge, the delight on the brim of merging with the divine, the flirtatious touch of bewilderment.

There is often a strong sense in Rumi's poetry of being in between: spirit and animal, full-zero surrender and the pang of desiring, praise and renunciation. *La!* ("Nothing!") No. *Illa* ("Only God.") Everything is God.

Rumi feels it is a deep necessity, if our lives are to be real, that we experience the *energy* of essence. Cups floating in the ocean, don't keep your rims dry! Night riders, get to know the horse that's carrying you through the darkness, the long muscular currents that bear us through events.

There's a passage in the *Masnavi* (VI, 84 ff.) in which the life of the soul is felt as an apple orchard; language, a thick morning fog covering it. Gradually, as the sun comes up and burns off the mist, we see through to the *taste,* unsayable beauty.

YOU ARE NOT YOUR EYES

Those who have reached their arms
into emptiness are no longer

concerned with lies and truth, with
mind and soul, or which side of

the bed they rose from. If you
are still struggling to understand,

you are not there. You offer your
soul to one who says, "Take it to

the other side." You're on neither
side, yet those who love you see

you on one side or the other. You
say *Illa*, "only God"; then your

hungry eyes see you're in "nothing,"
La. You're an artist who paints

both with existence and non. Shams
could help you see who you are, but

remember, *You are not your eyes.*

PRAYER TO BE CHANGED

You change one piece of ground to gold. Another you shape
into Adam. Your work

transforms essence and reveals the soul. My work is
forgetfulness and making

mistakes. Change those to wisdom! I am all anger. Turn
that to loving patience. You

that lift the bitter earth into dough and baked bread to
human energy, you

that appoint a distracted man guide, a lost man prophet,
you that arrange random

patches in an elegant design, we've changed from our first
condition a hundred thousand

times, with each unfolding better than the last, let our
heart's eye see this: all

change coming from the changer. Ignore intermediaries! As
they diminish, delight increases.

When we meet the mystic go-betweens that are helping us,
bewilderment dissolves. But

it's that confusion that takes us deeper into presence!
Successive lives grow from

successive deaths. Help us stay in that succession, the way
in. Don't let us love

one life-form so much we stop there like a rat in a granary.
Mineral to vegetable to animal

to this walking human being whose footprints on the beach lead
into the ocean, gone! Muhammad said,

"Three kinds of people are particularly pathetic: the powerful
man who is out of power, the

rich man with no money, and the learned man laughed at." Yet
these are those who badly want

change! Some dogs sit satisfied in their kennels. But someone
who last year drank ecstatic

union, the pre-eternity agreement, who this year has a hangover
from bad desire wine, the way

he cries out for the majesty he's lost, give me his longing!

A SMALL MARKET BETWEEN TOWNS

There's a town where the soul is fed, where love hears
truth and thrives, and

another town that produces lies that degrade and starve
love. Your voice is

a small market set up between the two towns. Goods arrive
from both directions, flimsy,

fake items and honestly made, wholehearted tools and wares.
Some travelers immediately know

which is which. Some voices open a shop and spend sixty
years cheating customers,

gossiping when they leave, and flattering women to get their
attention. Others weary

of the marketplace altogether and rarely go there.

LOVERS IN LAW SCHOOL

Speak Persian, Husam, though Arabic is very sweet. Love has
a hundred other languages

besides these two. A fragrance, a silence, the talking when
we're all ear. Lovers

leave for Bukhara, but not to listen to learned lectures.
They go there to explore

the face of the Friend. They study law, but really they're
whirling in ecstasy. They

add and subtract sums of money, when actually they're mining
for spirit treasure. They

talk about divorce and separation, but really they're leaning
back, riding in a wagon

on the Bukhara road, soul beauty their only expertise.

CUP AND OCEAN

These forms we seem to be are cups floating in an ocean
of living consciousness.

They fill and sink without leaving an arc of bubbles or
any good-bye spray. What we

are is that ocean, too near to see, though we swim in it
and drink it in. Don't

be a cup with a dry rim, or someone who rides all night
and never knows the horse

beneath his thighs, the surging that carries him along.

24. The Joke of Materialism: Turning Bread into Dung

There are the problems of location and identity, where we are and who we are, here sneezed into form, put in a bag, then told to tear out of the bag. So there's transcendence, but where are we then? Somewhere beyond the sky's blue bag, still looking for a key, turning toward India or Turkestan. Yet somehow, Rumi says, we are the ground the enlightened ones walk! We are part of the world's uproarious material, as well as this evolving language revealing the mystery of it. Dung does mix with other elements to become fertile soil, which mixes with sunlight and rain and seed to be grain and bread and the light in human eyes again. As Rumi says, a joke can carry deep truth.

Rumi considers the quoting of texts to attract compliments as an especially ugly form of materialism. Consider "Book Beauty." An aging woman tries to make herself more attractive by mixing a paste of pages from the Qur'an to fill the deep creases on her neck and face with. A less grotesque and truer beauty comes as we do what Rumi calls *polishing the heart*: going within to quietness and meditation that help the soul grow generous and handsome.

A man on horseback is Rumi's image of the mistaken inflation of personality, the ego with its gallant pose and sentimental memories, who prances to a stop asking the whereabouts of Death. "Hello, jackass," says Death. Splat. Rumi continues, "I am that mounted man, his illusion. How long shall I keep pointing to others? Shams of Tabriz is a fountain. We wash in the water of his eyes."

MOUNTED MAN

Look at this figure of a man on
horseback, his turban with gold

thread, striking a gallant pose,
asking, "Where *is* death? Show

me!" He seems powerful, but he's
a fake. Death attacks from six

sides. *Hello, jackass.* Where's
your magnetism now, the famous

temperament? The jokes you told,
the carpets you gave relatives?

It's not enough to spend your
life turning bread into dung.

We are pawing through manure to
find pearls. There are people

with the light of God on them.
Serve those. Don't trivialize

any suffering. I say this to
myself. I am that mounted man,

his illusion. How long shall I
keep pointing to others? Shams

of Tabriz is a fountain. We
wash in the water of his eyes.

THIS DISASTER

Why am I part of this disaster, this
mud hole for donkeys? Is this the place

where Jesus spoke? Surely not. A table
has been set, but we have not been served

sweet spring water yet. Evidently we came
here to be bound hand and foot. I ask

a flower, "How is it you are so wise so
young?" "With the first morning wind and

the first dew, I lost my innocence." I
follow the one who showed me the way. I

extend one hand up, and with the other I
touch the ground. A great branch leans

down from the sky. How long will I keep
talking of up and down? This is not my

home: silence, annihilation, absence!
I go back where everything is nothing.

SNEEZING OUT ANIMALS

I look for the light I used to
see. The key is hidden here

somewhere. I face toward India,
then Turkestan. I am the ground

you walked on. There's an old
story about Noah's ark when the

garbage began piling up. Yes!
That scow was in deep trouble.

Noah scratched a pig's back:
the pig sneezed out a rat, two

rats: the rats ate the garbage:
then Noah scratched a lion who

sneezed out cats which ate the
rats. I was sneezed out by a

lion and put in a bag, where I
heard, *If you're a lion cub, tear*

the bag. I did. Shams Tabriz
lives beyond the blue bag of sky.

NOT INTRIGUED WITH EVENING

What the material world values does
not shine the same in the truth of

the soul. You have been interested
in your shadow. Look instead directly

at the sun. What can we know by just
watching the time-and-space shapes of

each other? Someone half awake in the
night sees imaginary dangers; the

morning star rises; the horizon grows
defined; people become friends in a

moving caravan. Night birds may think
daybreak a kind of darkness, because

that's all they know. It's a fortunate
bird who's not intrigued with evening,

who flies in the sun we call Shams.

HOW ATTRACTION HAPPENS

Moses is talking to someone drunk with worshiping the golden
calf. "What happened to your

doubt? You used to be so skeptical of me. The Red Sea parted.
Food came every day in the

wilderness for forty years. A fountain sprang out of a rock.
You saw these things

and still reject the idea of prophethood. Then the magician
Samiri does a trick to make

the metal cow low, and immediately you kneel! What did that
hollow statue say? Have you

heard a dullness like your own?" This is how attraction
happens: people with nothing

they value delight in worthlessness. Someone who thinks
there's no meaning or purpose

feels drawn to images of futility. Each moves to be with
its own. The ox does not turn

toward a lion. Wolves have no interest in Joseph, unless
to devour him. But if a wolf

is cured of wolfishness, it will sleep close by Joseph,
like a dog in the presence of

meditators. Soul companionship gives safety and light
to a cave full of friends.

BOOK BEAUTY

Here's the end of that story about the old woman who wanted
to lure a man with strange

cosmetics. She made a paste of pages from the Qur'an to fill
the deep creases on her face and

neck with. This is not about an old woman, dear reader. It's
about you, or anyone who tries

to use books to make themselves attractive. There she is,
sticking scripture, thick with

saliva, on her face. Of course, the bits keep falling off.
"The devil," she yells, and

he appears! "This is a trick I've never seen. You don't need
me. You are yourself a troop

of demons!" So people steal inspired words to get compliments.
Don't bother. Death comes

and all talking, stolen or not, stops. Pity anyone unfamiliar
with silence when that happens.

Polish your heart with meditation and quietness. Let the inner
life grow generous and handsome

like Joseph. Zuleikha did that and her "old woman's spring
cold snap" turned to mid-July. Dry

lips wet from within. Ink is not rouge. Let language lie
bygone. *Now* is where love breathes.

An old man goes to a doctor, "My mind is not what it
used to be." "Mental

weakness comes at your age." "Sometimes I see dark spots."
"Age, old man." "I have

stiffness and a sharp pain in my back." "Age." "I can't
digest what I eat."

"Indigestion also comes with growing older." "Sometimes
I can't breathe well."

"Asthma. There are two hundred diseases that begin with
the onset of the last part

of life." "Fool!" cries the old man. "Do you have one
answer for everything? You

sew your one stitch in the same place over and over! Is
this all you've learned

of medicine! You quack, don't you know that God has given
a cure for every pain?"

The doctor replies, "This sudden anger is symptomatic of
being past sixty." The old

man sputters wordlessly and leaves. Not every elderly man,
and not every doctor, is like

this. The blessed grow externally old, and inwardly young.
They *live* the resurrection.

Why should they care about the plots, the hatred and heroism,
of the world? Their deep

core is the love of a soul guide. God lives there. A child
is weeping on the coffin

of his father. "Why are they taking you under the ground to
such a narrow room with no

doormat and no rug, no lamp, no bread, no smell of food being
cooked, no door with a working

latch, no way up to the roof, no neighbors to call to for help.
Your body, which people

loved to touch and kiss, why should it go to a damp place
where nothing lasts?" The son

keeps describing the grave-house, and weeping. Young
Nasruddin comes along, listening.

"They're taking the dead man to *our* house!" "Don't be
foolish," says his father.

"But listen to what he's saying! No lamp, no food, no door
in good repair. A rotten

roof. It sounds like our house!" In the same way, people
have the marks of their

willfulness on them, but they can't see the evidence, in
their houses narrow and dark,

unlit, under the hill and out of the sunlight.

25. Fana: *Dissolving Beyond Doubt and Certainty*

Fana moves in the night sky like a star with no name. Clear bead at the center, love with no object, one swaying being, the knack of compassion without attachment. Lovers love death because it keeps them moving beyond limits.

When I was a sophomore in high school, the Billy Graham Crusade came to town (Chattanooga), and I went up front for the invitation. I gave my heart to Jesus and went back behind the stage, where a group called the Navigators were doing follow-up. I began with Chuck Bovee a program of memorizing Bible verses, 227 of them, mostly the King James New Testament. I could say them all at once. I loved the transmission feel of it. I carried whatever 25 passages I was working on in a black leather packet in my back pocket. One day scuffling with my archrival, Billy D. Pettway, the verse wallet fell out on the ground. He picked it up. "What's this? Rubbers?" It was 1953, and there was no explanation for such a weird little *fana*-leap as I had taken. "Those are Bible verses I'm memorizing," said I in dismay.

Now I think of making such a pack for my nine-year-old granddaughter Briny, of lines from Shakespeare, Keats, Wordsworth, maybe some Bible, C. K. Williams, Agee, Yeats, Hopkins, Dickinson, Mary Oliver. For this open-air sanctuary without buildings, doctrine, or clergy, the one that some of us live in now where the Lord is *what is*, nothing less than that.

The experiment to live without religion, or rather to live in friendship with all religion and literature simultaneously, is the brave American try for freedom and flow: Thoreau's retreat to Walden Pond, Jake Barnes (in Hemingway's *The Sun Also Rises*) slipping into old Spanish churches to lis-

ten to his thoughts, Joe Miller's walks in Golden Gate Park, Joe Camp-
bell's lifework on mythology, Osho Rajneesh's brilliant attention to many
lineages, Huck out on the river at night, R.E.M.'s Michael Stipe up on
stage, *Losing my religion.* ..." There are many powerfully inclusive ges-
tures, figures, and journeys that inquire into mystery outside the structure
of any belief system. That's *fana.*

IN THE WAVES AND UNDERNEATH

A man is wandering the marketplace at noon with a candle
in his hand, totally ecstatic.

"Hey," calls a shopkeeper, "is this a joke? Who are you
looking for?" "Someone breathing

Huuu, the divine breath." "Well, there are plenty to choose
from." "But I want one who

can be in anger and desire and still a true human being in
the same moment." "A rare thing!

But maybe you're searching among branches for what appears
only in the roots." There's

a river that turns these millstones. Human will is an
illusion. Those who are proud

of deciding and carrying out decisions are the rawest of
the raw! Watch

the thought-kettles boiling, then look down at the fire.
God said to Job, "You

value your patience well. Consider now that I gave you that
patience." Don't be absorbed

with the waterwheel's motion. Turn your head and gaze
at the river. You say, "But

I'm looking there already." There are several signs in eyes
that see all the way to

the ocean. Bewilderment is one. Those who study foam and
flotsam near the edge

have purposes, and they'll explain them at length! Those who
look out to sea become the sea,

and they can't speak about that. On the beach there's
desire-singing and rage-ranting,

the elaborate language-dance of personality, but in the waves
and underneath there's no

volition, no hypocrisy, just love forming and unfolding.

INFIDEL FISH

The ocean way is this fish way
of the water-souls of fish who

die becoming the sea. Fish do
not wait patiently for water!

In this world full of shape,
there you are with no form!

You've made a universe from a
drop of my blood! Now I'm

confused. I can't tell world
from drop, my mouth and this

wine glass, one lip. I am
Nobbdy, the fool shepherd.

Where's my flock? What shepherd?
When I talk of you, there are no

words. Where could I put you,
who won't fit in the secret world,

or this? All I know of spirit
is this love. And don't call me

a believer. *Infidel* is better.

A STAR WITH NO NAME

When a baby is taken from the wet nurse, it easily forgets
her and starts eating

solid food. Seeds feed on ground awhile, then lift up into
the sun. So you should taste

filtered light and work toward what has no personal covering.
That's how you came here,

like a star with no name. Move in the night sky with those
anonymous lights.

RUSH NAKED

A lover looks at creek water and wants to be that quick
to fall, to kneel, then all

the way down in full prostration. A lover wants to die of
his love like a man with

dropsy who knows that water will kill him, but he can't deny
his thirst. A lover loves

death, which is God's way of helping us evolve from mineral
to vegetable to animal, the one

incorporating the others. Then animal becomes Adam, and the
next will take us beyond what

we can imagine, into the mystery of *we are all returning.*
Don't fear death. Spill your

jug in the river! Your attributes disappear, but the essence
moves on. Your shame and fear

are like felt layers covering coldness. Throw them off, and
rush naked into the joy of death.

Love's sun is the face of the Friend. This other sunlight
covers that. The day

and the daily bread that come are not to be worshiped for
themselves. Praise the great

heart within those, and the loving ache in yourself that's part
of that. Be one of God's fish

who receives what it needs directly from the ocean it swims—
food, shelter, sleep, medicine.

A lover is like a baby at its mother's breast, knowing
nothing of the visible or

invisible worlds. Everything is milk, though it could not
define that. It can't talk!

This is the riddle that drives the mind crazy: that the opener
and what is opened are the same!

It's the ocean *inside* the fish that bears it along, not the
river water. The time river

spreads and disappears into the ocean with the fish. Seeds
break open and dissolve in

ground. Only then do new fig trees come into being. So you
must *die before you die*.

REFUGE

I see the lamp, the face, the eye,
an altar where the soul bows, a

gladness and refuge. My loving says,
"Here. I can leave my personality

here." My reason agrees! "How can
I object when a rose makes the bent

backs stand up like cypresses?" Such
surrender changes everything. Turks

understand Armenian! Body abandons
bodiness. Soul goes to the center.

Rubies appear in the begging bowl.
But don't brag when this happens.

Be secluded and silent. Stay in
the delight, and be brought the

cup that will come. No artfulness.
Practice quiet and this new joy.

LOVE WITH NO OBJECT

There is a way of loving not attached to what is loved.
Observe how water is with

the ground, always moving toward the ocean, though the ground
tries to hold water's foot

and not let it go. This is how we are with wine and beautiful
food, wealth and power,

or just a dry piece of bread: we want and we get drunk with
wanting, then the headache

and bitterness afterward. Those prove that the attachment took
hold and held you back. Now you

proudly refuse help. "My love is pure. I have an intuitive
union with God. I don't need

anyone to show me how to be free!" This is not the case.
A love with no object

is a true love. All else, shadow without substance. Have you
seen someone fall in

love with his own shadow? That's what we've done. Leave
partial loves and find one

that's whole. Where is someone who can do that? They're
so rare, those hearts that carry

the blessing and lavish it over everything. Hold out your
beggar's robe and accept

their generosity. Anything not coming from that will damage
the cloth, like a sharp stone

tearing your sincerity. Keep that intact, and use clarity;
call it reason or discernment,

you have within you a deciding force that knows what to
receive, what to turn from.

THE ROAD HOME

An ant hurries along a threshing floor with its wheat grain,
moving between huge stacks

of wheat, not knowing the abundance all around. It thinks its
one grain is all there is to

love. So we choose a tiny seed to be devoted to. This body,
one path or one teacher. Look

wider and farther. The essence of every human being can *see*,
and what that essence-eye takes

in, the being becomes. Saturn. Solomon! The ocean pours
through a jar, and you might say it

swims *inside* the fish! This mystery gives peace to your
longing and makes the road home home.

COME OUT AND GIVE SOMETHING

Every prophet is a beggar calling, "Something for God's sake!
Please, lend something

to God." The people they ask this of are truly destitute, but
still prophets and teachers

go from door to door. Though all the doors of heaven are open
to them, they beg for

pieces of bread. They eat the bread they get, but they didn't
ask from appetite. In fact,

don't say they eat bread; they eat light. God has said *be
moderate* when eating and

drinking bread and wine, but God never said *be satisfied*
when taking in light.

God offers a teacher the treasures of the world, and the
teacher responds, "To be

in love with God and expect to be paid for it!" A servant
wants to be rewarded for what he does.

A lover wants only to be in love's presence, an ocean whose
depth will never be known.

This cannot be said! Let us return, Husam, to the story of the
teacher begging in the street.

Listen to him: "Love is reckless. Love makes the sea boil
like a kettle. Love crumbles

a stone mountain to sand. Out of love God says to Muhammad,
'But for you, I would not have

created the universe.' Love says, 'This world is the egg. You
are the chick.' Everything

helps us understand this." The ground is low to give some
notion of humility. Spring's

green comes to reveal an alchemy that happens *inside* us.
Every experience begs

like a dervish for us to come out and give something.

TWO HUMAN-SIZED WEDDING CANDLES

A message comes like honey to your
heart: seven friends and a dog have

slept three hundred and nine days
with God's wind turning them to rest

on one side, then the other. There's
another way of sleeping I pray we

avoid, the kind that's running after
joy with its grief shadow behind it,

or the other, persistently trailing
grief, meeting chance elation at the

corner. Help us to give up back-and-
forth, matter-illusion alternating

with the mind's calibration of what's
good and bad, wet and dry. Anything

alligator swallows becomes alligator.
Two human-sized wedding candles walk

toward fire. A piece of paper covered
with numbers and curving color streaks

drops in water, blurs, and flows away.

BLESSING THE MARRIAGE

This marriage be wine with halvah,
honey dissolving in milk. This

marriage be the leaves and fruit
of a date tree. This marriage be

women laughing together for days
on end. This marriage, a sign

for us to study. This marriage,
beauty. This marriage, a moon in

a light blue sky. This marriage,
this silence fully mixed with spirit.

ONE SWAYING BEING

Love is not condescension, never
that, nor books, nor any marking

on paper, nor what people say of
each other. Love is a tree with

branches reaching into eternity
and roots set deep in eternity,

and no trunk! Have you seen it?
The mind cannot. Your desiring

cannot. The longing you feel for
this love comes from inside you.

When you become the Friend, your
longing will be as the man in the

ocean who holds to a piece of
wood. Eventually wood, man, and

ocean become one swaying being,
Shams Tabriz, the secret of God.

There is a shredding that's healing, that makes us more alive, a grieving required to enter the region of unconditional love.

The heat in the oven cooks us to a loaf that's tasty and nourishing for the community. Rumi is always affirmative about grief and disappointments, mad with the *yes* inside all *no's*.

Rumi eats grief and the shadow and metabolizes them into his bewildered, surrendered self, then tries to live simply and generously from there.

> I've broken through to longing
> now, filled with a grief I have
>
> felt before, but never like this.

> The center leads to love.
> Soul opens the creation core.
>
> Hold on to your particular pain.
> That too can take you to God.

THIS BATTERED SAUCEPAN

Whatever you feel is *yours* the Friend
pulls you away from. That one does not

heal your wounds or torment you more.
Neither sure, nor uncertain, that one

keeps you *moving.* Decisions made at
night seem strange the next day. Where

are you when you sleep? A trickster
curls on the headboard. Restless in

the valley, you go to the ocean. Then
turning toward the light, you fall in

the fire. Who jiggles this battered
saucepan? The sky puts a yoke on you

to help with turning around a pole.
Teachers get dizzy like students. The

lion that killed you now wonders whether
to drag you off or tear you to pieces

here. There's a shredding that's really
a healing, that makes you more *alive!*

A lion holds you in his arms. Fingers
rake the fretbridge for music. A

compass revolves around the metal foot
point. Some grow fond of battle armor;

some, satin clothing. Others, like me,
love the word bunches called poetry.

A DELICATE GIRL

The terrible grief of being human! Let
us drink it all, but with a difference.

We sit with Junnaiyd and Bestami. The
moon rising here cannot be covered with

cloud. There are no deaths for lovers.
Who is the *self*? A delicate girl that

flows out when we draw the sword of
selfless action. This earth eats men

and women, and yet we are sent to eat
the world, this place that tries to fool

us with *tomorrow*. *Wait until tomorrow*,
which we outwit by enjoying only this

now. We gather at night to celebrate
being human. Sometimes we call out low

to the tambourine. Fish drink the sea,
but the sea does not get smaller! We

eat the clouds and evening light. We
are slaves tasting the royal wine.

THE THREAT OF DEATH

For safekeeping, gold is hidden in a desolate place, where
no one ever goes, not

in a familiar, easy-to-get-to spot. The proverb goes, *Joy
lives concealed in grief.*

The mind puzzles with this, but that strong beast, the soul, a
lively animal, will break

such a tether. Love burns away difficulties, as daylight does
night phantoms. Look for

the answer inside your question. Cornered in the edgeless
region of love, you'll

see the opening that leads neither east nor west, nor any
direction. You're a mountain

searching for its echo! Whenever you hurt, you say, *Lord
God!* The answer lives in that

which bends you low and makes you cry out. Pain and the threat
of death, for instance, do this.

They make you clear. When they're gone, you lose purpose. You
wonder what to do, where

to go. This is because you're uneven in your opening:
sometimes closed and unreachable,

sometimes with your shirt torn with longing. Your discursive
intellect dominates for a

time; then the universal, beyond-time intelligence comes. Sell
your questioning talents, my

son; buy bewildering surrender. Live simply and helpfully
in that. Don't worry about

the University of Bukhara with its prestigious curriculum.

There was a woman who bore a child almost every year, but the
children never lived longer

than six months. Usually after three or four months they would
die. She grieved long and

publicly. "I take on the work of pregnancy for nine months,
but the joy vanishes quicker

than a rainbow." Twenty children went like that, in fevers to
their small graves. One night

she had a revelation. She saw the place of unconditional love,
call it the garden or source

of gardens. The physical eye cannot see its unseeable light.
Lamp, green flower, these

are just comparisons, so that some of the love-bewildered may
catch a fragrance. The woman

saw pure grace and, drunk with the seeing, fell to the ground.
Those who gave the vision said

then, "This morning meal is for those who rise with sincere
devotion. The tragedies you've

had came from other times when you did not take refuge."
"Lord, give me more grief.

Tear me to pieces, if it leads here." She said this and
walked into the presence

she had seen. Her children were all there, "Lost to me," she
cried, "but not to you."

Without this great grieving no one can enter the spirit.

I saw grief drinking a cup of sorrow
and called out, "It tastes sweet, does it not?"

"You've caught me," grief answered, "and
you've ruined my business. How can I

sell sorrow, when you know it's a blessing?"

SOUR, DOUGHY, NUMB, AND RAW

If we're not together in the heart,
what's the point? When body and soul

aren't dancing, there's no pleasure
in colorful clothing. Why have

cooking pans when there's no food in
the house? In this world full of

fresh bread, amber, and musk, so many
different fragrances, what are they

to someone with no sense of smell?
If you stay away from fire, you'll

be sour, doughy, numb, and raw. You
may have lovely, just baked loaves

 around you, but those friends cannot
help. *You* have to feel oven fire.

I could not have known
what love is if I had never

felt this longing. Anything
done to excess becomes

boring, except this overflow
that moves toward you.

27. Inner Sun: No More the Presence

Perhaps presence is so elusive because of those continually disintegrating and reconstituting motions called *fana* and *baqa:* the wild longing to dissolve in God and then the coming back in the kind hand that reaches to help.

That motion is the subject of Rumi's poetry, or it might be better to say that his poetry enjoys the play of presence and absence, through the mind, through desire, love, deep silence, the whole conversational dance of existence, the being of Being.

Flowers and fish are doing calligraphy with their moving about. The great sun outside and the sun inside each human hum together. The bright core of their resonance is who we are. I love this Hasidic story about the transmission of such fire:

> When the Baal Shem Tov had difficult work to do, he would go to a certain place in the woods, where he made a fire and meditated. In the spontaneous prayers that came through him then the work that needed to get done was done.
>
> A generation later the Maggid of Meseritz was given the same work. He went to the place in the forest and said, "I no longer know how to light the fire and meditate, but I can say the prayers." What needed to happen, happened.
>
> A generation after that it came to Moshe Leib of Sassov to do the work. He went into the woods and spoke, "I do not know the fire meditation or the prayers, but I still come to this place where the Baal Shem and the great Maggid came. I hope that's enough." And it was.
>
> After another twenty years, Israel of Rishin was called to the task. "I do not know the place, the fire, the meditation, or the prayers, but here, inside, sitting at table I can tell the story of how it used to go." The story had the same effect as the wilderness retreat, the fire meditation, and the prayers that came to the Baal Shem Tov, the Maggid, and Rabbi Moshe Leib.

One might follow the sequence of the anecdote and say that it shows the diminishing of a living tradition. Or one can hear in it that the mystery of doing work takes many forms, and the same continuous efficacy is there no matter whether it's the Baal Shem in solemn silence before the fire in the woods or, generations later, Israel of Rishin indoors telling the story to a table of friends.

The vital God-human or human-God connection can break through anywhere at any time. There's no diminishing of it and no fading of grace. I like to hope that Rumi's poems, even in translation, carry the essence of the transforming friendship of Rumi and Shams, that that sun can reappear, whole and radiant in any one of us at any moment.

THE BREAST MY HEART NURSES

You are the breast my heart nurses
now, God's shadow, sun that casts

no shadow. You stir the particles
of this universe, giving love to

lovers, laughter, and dance steps.
You burn thought to ash. You turn

where you wish. Soul saw a bit
of light in an eye and went there.

Toothless geezers sing love songs.
Mind loses track. Beyond existence,

beyond absence, Shams of Tabriz,
the mountain of gentleness we're

hidden in, watches through a cleft.

NO MORE *THE PRESENCE*

No more meanings! My pleasure now
is with the inner sun, the inner

moon. No longer two worlds signaling
each other. Shapes do not come to

mind. This giving up has nothing to
do with exhaustion. I walk from

one garden into another, waves against
my boat, ocean flames refining, as

fresh as flowers and fish calligraphy.
Let's see what they're writing. No

more *the presence!* Green itself begs
me dive in this that Shams has given.

OUT IN THE OPEN AIR

Tell me, is there any blessing that someone's not excluded
from? What do donkeys

have to do with fancy desserts? Every soul needs a
different nourishment, but

be aware if your food is accidental or habitual, or
something that feeds your

real nature. It may be, like those who eat clay, that human
beings have forgotten what

their original food is. They may be feeding diseases.
Our true food is the sun.

But we receive nourishment from everyone we meet. The body
and the personality form a cup.

You meet someone, and something is poured in. Planet
approaches planet, and both

are affected. A man and a woman come together, and there's
a new baby! Iron and stone

converge: sparks. Rain soaks the ground and the fruits get
juicy. We walk into a ripe

orchard, and laughter enters our souls. From that emerges
generosity. From being out

in the open air, appetites sharpen. Flushed faces come from
the sun, that rose red,

the most beautiful color on earth. There is majesty in
these connections, invisible

grandeur. Live in that place of pure being. Don't worry
about having ten days of

famousness. Revolve with me around the sun that never sets.
The sun I mention is Shams.

I could not live without his light, as a fish needs water, as
a worker appears in his

work, as every living being pastures on the meadow of the
absolute: Muhammad's horse

Boraq, Arabian stallions, even donkeys, every creature grazes
there, whether they know it

or not. Husam, heal the madness of those who feel jealous
of the sun! Put salve in

their eyes and let them see that what they are wanting
is the extinction of light!

THE EYE OF THE HEART

A beautiful woman may turn into a nightmare for you, as
also the dank bottom of

a well can start to feel like a thriving garden. The eye
of your heart continually

opens and closes, working its alchemy, and there is one
behind these illusions

who holds your loving between thumb and forefinger:
what creates every

appearance can consume any morsel in a fiery instant!

A DEEP NOBILITY

There are degrees of nearness. Simply by existing,
every creature lives near

the creator, but there's a nobility deeper than just
being. The sun warms

generally the mountainside, but it *illuminates* the shaft
of a gold mine. The bush will

never know how the sun is with gold. There are dead
branches and live branches

full of sap. The sun brings flowers and fruit from one
and more withering to the

other. Don't be the kind of ecstatic who feels ashamed
when he or she comes

back to normal. Be a clear and rational lunatic whom
the most intelligent human

beings follow. Don't be a cat toying with a mouse. Go
after the love lion. You have

inflated yourself with imagination. Drink in rather the
soul of Khidr, who doesn't

flinch when it's time to die. All winter you carved
water jars out of ice.

How well will they hold the summer snowmelt?

28. *Sacrifice: Remember Leaving Egypt*

There are comforts in staying in a condition of slavery, and there are long-wandering dry times when we leave those solaces behind to begin the pilgrimage to freedom.

REMEMBER EGYPT

You that worry with travel plans,
read again the place in the Qur'an

where Moses is taking the Jewish
nation out of slavery. You so

frantic to have more money, recall
what they abandoned to wander in

the wilderness. You who feel hurt,
remember the pavilions and houses

left behind. You that lead the
community through difficulties, read

about the abundant fountains they
walked away from to have freedom.

You who dress in clothes that appear
to have elegant meaning, you with so

much charm, remember how your face
will decay to dirt. You with lots of

property, "They left their gardens
and the quietly running streams."

You who smile at funerals going by,
you that love language, measure wind

in stanzas and recall the exodus,
the wandering forty-year sacrifice.

The doctor leans close to the yellow
ones in his garden. "A little water

will turn you rose." Red and saffron
are things we control, and yet earth

beauty steals from us, from our kind-
ness and grace. Earth beauty withers

and fails. That's what happens to
thieves in this community. It's morning.

Time to give back what you took. Then
night comes, and the stars begin talking.

Venus: *This section of sky is mine.*
The moon: *But this over here is my*

territory. Jupiter pulls out a unique
coin and shows it to Saturn. Mercury

at the head of the table says, *The*
whole sky belongs to me since all signs

begin here at the top. We're beyond
these astrological bickerings. Jupiter

begs for *our* help. The sun rides his
horse into the courtyard; we wave him

away. *Come back tomorrow.* Whoever gets
sacrificed rises again as a ceremony and

a holiday. Shams-i Tabriz went through
that change, but what he is now cannot

be said. It's as though a remote star
grew on the low branch of an olive tree.

EXTRACT THE THORN

The prophet said, "In these days the breath of God is breathing
through. Keep your ear

and mind attentive to influences and catch them!" So the divine
breath came and looked at you

sleeping and left to blow its life into someone else. Now
another breathing comes!

Don't miss this one. Your fieriness feels its extinguishing
near, as a dead soul feels

life approaching. When this breathing arrives, the animals
will pee on themselves in fear.

They won't accept it. The Qur'an says, *They refused it. They
shrank.* The center of a mountain

fills with blood. Last night this came in different images,
but some food I had eaten kept it

away! The things we forget, the people we don't meet, and the
spirit gardens we do not enter

because of food! As a camel with a great Muhammad-soul on its
back goes toward the thorn thicket

moaning, "Where is the rose garden? Where?!" While on its back
it has a bale of roses, perfume

from which could grow a thousand gardens. How long will we
keep searching for rose gardens?

What cannot be contained by the universe is hidden in the point
of a thorn! Extract the thorn and see.

29. *When Friends Meet: The Most Alive Moment*

If matter itself is ecstatic, what use is language? Consider now the inner, where the energies of singing souls see each other and talk, and walk along. I lose my place.

In the meeting of Rumi and Shams, in that vital encounter, healing and the truest life begins. Any form of beauty or wisdom or celebration that puts one back in friendship with the soul is where the opposites find rest. "How can I be separated and yet in union?"

Who is this Shams of Tabriz? The question is often asked if Rumi and Shams were lovers in the sexual sense. No. Their meeting in the heart is beyond form and touch and time.

The poet Robert Bly and I were flown over to Ankara and Konya by the Turkish government in December 2000 to help celebrate the 727th anniversary of Rumi's death, his *urs*, or wedding night. Robert in 1976 had started me out on this Rumi work by handing me some scholarly transla-

Photo by Judith Orloff

tions and saying, "These poems need to be released from their cages." As we came out of the tomb area in Konya, we sat on a stone bench to put our shoes back on. Sort of solemn with the moment, I leaned against him, "Thanks for giving me this." He looked back, "That's like thanking a bird for the wind." That broke the holy and left us laughing. Why do we visit tombs of great souls? Surely there's a resonance that feeds us, a field, a wind the freed birds rest on and ride.

One of the startling prospects that Rumi and Shams bring to the world of mystical awareness, which turns out to be ordinary consciousness as well, is the suggestion that we "fall in love in such a way that it frees us from any connecting." What that means is that we become friendship. "When living itself becomes the Friend, lovers disappear." That is, a human being can become a field of love (compassion, generosity, playfulness), rather than being identified with any particular synapse of lover and beloved. The love-ache widens to a plain of longing at the core of everything: the absence-presence center of awareness. Rumi went in search of the missing Shams. The story is that he was on a street in Damascus when the realization came that he *was* their Friendship. No separation, no union, just he was that at the silent core. I'd have to say that's the *baraka* (a blessing, the particular grace of taking in presence), the mystery of the ecstatic life.

THE MOST ALIVE MOMENT

The most living moment comes when
those who love each other meet each

other's eyes and in what flows
between them then. To see your face

in a crowd of others, or alone on a
frightening street, I weep for that.

Our tears improve the earth. The
time you scolded me, your gratitude,

your laughing, always your qualities
increase the soul. Seeing you is a

wine that does not muddle or numb.
We sit inside the cypress shadow

where amazement and clear thought
twine their slow growth into us.

THE SOUL'S FRIEND

Listen to your essential self, the Friend: *When you feel
longing, be patient, and*

*also prudent, moderate with eating and drinking. Be like
a mountain in the wind.*

*Do you notice how little it moves? There are sweet
illusions that arrive*

*to lure you away. Make some excuse to them, "I have
indigestion," or "I need*

*to meet my cousin." You fish, the baited hook may be fifty
or even sixty gold pieces, but*

*is it really worth your freedom in the ocean? When traveling,
stay close to your bag.*

I am the bag that holds what you love. You can *be
separated from me! Live*

carefully in the joy of this friendship. Don't think,
But those others love me

*so. Some invitations sound like the fowler's whistle
to the quail, friendly, but*

not quite how you remember the call of your soul's Friend.

INSIDE SHAMS'S UNIVERSE

Inside a lover's heart there's
another world, and yet another

inside the Friend of this community
of lovers, an ear that interprets

mystery, a vein of silver in the
ground, another sky! Intellect and

compassion are ladders we climb,
and there are other ladders: as we

walk in the night, the voice that
talks of forgiveness; inside Shams's

universe candlelight itself becomes
a moth to die in his candle.

LIKE LIGHT OVER THIS PLAIN

A moth flying into the flame says
with its wingfire, *Try this.* The

wick with its knotted neck broken
tells you the same. A candle as

it diminishes explains, *Gathering
more and more is not the way. Burn,*

become light and heat and help.
Melt. The ocean sits in the sand

letting its lap fill with pearls
and shells, then empty. A bittersalt

taste hums, *This.* The phoenix gives
up on good-and-bad, flies to rest on

Mt. Qaf, no more burning and rising
from ash. It sends out one message.

The rose purifies its face, drops
the soft petals, shows its thorn, and

points. Wine abandons thousands of
famous names, the vintage years and

delightful bouquets, to run wild
and anonymous through your brain.

The flute closes its eyes and gives
its lips to Hamza's emptiness.

Everything begs with the silent rocks
for you to be flung out like light

over this plain, the presence of Shams.

WAKE AND WALK OUT

If I flinched at every grief, I
would be an intelligent idiot. If

I were not the sun, I'd ebb and
flow like sadness. If you were not

my guide, I'd wander lost in Sanai.
If there were no light, I'd keep

opening and closing the door. If
there were no rose garden, where

would the morning breezes go? If
love did not want music and laughter

and poetry, what would I say? If
you were not medicine, I would look

sick and skinny. If there were no
leafy limbs in the air, there would

be no wet roots. If no gifts were
given, I'd grow arrogant and cruel.

If there were no way into God, I
would not have lain in the grave of

this body so long. If there were no
way from left to right, I could not

be swaying with the grasses. If
there were no grace and no kindness,

conversation would be useless, and
nothing we do would matter. Listen

to the new stories that begin every
day. If light were not beginning

again in the east, I would not now
wake and walk out inside this dawn.

FORM *IS* ECSTATIC

There is a shimmering excitement in
being sentient and shaped. The

caravan master sees his camels lost
in it, nose to tail, as he himself is,

his friend, and the stranger coming
toward them. A gardener watches the

sky break into song, cloud wobbly with
what it is. Bud, thorn, the same.

Wind, water, wandering this essential
state. Fire, ground, gone. That's

how it is with the outside. Form
is ecstatic. Now imagine the inner:

soul, intelligence, the secret worlds!
And don't think the garden loses its

ecstasy in winter. It's quiet, but
the roots are down there riotous.

If someone bumps you in the street,
don't be angry. Everyone careens

about in this surprise. Respond in
kind. Let the knots untie, turbans

be given away. Someone drunk on this
could drink a donkeyload a night.

Believer, unbeliever, cynic, lover,
all combine in the spirit-form we are,

but no one yet is awake like Shams.

30. *The Reedbed of Silence: Opening to Absence*

This section is meant to encourage a move into silence, to suggest that every so often, say at four-month intervals, we block out a couple of days to spend without talking or reading, without checking e-mail. No telephones or television. We get yard work done. We crawl around on the ground like lizards basking in the reptile mind, like puppies nursing the mammal slope. Touch becomes more profound and exciting. But there is an even more compelling reason for intentionally quieting down.

Rumi says silence brings a chance to taste the core of our being, to go deeper and experience the *oil* of the walnut rather than its rattling noise on the shell wall. Talking, in his metaphor, is proof we're not as free as we might be ("The Taste").

I had a dream recently about Shams Tabriz. I am shown a cave, a tunnel curving up into a shaft chamber that is called *Rasa Shamsi* (a Sanskrit word I have since learned means the "essence" or the "way" of Shams, the taste of fulfillment in the soul); I saw that spelling in the dream. Galway Kinnell, a living soul poet, has his left arm extended pointing me into the cave. I enter. Up and down the shaft of the room great beings are seated on shelf niches, sconcelike ledges, as though they were robed candles, meditating. Midway, where the entrance tunnel opens into the shaft is a wider ledge with a railing and an empty chair on it, a square, rough wooden throne. It is Shams's place, vacant. I sit on the floor to the left of the chair, facing out. To the right a man stands up to say that the most appropriate way for us to be here is to sing with strong voices. I stand and declare, "No. Silence is better." That is the end of the dream, but the feel of the cave chamber stays with me as inner depth, an absence-emptiness; not an emotion, more of a core place inside, vital and given.

The mysterious conversation (*sohbet*) of Rumi and Shams surely rests on a bedrock of silence. Carl Jung's Bollingen tower in Switzerland was deeply connected to the healing power of being quiet:

> Solitude is a fount of healing which makes my life worth living. Talking is often a torment for me, and I need many days of silence to recover from the futility of words.
>
> Letter, May 30, 1957.

The stone tower, which he retreated to and worked on from 1923 until his death in 1961, was associated with the visionary gnostic figure Jung experienced as an inner guide, Philemon. The tower is called, in a stone carving done by Jung, *Philemon's Shrine*. The Bollingen tower was Jung's celebration of the beauty of retreat and also of the importance of handwork in the soul-making process. It was where he did his own cooking, wood chopping, and building with stone, sometimes under the instruction of Italian master masons. There is a spring there he tended. He loved to make small alterations with a stick in the channels through which the water found its way into Lake Maggiore. It was not an entirely solitary place. He enjoyed having friends in for a meal and to share in the work. Jung's tower is a solid, tutelary image, a reminder of Solomon's *far mosque*, the psyche's retreat space so necessary for everyone. The *Rasa Shamsi* cave in my dream is the most powerful example I've experienced of the space.

A man once asked Rumi, "Why is it you *talk* so much about silence?" His answer: "The radiant one inside me has never said a word."

BACK INTO THE REEDBED!

Time to ignore sensible advice,
to untie the knots our culture

ties us with. Cut to the quick!
Put cotton in both sentimental

ears. Go back into the reedbed.
Let cane sugar rise again in you.

No rules or daily duties. Those
do not bring the peace of silence.

A VAGUE TRACE

Soul gave me this box of emptiness.
What I say is one truth I know. I

go to neither side of any argument. I
stay in the center letting explanations

rise from failure, this weeping witness
face, this saffron tulip, a vague trace.

Whoever understands me like Saladin
does, this is for you, this opening.

THE TASTE

A walnut kernel shaken against its shell makes
a delicate sound, but

the walnut taste and the sweet oil inside makes
unstruck music. Mystics

call the shell rattling *talk;* the other, the taste
of *silence.* We've been speaking

poetry and opening so-called secrets of soul growth
long enough. After

days of feasting, fast; after days of sleeping, stay
awake one night; after these

times of bitter storytelling, joking, and serious
considerations, we should

give ourselves two days between layers of baklava
in the quiet seclusion where

soul sweetens and thrives more than with language.

I hear nothing in my ear
but your voice. Heart has

plundered mind of all its
eloquence. Love writes a

transparent calligraphy, so
on the empty page my soul

can read and recollect.

31. *The Uses of Community: The Plural* You

I get nostalgic for community when I think of Rumi's *medrese*, the dervish college he met with; it's the same remembering how it went in Bawa Muhaiyaddeen's room. I long again for that *satsang*, or *darshan*, whatever you call hanging out with an enlightened being. Bawa called the ones gathered there "precious jewel-lights of my eyes." That kind of inner-outer community, though, does not seem to be what I am part of any-more, not in that form.

Or maybe it's nostalgia for the agreement even further back. In either case, the web of connection feels wider now, more fluid, more imagina-tively alive, and without an acknowledged focus, or exemplar. What shall we call this new kind of gazing-house, *this* way of being together? Books, film, paintings, e-mail and Internet, the cell phone, poetry readings, infor-mal gatherings of many kinds that hold us in community.

The world's longest, as far as I know, *ghazal* ("Bowls of Food") in its wandering wonders what's hidden in language, in the talk of plants, and in *the moment*, which, it says, is an embryo inside an eggshell that shatters into birth to become birdsong, and God! Such an astonishing image for the transformative edge of the present. Maybe community is in the gift of these moments, and ways we have to give voice in them, the birdsong. I have noticed how birds love to socialize and gab inside a hedge. Maybe there's a morphic resonance from other communities we can share and learn from, the essence of their moment. Maybe the invitation to meet with great souls has come, and there's a conversation for us to join in, now.

LOVE DERVISHES

It takes the courage of inner majesty
to stand in this doorway, where there's

no celebrating good fortune, where talk
of luck is embarrassing. However your

robe of patches fits is right. If you
are God's light, keep moving east to

west as you have been. Don't pretend
something other than truth. Measuring

devices don't work in this room where
the love dervishes meet. No tradition

grows here and no soup simmers! We sit
in pure absence without expectation.

THE COMMUNAL HEART

This is what grace says to the communal heart we share:
"When a gnat falls in

a vat of buttermilk, it becomes buttermilk, no longer a
gnat, so you have become

nourishment. Not drunk anymore, you *are* the wine.
Vultures learn from you

how to fly, riding a thermal of witness. Mountains get
woozy when they see you

coming, so let this love move out like music." Husam, if
I had a hundred mouths,

I would sing choral praise, but I have just this solo
tongue, which is timid and

confused with the energy wanting to come through. I
faint in the urgency.

As dust rises in wind, as a ship slides on the ocean, as
travelers get drawn along

a path, those are ways I'm lost in the presence. You are
the spring source that

makes a garden happy, and you are inside the continual
dying and coming back.

The body's death means no more than going to sleep. The
majesty you give is the

plural *you*: courage, artistic daring, and practical
guidance shine here at

the end of Book V like constellations sailors follow.

BOWLS OF FOOD

Moon and evening star do their
slow tambourine dance to praise

this universe. The purpose of
every gathering is discovered:

to recognize beauty and to love
what's beautiful. "Once it was

like that; now it's like this,"
the saying goes around town, and

serious consequences too. Men
and women turn their faces to the

wall in grief. They lose appetite.
Then they start eating the fire of

pleasure, as camels chew pungent
grass for the sake of their souls.

Winter blocks the road. Flowers
are taken prisoner underground.

Then green justice tenders a spear.
Go outside to the orchard. These

visitors came a long way, past all
the houses of the zodiac, learning

something new at each stop. And
they're here for such a short time,

sitting at these tables set on the
prow of the wind. Bowls of food

are brought out as answers, but
still no one knows the answer.

Food for the soul stays secret.
Body food gets put out in the open

like us. Those who work at a bakery
don't know the taste of bread like

the hungry beggars do. Because the
beloved wants to know, unseen things

become manifest. Hiding is the
hidden purpose of creation: bury

your seed and wait. After you die,
all the thoughts you had will throng

around like children. The heart
is the secret inside the secret.

Call the secret *language,* and never
be sure what you conceal. It's

unsure people who get the blessing.
Climbing cypress, opening rose,

nightingale song, fruit, these are
inside the chill November wind.

They are its secret. We climb and
fall so often. Plants have an inner

being, and separate ways of talking
and feeling. An ear of corn bends

in thought. Tulip, so embarrassed.
Pink rose deciding to open a

competing store. A bunch of grapes
sits with its feet stuck out.

Narcissus gossiping about iris.
Willow, what do you learn from running

water? Humility. Red apple, what has
the Friend taught you? To be sour.

Peach tree, why so low? To let you
reach. Look at the poplar, tall but

without fruit or flower. Yes, if
I had those, I'd be self-absorbed

like you. I gave up self to watch
the enlightened ones. Pomegranate

questions quince, Why so pale? For
the pearl you hid inside me. How did

you discover my secret? Your laugh.
The core of the seen and unseen

universes smiles, but remember,
smiles come best from those who weep.

Lightning, then the rain-laughter.
Dark earth receives that clear and

grows a trunk. Melon and cucumber
come dragging along on pilgrimage.

You have to *be* to be blessed!
Pumpkin begins climbing a rope!

Where did he learn that? Grass,
thorns, a hundred thousand ants and

snakes, everything is looking for
food. Don't you hear the noise?

Every herb cures some illness.
Camels delight to eat thorns. We

prefer the inside of a walnut, not
the shell. The inside of an egg,

the outside of a date. What about
your inside and outside? The same

way a branch draws water up many
feet, God is pulling your soul

along. Wind carries pollen from
blossom to ground. Wings and

Arabian stallions gallop toward
the warmth of spring. They visit;

they sing and tell what they think
they know: so-and-so will travel

to such-and-such. The hoopoe
carries a letter to Solomon. The

wise stork says *lek-lek*. Please
translate. It's time to go to

the high plain, to leave the winter
house. Be your own watchman as

birds are. Let the remembering
beads encircle you. I make promises

to myself and break them. Words are
coins: the vein of ore and the

mine shaft, what they speak of. Now
consider the sun. It's neither

oriental nor occidental. Only the
soul knows what love is. This

moment in time and space is an
eggshell with an embryo crumpled

inside, soaked in belief-yolk,
under the wing of grace, until it

breaks free of mind to become the
song of an actual bird, and God.

BLADE

The soul of this community is coming
toward us, the sun on his forehead,

wine jar in right hand, stride by
stride. Don't ruin this chance with

politeness and easy promises. The
help we called for is here, the

invitation to join with great souls.
Any place we gather becomes a ceremony

on the approach to the Kaaba. Meaning:
pass quickly through your being into

absence. The self of your name and fame
secures you with a new knot every moment.

Personal identity is a sheath. The
creator of that, a sword. The blade

slides in and unites: worn covering
over bright steel, love purifying love.

32. Eye of Water: Clairvoyance, Being Several Places at Once, and the Rainpaths of Inspiration

To use a current parapsychological research term, Rumi has a *nonlocal* dynamic in his being. In one famous poem he claims to be sitting with Shams in Konya, and also at the same time they're in Khorasan and Iraq ("Sitting Together"). I have never experienced such a thing, though my teacher, Bawa Muhaiyaddeen, told me that one could travel without an airplane! The cosmos, he said, is a tiny speck in which one can move about at will. He was able to visit me, consciously on his part, in dream. I've no doubt about that. It happened several times. My dream notebook records this one: Bawa is teaching me how to take microscopically small sips from a glass of water and also how to bow completely down. My back is stiff. When I go to Philadelphia and begin to tell him the dream, he waves me on. No need to hear about it; he was there. What did I want to know?

"What do the tiny sips mean?"

"You want to be wise too quickly. Take in a small portion of wisdom, assimilate it in your life, then take in another."

Because the evidence is not consistently replicable, institutional science will not consider what many of us know to be actual experience. We have a range of perceptions that conventional science does not admit are possibilities. Rumi's poetry very naturally speaks of telepathy, precognition, communion with the dead, remote vision, and travel in the spirit.

Whitman is on target when he says, "I am not contained between my hat and my boots." Consciousness roams about through time and space, and beyond those. We are not discretely separate in hermetically sealed units. There's overlap, and the scope of our powers has not been fully mapped. It does seem, though, that those powers have not been equally distributed among us. We may all have the potential, but not the opportunity, grace, or compassion, to develop them. We are lovers at varying depths. Rain comes, and the rainpaths follow various circuitous, direct, blurry, and sure ways into reservoirs.

My teacher tried to explain how he knew Rumi and Shams, not as historical personages or as the imagination knows characters in books, but "like I know you, like we're here together now." With enlightened beings the appearance of a gathering must be much different than it is for those of us who are not enlightened. For them, other lighted beings may be present, as well as spirit entities, and maybe even our own potential selves. There is a photograph of Bawa in a turban looking away with a severe and regal countenance. When showed the picture, he said, "That's the mood of Gilani." Abd al-Qadir Gilani is a lineage he brings forward. Some humans have one foot in timeless regions and one solidly here. The rules of a rational universe, if there be such a thing, do not always apply with them or with their poems. Rumi's poetry explores the human soul, the work it does, and many aspects of the knowing it has. The space his poetry inhabits feels like the galactic emptiness teeming with interpenetrating beings.

COOKED HEADS

I have been given a glass that has the
fountain of the sun inside, a Friend

in both worlds, like the fragrance of
amber inside the fragrance of musk. My

soul-parrot gets excited with sweetness.
Wingbeats, a door opening in the sun.

You've seen the market where they sell
cooked heads: that's what this is: a

way of seeing beyond inner and outer.
A donkey wanders the sign of Taurus.

Heroes do not stay lined up in ranks
for very long. I set out for Tabriz,

even though my boat is anchored here.

FLOAT, TRUST, ENJOY

Muhammad said no one looks back and regrets leaving this
world. What's regretted

is how real we thought it was! How much we worried about
phenomena and how little

we considered what moves through form. "Why did I spend my
life denying death? Death

is the key to truth!" When you hear lamenting like that,
say, not out loud, but

inwardly, "What moved you then still moves you, the same
energy. But you understand

perfectly now that you are not *essentially* a body, tissue,
bone, brain, and muscle. Dissolve

in this clear vision. Instead of looking down at the six
feet of road immediately

ahead, look up: see both worlds, the face of the king, the
ocean shaping and carrying

you along. You've heard descriptions of that sea. Now
float, trust; enjoy the motion."

LIGHT BREEZE

As regards feeling pain, like a hand cut in battle,
consider the body a robe

you wear. When you meet someone you love, do you kiss
their clothes? Search out

who's inside. Union with God is sweeter than body comforts.
We have hands and feet

different from these. Sometimes in dream we see them.
That is not

illusion. It's seeing truly. You do have a spirit body;
don't dread leaving the

physical one. Sometimes someone feels this truth so strongly
that he or she can live in

mountain solitude totally refreshed. The worried, heroic
doings of men and women seem weary

and futile to dervishes enjoying the light breeze of spirit.

SITTING TOGETHER

We sit in this courtyard, two forms,
shadow outlines with one soul,

birdsound, leaf moving, early evening
star, fragrant damp, and the sweet

sickle curve of moon. You and I in a
round, unselved idling in the garden-

beauty detail. The raucous parrots
laugh, and we laugh inside laughter,

the two of us on a bench in Konya, yet
amazingly in Khorasan and Iraq as well,

friends abiding this form, yet also
in another outside of time, you and I.

SEEING WITH THE EYE OF WATER
WE FLOAT ON

My mention of Moses may block the message, if you think
I refer to something in

the past. The light of Moses is here and now, *inside* you.
Pharaoh as well. The ceramic

lamp and wick change, but the light's the same. If you
focus on the translucent

chimney that surrounds the flame, you will see only the many,
the colors and variations.

See the light within the flame. You *are* that. Where you
perceive from should not

change what you perceive, unless you're in a dark room. Some
Hindus brought an elephant to

exhibit. They kept it in a dark house. People went in and
out. They couldn't see anything.

They felt with their hands. One person touched the trunk.
"It's like a downspout."

One, an ear. "More like a fan." The leg. "I find it round
and solid like a column

on a temple." One touches the back. "An enormous throne."
One says, "Straight," another,

"Crooked." If each had a candle and if they went in together,
the differences would disappear.

Sense knowledge is the way the palm knows the elephant in the
total pitch-dark. A single

hand cannot know the whole animal at once. The ocean has an
eye. The foam bubbles

of phenomena see separately: we bump against each other,
asleep in the bottom of

our body-boats. We should wake and look with the clear
eye of water we float on.

SOLOMON'S SIGHT

Wisdom is Solomon's seal: the whole world, a form
wisdom animates. Or call it

the soul that collects in human beings and lets them reign
over the leopard, the lion,

and the crocodile in the river. What threatens a person
more than those, though,

are the invisible forces that fight in his or her heart.
You wade in a river to wash.

Something cuts your foot, a thorn, a piece of shell. You
cannot see what, but you

know you're hurt. When wisdom transforms the senses, you
will *see* and feel whose

words fall away and whose remain inside you to guide.

33. Music: Patience and Improvisation

We *are* a music that longs to be free and set others free. What happens when we listen to music and just after? Music mixes and becomes part of our waiting and opening to improvisation. Listening was central to Rumi's practice.

There's an inner patience that allows inspiration. We wait to learn the timing of art. I have a friend who as a child when she took piano lessons would sometimes go back and add a note she hadn't played. "The time for that note is over," said her teacher.

Was it a *New Yorker* cartoon? There's a kid in the subway listening to a man noodling on the sax. His mother is pulling on him. "Come on honey. That's not real music. He's just making it up." Following inspiration and the nudges of intuition sets the vitality of our unique music in motion.

WE NO LONGER SEE THE ONE
WHO TEACHES US

Musician, play this moment's music as grace
for those who block our road, grace for

bandits! Musician, you learned this from
a true bandit. I hear the teacher's accent

in the student's art. Musician, turn your
face to absence, because existence is

deceitful and afraid. The soul knows it is
not from here. It feels bound in a body,

yet also knows the pleasure of absence.
Absence is the ocean we swim! Existence, a

fish hook. Anyone caught loses the joy
of freedom. Being nailed to the four

elements is a crucifixion. If you keep
running after your wishes and desires,

that's *your* crucifixion, be sure of it!
There is a fire in patience that burns

what of you is born to fine ash. Strike
the flint of Sura 100, *Honor the one*

who loses breath. And, *Fire rises*
where they walk. These are brave souls,

musician igniting musician. What's the
point of the chess-game world where a

pawn cuts off a king? I walk awkwardly,
but the smoke goes straight up.

Sometimes a pawn makes it to the other
side and redeems a queen. The knight

says, "Your plodding is one or two moves
for us." Judgment Day is closer than

that for everyone, one step away. The
chess king says, "Without me this motion

and figuring mean nothing. The bishop
might as well be a mosquito." Winning

and losing are the same. There's *check-*
mate in both. We no longer see the one

who teaches us. You could say we've
been checkmated. What happens now?

MUSIC LOOSENS DEAFNESS

You that pour, people don't see
the beauty anymore of this joy

we call wine. The clear saying
of wisdom cannot now be easily

213

heard by the soul. And sign
language won't help. We need

the sword of Shams to free us.
We have wanted material things

more than the deep connection
of this circle, bread more than

wine. You've heard how Moses
was with God on Sinai. That

closeness is far away now. Look
at the overcast sky: it's not

the splendor of feeling near.
We've been lazy. We should

either disband altogether or
not stay apart so long. Let

music loosen our deafness to
spirit. Play and let play.

This is Jami's (1414–92) story about the song power of the ache for
freedom.

JAMI'S THE CAMEL DRIVER'S SONG

A sufi was on the path of clarity. Every day he walked
the desert, and every night

he walked and slept in the emptiness of God's custody.
One night he came upon

a merchant's tent and felt the need for conversation. He
lifted the tent flap

and saw a black slave in chains, unable to move, but shining
with intelligence like

the moon. "Help me," the slave whispered. "My master will
not refuse a guest. Ask

him to set me free." The merchant welcomed the sufi
to his tent and brought

food. "I cannot accept your generosity until you release
this poor man." "I will.

But first listen to what I have suffered because of him!
I used to have many purebred

camels, beautiful animals with humps like mountains, swift
as the wind over steep

and flat, powerful as rhinoceri, tall and dignified as
elephants. Their crossing

and recrossing this desolation were the source of my
existence, their bells my most

wished-for sound. As they traveled, this camel driver sang
songs. The camels heard

and carried their loads with courage and discipline. This time,
though, when we unloaded

them, they fled in every direction, vanished in the desert,
all but the one still

tied outside my tent." The sufi said, "Let me hear the camel
driver's song." The master

gestured, and the slave began. The visitor sat politely
watching the tethered animal,

but as longing deepened in the song, the night walker
tore his clothes and fell

on the ground, while the last camel snapped its rope and
escaped into the darkness.

34. Gratitude for Teachers: The Lesson of Dogs

I am very grateful for the gifts my soul teachers have given. Jim Hitt's (high-school English) love for the place where writing and living intersect, sitting out on the bluff talking that, the dirt road on the island going down inside the river. James Pennington (Latin) and his *cuties*, the elegant Virgilian phrasing, crystal cabinets. *Hac iter Elysium nobis: the journey is the kingdom!* Alvaro Cardona-Hine, James Dickey, Robert Bly, Galway Kinnell, C. K. Williams, Robert Hass, Annie Dillard. Now that I start with names, I might go on filling the air like an assembly field in a Tibetan mandala. Henry Miller, Dostoyevsky, Rinzai, Gary Snyder. Surely if we could *see*, we are each a swarm of teachers and learners.

It was Bawa Muhaiyaddeen who told me to do the Rumi work and led me to the edge of the awareness the poems come from. Osho Rajneesh warned that these poems could, for me, become *ecstatic self-hypnosis*, which was helpful, though I haven't absorbed the whole lesson yet. I keep listening to Osho's wonderful tapes. Joe Miller said that if I spoke Rumi's poems enough out loud, my heart would melt. I'm certainly giving *that* a shot.

Forgive the absurd anachronism of the Three Stooges in the opening poem of this section. Michael Green once asked our teacher Bawa about the puzzling combinations of Arabic letters at the beginning of certain suras in the Qur'an. Bawa leaned close and whispered, "The Three Stooges!" He was joking with Michael's esotericism, but he may have been communicating some subtlety that will resonate with someone who knows the Qur'an more devoutly than I. I include those movie rascals in this poem to give a taste of Bawa's humor, and because they seem to want to be here.

THE THREE STOOGES

When eternity touches anything temporal, silence deepens
and becomes one zeroed thing

made of both. Dervishes can find a hundred ways to say
how this happens. I've

no interest in more poetic images. Mysterious combinations
of Arabic letters stand

at the beginning of certain Qur'anic chapters: *alif lam
mim ha-mim*. They seem

like other letters, but only as biscuits resemble the
moon! A true feeling of

what comes from the presence can free the imprisoned
and resurrect the helpless.

Some word combinations, like skin-and-bone arrangements,
have sublime qualities. These

three people talking in the street are ordinary young
men, but *Alif, Lam,* and

Mim have an exchange more like Larry, Curly, and Moe.

LISTEN TO THE DOGS

Those who don't appreciate what they've been given are worse
than dogs. When a dog gets

fed at a certain door, he becomes a guardian there. He'll
risk his life protecting

it. And if a strange dog comes, he teaches him to go where
he was first fed. "Go

back and do your duty!" It's the same with those who have
eaten at a spirit door

and drunk its water. You've been given mystical knowledge
and selflessness in

your soul, but still you sniff like a bear at other shops.
For bread soaked in gravy

you walk the town, but it's not material food that makes you
flourish. The table you love

is in the room of Jesus where people gather at dawn: the
blind, crippled, palsied, and

poor. Jesus finishes his morning practice and comes out.
Whatever you wanted, you've been

given. Now go and live in that kindness. They get up
quickly like camels that have

been untied. You have lived through many diseases because
of the teachers you've known.

Your limp has turned to a smooth step. Tie a cord around
your ankle, so you don't

forget what you've been given. Ingratitude and forgetfulness
block the further blessings

they could give. Run after and catch up and beg for
mercy. Stay near the door.

Don't be less than dogs! This brings up the question of who
to be more faithful to,

your parents or your soul. Your father joined with your
mother and your form began

inside her. For a while she felt you as part of herself;
then you separated. The right

of the soul is prior to the right of parents and more
powerful. Anyone who

doesn't understand this is dumb and stubborn as a donkey.

THE BOW TO ADAM

What is a living death? To forget the one who teaches you,
which is often the

wisdom that comes in suffering and difficulties. The more
of that you have, the more

soul. In what way are we above the animals? With that
same consciousness that builds

in us then, in humbling circumstances. There is a
hierarchy: human over

animal, angel over human, with the true human being's soul
over those. Why else would

angels be commanded to bow to Adam? The soul of all things
follows the one-pointedness

of a true human being as thread follows needle.

TO TRUST THE OCEAN

A stranger criticizes a certain teacher, "This man is not on
the path. He drinks wine.

He's a hypocrite and something of a scoundrel. How can he be
helpful?" One of the students

replies, "This is not true, but even if it were, someone who
is a friend of God cannot

be judged by any standard. The Red Sea is not polluted by
one dead bird." Conventional

signposts do not guide someone who with every step gets lost
again in the desert. One who

lives in union sees with the lamp of intuition. There is no
road for such a being. If he

or she points a particular way, it's only to say something to
dialecticians, those who

understand through opposition. To the newborn, the
father babbles language noise, while

the child with his pure intellect scans the universe. The
nobility of a master is not

diminished by some misplaced diacritical marking. Try to go
inside the infant's vast

wordlessness, which is the same as the silence of a teacher.
Criticism and mistrust have

a small range. Where there is only the face of God, all
judging of betrayal and

disobedience fades. This body head is a screen for mystical
awareness, a big jar put down

over a lantern. What is mistrust? Forgetting your teacher.
Who is alive? Someone who knows

and trusts the ocean where the teacher lives. Such awareness
includes and directs angels

and humans, birds and fish. The fish, in fact, bring gold
needles in their mouths

for him to patch his robe with, as they did for Ibrahim.
Do you remember that story?

STRANGE GATHERING

This man holds up a tambourine
and an entire musical mode comes

into the air! Prepare to travel;
tie the pack; open out the flag.

John the Baptist and David and
Joseph are turning somersaults!

Jesus and Moses watch Gabriel by
the door casting spells. Abraham

looks lost in his longing, holding
a sword over Ishmael *and* Isaac.

They bow down. Muhammad says to
God, "My true brothers are those

who believe, though they do not
see me. I wish I could *see* them."

Abu Bakr, "True. It's true." Layla
and Majnun, Husrev and Shirin

stay glass-bright in the world of
pleasure; Rustam, warrior, Hamza,

Muhammad's uncle, arrows, shield,
and Ali's sword: who could stand

against that blade or throw it and
split the moon? Husamuddin here

is love's king. He bows at the
name of Shams Tabriz and says

again, *I am the truth*. The soul
is tremendously honored by that.

AUCTION

As elephants remember India
perfectly, as mind dissolves,

as song begins, as the glass
fills, wind rising, a roomful

of conversation, a sanctuary
of prostration, a bird lights

on my hand in this day born of
friends, this ocean covering

everything, all roads opening,
a person changing to kindness,

no one reasonable, religious
jargon forgotten, and Saladin

there raising his hand to bid
on the bedraggled boy Joseph!

SCATTERBRAIN SWEETNESS

There is a glory that breathes life back
in a corpse and brings strangers together

as friends. Call that one back who fills
the held-out robe of a thornbush with

flowers, who clears muddied minds, who
gives a two-day-old infant wisdom beyond

anyone's learning. "What baby?" you ask.
There is a fountain, a passion circulating.

I'm not saying this well because I'm too
much in the scatterbrain sweetness. Listen

anyway. It must be said. There are eyes
that see into eternity. A presence beyond

the power and magic of shamans. Let that
in. Sink to the floor, full prostration.

EVERY SECTION OF ROAD

Move about. Take trips. Travel as a pawn goes one slow move
at a time to redeem

the wide-ranging nobility of the queen. Joseph traveled, and
everything came to him.

A man goes to live in the country because his friend lives
there, taking his whole family

with him. By day under the scorching sun; by night, learning
to plot the stars.

Every section of road seems amazing because of the one they
go to see. Bitter,

complaining people sound dear. Thorns have charm. A
narrow room grows vast.

Thin sticks turn to plump figs. Straps cut a load carrier's
back. Smoke blackens

the ironsmith's face. A shopkeeper sits on his bench
in a torture of boredom.

Pain gets lived through, because somewhere nearby
there's a Friend. A

merchant goes on a long land-and-sea journey for the sake
of those at home.

A CAP TO WEAR IN BOTH WORLDS

There is a passion in me that doesn't
long for anything from another human

being. I was given something else, a
cap to wear in both worlds. It fell

off. No matter. One morning I went
to a place beyond dawn. A source of

sweetness that flows and is never less.
I have been shown a beauty that would

confuse both worlds, but I won't cause
that uproar. I am nothing but a head

set on the ground as a gift for Shams.

35. Forgiveness: As a Christian Disappears into Grace

Every religion has times of renewal, of emptying out and beginning again, times of forgiveness. Surely this is at the core of Christianity.

Rumi's connection with Jesus stays strong. Christians feel it when he speaks of the Friend. My friend, the writer Jim Kilgo, says that the Christian idea that God is available to human beings as a friend is what he hears when he reads Rumi—that inner friendship.

In the Sufi tradition they sense that the energy in Jesus reappeared in the form of Rumi. Rumi is known to the Sufis as the pole of love, the *qutb*. This traditional invitation into Rumi's community sounds very like what I heard in the Christian gatherings of my youth.

> Come, come, whoever you are,
> wanderer, worshiper, lover of leaving.
> This is not a caravan of despair.
> It doesn't matter that you've broken
> your vow a thousand times, still
> come, and yet again, come.

THE SPRING

A Christian goes to his priest and tells a year's worth of
sin: fornication, meanness,

hypocrisy. He wants to be forgiven, and he hears the
priest's absolving as grace.

The priest himself may have no experience of that mercy,
but the Christian's imagination

gives it to him. Love and imagination do many things. They
conjure up a sweetheart's form,

so that you can speak to it, "Do you love me?" *Yes, yes.* A
mother beside the new grave

of her son says things she never said when he was alive. The
ground there seems to have

intelligence. She lays her face on the fresh earth, giving
her love as never before.

Days and weeks go by. Grief for the dead diminishes. Soon
there is nothing but

oblivion at the grave site. Let your teacher be love itself,
not someone with a white

beard. In the state of *fana*, love without form says, *I am
the source of sober clarity*

*and drunken excitement. You have loved my reflection in forms
so well that now there's*

no mediating. When a Christian longs to be forgiven,
the priest disappears

in that longing. Water flows out of the ground over a stone.
No one calls it *a stone*

anymore. It's the pure substance pouring over it, *a
spring.* These forms we're

in are like bowls. They acquire value from what pours
through to serve as nourishment;

then they're washed and put away for the next use.

THE WAY THAT MOVES AS YOU MOVE

Some commentary on the verse, *As you start on the way,
the way appears. When*

you cease to be, real being comes. Zuleikha shut every
door, but Joseph kept

rattling the locks. He trusted and kept moving back and forth, and somehow he

escaped. This is the way to slip through to your non-spatial home. Think how

you came into this world. Can you explain how that was? No? The same way you came, you

leave. You wander landscapes in your dreams. How did you get there? Close your eyes

and surrender. Find yourself in the city of God. But you're still looking for

admiration! You love how your customers look at you. You sit at the head of the assembly.

When you close your eyes, you see people applauding, as surely as an owl shuts its

eyes and sees the forest. You live in an admiration-world, but what do you offer admirers?

If you had true spirit gifts to give, you would not think of customers. There was once

a man who said, "I am a prophet. In fact, I am the edge of prophecy moving through time."

People surround him and tie him up and bring him before the king. "What right

does this man have to say that he lives in the place of revelation?" The man himself

speaks up, "Think how an infant sleeps and grows unconsciously into awareness.

Prophets are not like that. They pass *awake* from the source to this up-and-down of the five

senses, this left-right back-and-forth." "Put him on the rack," they scream.

But the king sees that the man is thin and fragile. He
speaks gently. Kindness

is his way. He disperses the crowd, sits the man down, and
asks where he lives. "My home

is the peace of God, but I have come to this judging place
where no one knows me.

I feel like a fish upon sand." The king keeps trying to
joke him out of his state. "But

why did you make these claims *today?* Was it something you
ate?" "I don't care about

world-food. I am tasting God's honey, but what is that to
these people? They're like

mountain rocks. They scoff at me by echoing what I say. If
I brought them news of money,

or a love note from a sweetheart, they would welcome me. But
not with this prophecy talk.

It's like a blood-soaked bandage on a donkey's back. The one
who removes it is being helpful,

but he's going to get kicked! No one here wants to be
healed. Show me someone who

wants what I have!" The king becomes more curious about the
man. "What is it *exactly*

that you who have come as messengers have to give?" "What do
we not have! But let's

suppose for a moment that my inspiration is not divine.
Still, you would agree, my

speaking is not inferior to the workings of a bee? The
Qur'an says, *God has inspired*

the bee. This universe is filled with honey. Human beings
feed on it and evolve upward

with the same, but more profound, inspiration as the bee."
So the man defends his claim.

You have read about the inspired spring. Drink from there.
Be companions with those

whose lips are wet with that water. Others, even though
they may be your father

or your mother, are enemies. Leave, before they kill you!
The pathless path opens

whenever you genuinely say, *There is no reality but God.*
There is only God.

WE PRESCRIBE A FRIEND

We are wisdom and healing, roasted
meat and the star Canopus. We're

ground and spilled wine soaking
in. When illness comes, we cure

it. For sadness we prescribe a
friend. For death, a friend. Run

to meet us on the road. We stay
modest, and we bless. We look like

this, but this is a tree, and we
are morning wind in the leaves that

makes the branches move. Silence
turning now into this, now that.

How can we know the divine qualities from *within?* If we
know only through metaphors,

it's like when virginal young people ask what sex feels like
and you answer, "Like candy,

so sweet." The *suchness* of sex comes with being *inside* the
pleasure. So whatever you

say about mysteries, *I know* or *I don't know,* both are close
to being true. Neither is

quite a lie. Someone asks, "Do you know the prophet Noah?"
You may answer, "Well, I've

read stories in school. I've heard the legends that have
come down." But only someone in

Noah's state can *know* him. Now I hear a theologian reacting,
"Don't get stuck in that ditch!

What you have just said is absurd." And that king of saints,
the *qutb,* replies, "Any state

other than what you have experienced seems absurd. You have
had certain visions. Before

them, did not mysticism sound ridiculous? What you've been
given has released you from

prison, ten times! And won't this empty desert freedom you
feel now someday be confining?"

Now I lay me down to stay
awake. Pray the Lord my soul

to take into your wakefulness,
so that I can get this one bit

of wisdom clear: grace comes to
forgive and then forgive again.

GRACE GOT CONFUSED

One maddening drop, then another,
you pour wine for us now like that.

Remember when you poured full light
all at once, a whole day! You put

your finger on your lips wanting
quiet, but those drops you drip

keep talking. It's not us! As you
were killing Junnaiyd, he said, *More,*

more! In each blood drop of his, a
new Bestami. The first that fell

on ground grew Adam. In the sky,
Gabriel. Those old days you poured

according to merit. Then grace got
confused, and you poured everybody

some. Bread does not deserve you,
yet you lived your life for bread.

You brought water and threw it at
the water carrier. What you showed

Moses was not fire, but a shape of
consciousness. Will that Friday

ever come again when you served
your close friends *individually?*

Each moment a stranger and friend
meet. Their bloods mix. Roses

drop petals in autumn. Shy. Offer
your friendship to the prophets!

Don't think they're ordinary people.
There's a huge difference in the

quality of praying, as between those
you bless and those you turn from.

36. Soul Art: The Hungry Animal and the Connoisseur

Many of these poems could go in several different sections. The poem I have called "If You Want to Live Your Soul," for example, has advice about the importance of meeting the Friend. It also has the wonderfully elaborate word-working image of rain and guttering, so I include it in this group.

How you love is the sky itself. When it rains (the grace of energy), an individual roof with its guttering (the personal self) conducts water flow like skill with language. Rumi says the most beautiful gardens grow from the rain collected in the barrel under your own roof, the one with your tears in it.

Soul artists guide the motions of energy that's given. One of the models of this for Rumi was Hakim Sanai (d. 1131). It is said he could hold two opposing energies in one gesture: his wildly instinctual, sudden leaps and his settled discernment walking with one stride. These poets, Rumi and Sanai, nourish us by pouring the genuinely ecstatic into our lives as surely as children do, or dogs or trees or river or rain.

I am given a six-foot snakeskin. A king snake has used my doorsill stone to snag on, rid himself of the old, and renew. It is strung out whole so that I must step over it to enter or leave. I lift the glassen tissue and lay it over my small cabin bookcase, like Indian braids hanging down each temple, some unpredictable denouement.

ONE HUMAN GESTURE

You have a source inside you, a cool spring that sometimes
stops flowing, frozen

or clogged with silt. A voice says, "Consider the situation
more deeply, my friend."

Such advice is not idle. It is immediate companionship with
a soul artist like David,

who works iron until it melts and he can shape it. Spirit
is the art of making what's

blocked start moving again. When your body dies, give
it to the death angel,

Israfil. If your heart feels numb and metallic, walk out
into the sun, or whatever

the mystery is that makes *your* inner spring well up. There
was once a sage who felt

this flow moving inside him. As he walked the garden
that was being restored with

spring water, he gave names to aspects of the vital dance
he was doing: *the animal's*

hungry agility and *the connoisseur's intelligent choice.*
Blessings on Hakim

Sanai, who could put those two in one gesture!

THE MANGY CALF

I went to the doctor who could cure me
and said, "I have a hundred things wrong.

Can you combine them into one?" *I thought*
you were dead! "I was, but then I caught

your fragrance and started to live again."
Gently he put his hand on my chest. *Which*

tribe are you? "This tribe." He began to
treat my illness. Whenever I was angry

and aggressive, he gave me wine: I quit
fighting; I took off my clothes. I sang

in the circle of drunkards. I roared and
broke cups, even big jars! Some people

worship golden calves. I am a mangy calf
who worships love. The healing one is

calling me out again from the hole I have
put myself in. My soul, if I'm agile,

or stumbling, confused, or if I'm in my
true being, it's all you. Sometimes I

am the sleek arrow; sometimes the worn
leather thumbguard. You brought me here

where everything circles. Now you put
a lid on the wine; I'll close my mouth.

BEGGARS

There's a voice in the beggar's ear that says, *Come close.*
Generosity needs you.

As beautiful people love clear mirrors, so abundance becomes
visible when you move near.

God reminded Muhammad not to shout and drive away the
beggars. *Approach the source*

with both hands out begging! There are two kinds of
mendicants: one grace causes

to call out for alms in the street, while the others are
given immediately more than

they need without saying anything. Both are mirrors for how
the absolute acts. Anyone else

is a fake. Don't hand a piece of greasy bread to the picture
of a dog! The beauty that a

true dervish hungers for is real. How can someone in love
with his own imagination also

be in love with the lord of all giving? I'll tell you.
There's a quality of sincerity in

some that leads them from metaphor to what's behind the
metaphor. I'm afraid to

elaborate on this. Weak minds may use the explanation
foolishly. Think of a sad

face drawn on paper. Can it learn from its grief? There is
a happiness and a sadness

that are just figures on a bathhouse wall. Move through the
world naked, noticing the pictures

that *live*. Inner joy and grief are different from artful
appearance. Take off your

phenomena-clothes when you enter the soul's steam bath: no
one comes in here with clothes on.

IF YOU WANT TO LIVE YOUR SOUL

The soul within our individual souls
loves the one who runs and falls down

more than the one who sits and watches.
The soul within soul lives in a lover.

Consider this metaphor: how you love is
the open sky. These personal selves are

the separate roofs of a town. Your tongue,
the guttering where words flow. If the

roof's not clean, the water-words get thick
and murky. Some people have elaborate

systems that drain water from other roofs.
This is not wise. There's a false eloquence

to it. A lover is one who waters a garden
from the rain barrel that fills under his

own roof. Roses that grow from that have
tears in them. Sometimes the scale pans may

weigh correctly, but the balancer is off.
A sweet doctor may give bitter medicine.

A foot finds the right shoe in the dark.
Love moves on its way through the pleasures

it feels. Even though the time you live in
is violent and frightening, you're safe in

Noah's boat. If you want to know who someone
is, hang around with those close by. They

know. The rule that covers everything is:
How you are with others, expect that back.

If you want to know God, enjoy the company
of lovers. If you want to be thought a great

person, learn some subtle point and say it
with many variations as the answer to every

question. If you want to live your soul,
find a friend like Shams and stay near.

37. More Pilgrim Notes: Habits That Blind the Psyche

Not all of Rumi's poems encourage ecstatic communion. Some are more like practical travel advice. In Bunyan's *Pilgrim's Progress*, the Slough of Despond (the swamp of feeling depressed) must be negotiated and Vanity Fair (the town that encourages talk-show ambitions and conspicuous luxury) passed through. On Rumi's pilgrimage there are dangers and distractions not so openly allegorical as Bunyan's. He warns against conduct that disorients the caravan, self-destructive passion, and whatever blocks kindness and one's connection with a teacher.

Any human action that turns cold can delay the soul's pilgrimage. Everything is about encouraging the deepening of love and compassion. Rumi advises specifically against jealousy, wanting world-power, and toying with fermented drink. His image of the so-called lovers who are cruel to each other is a scene of demented dolls pulling the stuffing out of one another. He also recommends we be slow to blame anyone other than ourselves.

And the corollary to that might be: when you give advice, be sure you can accept it for yourself. A story has come down about Rumi: a woman asks if he would say something to her young boy about his eating too much of a particular kind of white-sugar candy. Rumi tells her to come back in two weeks. She does, and he tells her again to come in two weeks. She does, and he advises the child to cut down on sweets.

"Why did you not say this a month ago?"

"Because I had to see if I could resist having that candy for two weeks. I couldn't. Then I tried again and was successful. Only now can I tell him to try not to have so much."

HABITS THAT BLIND THE PSYCHE

Are you so full of light you can recklessly court
unconsciousness? "Look

for shade on a bright day," they say, not on a cloudy
night when everything is

already obscure. Habits that blind the psyche throw
dust in the eyes of our

guides. Toying with fermented drink, for instance. No
need to honor a petty thief.

Keep his hands tied, or he will tie yours. The real
wine is your compassion.

The taste of that keeps the caravan pointed home. Be
reasonable! Don't give

morning energy to what clearly hurts you!

DOLLS THAT PULL THE STUFFING
OUT OF EACH OTHER

You that give nourishment and steadiness and freedom,
give the bent soul strength

to stand up straight in the work it knows it's here
to do. Give us patience and

generosity and clarity to see *through* the images that
appear. There is a coarse

desire that wants world-power; there are armies that
kill their own relatives;

and there is the bitter pleasure of dolls that pull the
stuffing out of each other.

Read the passionate love stories again. Notice how
everyone *perishes* in what is

not love. Love is when the holy nothingness loves itself.
Jealousies come as kindness

turns cruel. If there were no legal punishment, no threat
of prison, people would shred

their enemies, the so-called lovers. Envy connects deeply
with the old ambition of fallen

angels, who *do* exist, and they have human helpers who try
to destroy anyone who

has loved and received wisdom from a teacher.

BEING SLOW TO BLAME

The king asked his faithful servant Ayaz to give some
judgment on the accusers

who had broken into his room and found only Ayaz's old
work boots and tattered

sheepskin jacket. Ayaz delayed his decision, but when the
king urged him for a quick

decision, Ayaz answered, "All command is yours. What is
Venus, Mercury, or the rare

appearance of a comet when the sun is out? I hesitate to
blame anyone in this

matter. If I had not done my strange honoring of those old
earth-covered clothes, I would

not have triggered the imagination of these who love to
look for faults. Doing

that with me, though, is reaching into a river to find a
dry clod. How can a fish

betray the sea? They were looking for some mistrust in one
whose enveloping medium

is trust." I would comment on Ayaz's words if I didn't know
how many are waiting to

misquote me and cause confusion. There is a voice that
doesn't use words. Listen

to that as your personal self breaks open. Taste the
silence in the oil of a nut.

That sweet joy is the reason we bother with walnut-rattling
words at all. Hear the ecstatic

dumbness inside poetry and discourses on mystery. For
one day try *not* speaking!

CUISINE AND SEX

You risk your life to feed desires,
yet you give your soul only short

grazing spans and those grudgingly.
You borrow ten and repay fourteen.

Most of your decisions can be traced
back to cuisine and sex. The fuel

basket goes from one stoke hole to
the next. Six friends hoist your

handsomeness and carry it to the
cemetery. Food changes going from

table to latrine. You live between
deaths, thinking that's right enough.

Close these eyes to open the other.
Let the center brighten your sight.

The soul fell into the soup
of nature and started mixing

with all manner of delicious,
and not so tasty, ingredients.

Our actions take on a tinge
of those we're near. God

keep us from bitter company!

Be clear and smiling for those who
are glad to see you. Someone who's

not, let his way darken like a pen
leaving its faltering ink trail.

NO DISCUSSION

West or East, there has been no lover
like me: my sky bends back like a

bow at full draw for centuries. I am
the lucky one who wakes for a lover's

touch. With bitter medicine I taste
sweet juice. If you resent the cure,

you stay sick. Apprentice bows to
master in silence, no impudent banter.

Underwater, divers hold their breath.

ONE WHO CAN QUIT SEEING HIMSELF

I look for one simple and open enough
to see the Friend, not an intelligence

weighing several perspectives. I want
an empty shell to hold this pearl, not

a stone who pretends to have a secret
center, when the surface is all through.

I want one who can quit seeing himself,
fill with God and, instead of being

irritated by interruption and daily
resentments, feel those as kindness.

38. The Mystery of Renunciation: A Way of Leaving the World That Nourishes the World

Renunciation may be another way of listening better, listening within, without distractions; listening to the point of being here, near people with open hearts.

In the Sheikh Sarrazi story ("Sheikh Sarrazi Comes In from the Wilderness"), it is said there is only one rule: never be satisfied in your longing for light! Sarrazi's last job is to go door to door with an empty basket. He may seem to be begging, but he's really offering others a chance to listen for how they are prompted by inner guidance. The mystery of the voice that comes when we *listen* is the Friendship that is Sheikh Sarrazi's core of being, the wild presence celebrated in much of Rumi's poetry. That open heart is the empty basket Sarrazi takes door to door!

A WAY OF LEAVING THE WORLD

Some clouds do not obscure the moon, and there are mornings
when drops of rain descend

from an open sky. A saint is a cloud that's here, but
with its cloud nature

erased. Something in us wants no intermediary, no nurse,
just to be the wide blue

merged with the mother's breast, sublime emptiness. There
is a way of leaving the

world that nourishes the world. Don't do anything for
applause. Khidr scuttled

the fisherman's boat, but that demolishing was kindness.
What you are is a soul

that is both food and hunger, longing and what the
longing is for. Remember

that, and try then to experience renunciation.

ONE-HANDED BASKET WEAVING

There was a dervish who lived alone in the mountains,
who made a vow never to pick

fruit from the trees, or to shake them down, or to ask
anyone to pick fruit for

him. "Only what the wind makes fall." This was his way
of giving in to God's

will. There is a traditional saying of Muhammad that
a human being is like a

feather in the desert being blown wherever the wind takes
it. So for a while in

the joy of this surrender he woke each dawn with a new
direction to follow. But

then came five days with no wind, and no pears fell. He
patiently restrained

himself, until a breeze came just strong enough to lower a
bough full of ripe pears

close to his hand, but not strong enough to detach the
pears. He reached out and

picked one. Nearby, a band of thieves were dividing what
they had stolen. The authorities

surprised them and immediately began the punishments: the
severing of right hands

and left feet. The hermit was seized by mistake and his hand
cut off, but before his

foot also could be severed, he was recognized. The prefect
came. "Forgive these men.

They did not know. Forgive us all!" The sheikh said, "This
is not your fault. I broke

my vow, and the beloved has punished me." He became known as
Sheikh Aqta, which means

"the teacher whose hand has been cut off." One day a visitor
entered his hut without

knocking and saw him weaving palm-leaf baskets. It takes two
hands to weave! "Why have you

entered without warning?" "Out of love for you." "Then
keep this secret which you

see has been given to me." But others began to know about
this, and many came to

the hut to watch. The hand that helped when he was weaving
the palm leaves over and

under one another came because he no longer had any fear of
dismemberment or death. When

that anxious, self-protecting imagination leaves, the real
cooperative work begins.

NOT A FOOD SACK, A REED FLUTE

You that add soul to my soul, who
hear my night grief, timely, un-

likely fire in every grain of my
being, mountain sound harmonizing

with my song, magnet for form, you
have none! With your joy I live

my entire life in a small valley.
Without you, every natural pleasure,

of tasting, of intelligence, of
being outdoors, becomes a heavy

wooden hobble tied to my feet. I
untie it and see it's immediately

there again. Tonight is a night
when grace gives me a love book to

read. I empty out whatever blocks
a clear note. Not a food sack,

I'm a reed flute. There is no cure
for this soul but you, Averroës.

THE FLOWER'S EYE

Find me near the flower's eye
that takes in provocation

and begins to grow. Love a
baby that struggles and fights,

stops nursing, and runs out
through the door, escaping as

fire jumps to the next burn.

SHEIKH SARRAZI COMES IN FROM THE WILDERNESS

Sheikh Sarrazi, great ascetic and eater of vine tendrils,
is tired of existence. He

wants to know the beauty more directly. He prays in the
desert for death, but the voice

of the unseen comes, "Not yet. Go to the city and become
like Sheikh Abbas, the seller

of date syrup, the storyteller who begs from house to
house." Sarrazi is always

in conversation with this voice, and his devotion to it is
so complete he changes

his life. You can read about this in Shams's book of sermons,
the *Maqalat.* I won't say

more here. Someone might misunderstand. Sarrazi goes from
the desert to the city, his

face glowing with Friendship. The city elders come out to
welcome the saint and

to ask him to give discourses. "No. My mission now is
quietness and humility, not

self-advertisement. I shall carry this basket from door
to door, saying one

thing, 'If God prompts you to give something, be generous.'
I'll accept whatever

it is." Sheikh Sarrazi wants only intimacy with the voice
he hears. Love for the invisible

is enough. He needs no wages. There is nourishment like
bread that feeds one part

of your life and nourishment like light for another. There
are many rules about restraint

with the former, but only one rule for the latter, *Never be
satisfied.* Eat and drink

the soul substance, as a wick does with the oil it soaks in.
Give light to the company.

I THROW IT ALL AWAY

You play with the great globe of
union, you that see everyone so

clearly and cannot be seen. Even
universal intelligence gets blurry

when it thinks you might leave.
You came here alone, but you create

hundreds of new worlds. Spring is
a peacock flirting with revelation.

The rose gardens flame. Ocean
enters the boat. I throw it all

away, except this love for Shams.

39. Warrior Light: How One Embodies the Collective

This moment this love comes to rest in me,
many beings in one being.

There is a *power* that accumulates when someone does inner work. Moses communes with God in desert solitude, and Mt. Sinai begins to dance! Meditation and prayer and *sohbet* (inner conversation) are ways to align with the *Tao*, silence, the kindness of an open heart.

A chained bear may seem to be doing the trainer's bidding, but there is a wild motion *inside* the bear that has nothing to do with any exchange of coins or idle street entertainment. A natural warrior energy builds on retreat.

This has nothing to do with military fighting or the martial arts. No swinging of swords. The mystics agree, *If we fight within to make ourselves clear, once that inner war is over, there need be no outer war. The only war is within.*

Those doing soul work, who want the searing truth more than solace or applause, know each other right away. Those who want something else turn and take a seat in another room. Soul-makers find each other's company.

Jafar, Muhammad's cousin, was a warrior of concentrated
light. When he rode up

to a walled city, it was no more to him than a gulp of water
in his dry mouth. This

happened at Mutah. No one went out to fight him. "What's
to be done?" the king asked

his clairvoyant minister. "If you strap on your sword
with this one," replied

the advisor, "also wrap your shroud around you!" "But
he's only one man!"

"Ignore the singularity. Look with your wisdom. He
gathers multitudes, as stars

dissolve in sunlight." Human beings can embody a
collective, a majesty

of spirit, which is not like having a name or a body.
A herd of onagers may display

a thousand antler points; then a lion comes to the edge of
their field: they scatter.

INSIDE SOLITUDE

A human being is like the rod Moses held, or the words
Jesus said, the outer just

a piece of wood or mouth sounds from a country dialect.
But the inner can divide

the green ocean and make the dead sit up and smile. You
see the far-off tents of an

encampment: you go closer. There's a dust shape, someone
walking. Closer. Inside

that, a man, bright eyes and strength of presence. When
Moses returns from the

wilderness where he goes alone, Sinai begins to dance!

THE BEAR'S TRUE DANCE

Have you heard about the man in India who meets a desperate
crowd on the road? He

sees they have suffered a tragedy. They have no provisions,
no money, no hope. His

wisdom blossoms out of his love like a sudden rosebush. "I
understand what has happened

to you, but up ahead beside this road is a young elephant.
Do not kill and eat that

baby elephant. It would be an easy solution to your hunger,
so tender and weak it is,

and seemingly untended. But understand, the mother elephant
is there somewhere, even if

not visible. Elephants accompany their children as God his
lovers. Absence and presence

are identical states. Ravaged, orphaned, exiled, imprisoned,
these are not true

qualities of existence to the loving ones who stay inside
the Friendship. A

hundred million scattered dervishes do not act alone, but as
one magnificent body. Don't

touch the young elephant! You will regret it for generations
to come. Look farther down

the road. A chained bear dances for the merchant's greed,
but the bear's true dance

has nothing to do with honey or marks on paper documents."

40. *Choosing and Total Submission:* Both Are True

This cannot be understood by the rational mind:

> *Every human choice bows like a slave in submission to the absolute's creative*
>
> *will, yet this does not deprive us of freedom or of taking responsibility for what we choose.*

> (*Masnavi*, V, 3097–98)

We do make choices in time and space, yet they occur within the wider context of an absolute creative will. I can paraphrase Rumi's statement, but that's not to say I understand.

The only way to *know* the play of destiny and free will is to dance the mystery and die inside it. Reconciliation comes as hearts open within an art beyond any figuring.

CHOOSING AND TOTAL SUBMISSION

A philosophically minded thief was shaking down fruit
in an orchard when the owner

came by. "Have you no reverence for divine commandments?"
"But look at this abundance!

I am just the agent of its enjoyment." The owner tied the
man to a fruit tree and began

beating him. "This is a simple, uncomplicated cudgel. I am
merely the instrument of its justice."

"Wait! You're right. I recant the necessitarianism. There
is free will. We *do*

have choices! Please stop!" Everyone has the power to
choose, because the creator

chose to create, so that freedom is innate. And this is
the extraordinary truth:

every human choice bows like a slave in submission to
the absolute's creative

will, yet this does not deprive us of freedom or of taking
responsibility for what

we choose! You might get clever and say, "My doubting
God's existence was

willed by God." Only half true. You also *chose* to doubt.

THESE DECISIONS

The old argument continues about fate and free will with
the king and his advisors

talking. The king rebuts their contention that all actions
are predestined. "But

surely we must be responsible for what we do! Why else
would Adam admit guilt?

Rather, he would have used Satan's answer, *You led me
astray*. Adam did have a

choice." Yet somehow both are true, destiny and free will.
We vacillate between

journeys. Shall we go to Mosul for trade or Babylon to
learn occult science?

These decisions are real. One person drinks a lot of wine.
Does someone else wake up

nauseated? When you work all day, *you* get the wages. A
child born from your soul

254

and body holds on to *your* legs. When has it been otherwise?
And if the consequences fail

to show up here, be sure they have taken form in the unseen.

FRINGE

You wreck my shop and my house and now my heart, but
how can I run from what

gives me life? I'm weary of personal worrying, in love
with the art of madness!

Tear open my shame and show the mystery. How much longer
do I have to fret with

self-restraint and fear? Friends, this is how it is:
we are fringe sewn inside

the lining of a robe. Soon we'll be loosened, the binding
threads torn out. The beloved

is a lion. We're the lame deer in his paws. Consider what
choices we have! Acquiesce

when the Friend says, *Come into me. Let me show my face.*
You saw it once in preexistence;

now you want to be quickened and quickened again. We
have been secretly fed

from beyond space and time. That's why we look for
something more than this.

The *Masnavi*
Book IV

Introduction

RUMI'S WILD SOUL BOOK

In cave drawings there are sometimes X-ray, essence-energy lines drawn from the mouths of animals to their hearts.

The *Masnavi*[1] is Rumi's heart-breath community voice. This walking-around poem was spoken as Rumi strolled the streets and gardens and orchards of Konya with his scribe Husam Chelebi during the last twelve years of Rumi's life (1261–73). It has that peripatetic feel, a moving vicinity that filters many subjects. I am told that *upanishad* means a sheaf of notes taken by someone at the side of a master. The *Masnavi* is such a collection. Much of it too was spoken in the dervish college Rumi headed, its fluid form reflecting the way a master tends soul growth, sometimes individually, sometimes for the group.

The *Masnavi* is an ocean-openness. As we listen to it, a synchrony rises. They say that sufis don't pray, because they know that *everything* is God. What could they want? Take Rumi's book with you to the mountains. It has a motion that belongs there, a wildness beyond Thoreau or D. H. Lawrence or Nietzsche. This wildness is in the area of Bodhidharma and Niffari, Blake and Hafez. You feel it in the proliferation and in the fierce shards of its ruin. "All we sell here is *fana* and *baqa*" (VI, 1528).

MUD AND GLORY

There are scandalous episodes in Rumi's *Masnavi*,[2] so much so that one of them at least ("The Importance of Gourdcrafting") has caused a curriculum adoption of *The Essential Rumi* to be cancelled in Berkeley, California! Parents and teachers were offended.

Rumi's stories with their wild moments belong in the tradition of medieval *fabliaux*. They are very like those European and Near Eastern stories, but with a radiant difference. A *fabliau* (Old French, "a little fable") is a raucous peasant tale, often scatological (involving excrement) or lewd. People, mostly men, get themselves in absurd, humiliating postures similar to those assumed in defecation or copulation, but in *fabliaux* the cramped calisthenics take place out in the open for everyone to see. I have vivid memories of such scenes not because I read medieval French, but because in 1959 I took a graduate course at Berkeley with Alain Renoir (son of the movie director Jean, grandson of the painter Pierre Auguste). Alain was a great teacher and a solid medievalist. He retold a few *fabliaux* for us twenty first-semester graduate students in a classroom in Dwinelle Hall. He stomped about putting on shoes filled with imaginary shit, squishing obliviously through swamps and hatfuls of the stuff. He sidled, with his enormous virtual erection, into the chambermaid's pantry.

Perhaps you discovered, dear reader, as I, in your high-school library the naughty minx-wives and daughters of Chaucer's miller and reeve. The musical-bed capers, the snoring and the farts, O country lore of puberty in Nevill Coghill's translation:

> That's how the carpenter's young wife was plumbed
> For all the tricks his jealousy could try,
> And Absalon has kissed her nether eye
> And Nicholas is branded on the bum,
> And God bring us all to Kingdom Come.[3]

In the *Masnavi* a man is discovered by his wife with his thighs drenched with gism and the vaginal juices of their maid. The husband is pretending to do his daily prayers. "So this is how a man prays, with his balls!" the wife screams (V, 2203).

In another story, Nasuh, a virile young man, works as an attendant in the women's bathhouse. He has acted effeminate to appear harmless in this sensitive job. As the secret of his continuous hard-on is about to be revealed, just at the point of near humiliation, his awareness breaks open and expands beyond the personal.

> *At that moment his spirit grows wings and lifts. His*
> *ego falls like a battered*
>
> *wall. He unites with God, alive, but emptied of Nasuh.*
>
> (V, 2274–76)

Nasuh's breaking into an enlightened state through the *threat* of sexual embarrassment is perhaps a moment unique in literature. Rumi uses *fabliau* moments, always, to look into soul growth. A glutton has shit in his bed. Muhammad comes to wash the bedclothes. With shame comes an opening.

He's quiet and quivering with remorse. Muhammad bends over
and holds him and caresses

him and opens his inner knowing. The cloud weeps, and then
the garden sprouts. The baby

cries, and the mother's milk flows. The nurse of creation
has said, Let them cry

a lot. This rain-weeping and sun-burning twine together to
help us grow. Keep your

intelligence white-hot and your grief glistening, so your
life will stay fresh.

(V, 132–39)

An adulterous judge is hiding in a clothes chest being carried down the street. He talks to the porter:

"Tell the court deputy to come and buy this chest and take
it, unopened, to the judge's house."

"Is this the voice of God or a genii talking to me?"

(VI, 4493–95)

Like scenes from a Marx Brothers film or a Charlie Chaplin skit, or perhaps more accurately, from the raw, priapic interludes of Greek drama or, later, the Italian *Commedia del Arte*, such shenanigans we have with us always. Rumi uses them to look at, and love, our insistent, stubborn, insatiable desire-bodies, the hypocrisy of hiding them, and the wisdom of not identifying with them.

Bill Clinton, ole buddy, helped us feel something of this human crux more recently. The foolishness of those months in 1998 seems almost wistful now. Larry Flynt's roll call of matching Republican sleaze, the beautiful black clergy standing quietly in the Rose Garden. Wonder what the poor pasty, sexless slug Ken Starr is examining now, whose spattered dress?

Rumi lets the judge speak from within his box.

A lover of world-things has put himself in just such a box.
Though he appears to be free,

he can see nothing but the inside of his chosen chest.

(VI, 4496–97)

How do these ridiculous and sometimes horrifying incidents (a woman is killed having sex with a donkey [V, 1333–1405]) fit in this poet's wider vision? Beautifully, I would say, with an openness about experience that is still difficult for us to accept.

T. S. Eliot says of William Blake's poetry, "It is an honesty, against which the whole world conspires, because it is so unpleasant." The same is true of Rumi's details of embodiment. He uses grungy specifics to say truths about transcendence. Consider "Two Ways of Running," (V, 2163–2204), in which the agile energy with which a husband runs after his desire, the young maid, and the way the wife runs, who is trying to catch him at his lust, are contrasted; the former motion is like that of the lover of God and the latter like the heavy tread of the literalist or the rule enforcer. Rumi honors the direct, more necessary enthusiasm of the husband rather than the mean-spirited, "gotcha" mentality of the wife.

As the humbling, and healing, truth finds voice, the outrageous boxes of personae pretense (false egos) fall open, and the impulse is to laugh and weep at once. So Rumi's ecstatic vision includes this kind of *shadow work*, if it can be called that, attention to the *nafs* ("the wantings"), to the shame attached, and to its uncovering. He is a surgeon lancing infection, unbandaging armored crust, or at the least waving away the flies, his image for our self-protecting excuses.

> *Put your vileness up to a mirror and weep. That's when the real art, the real*
>
> *making, begins. A tailor must have a torn shirt to practice his expertise.*
>
> (I, 3205–9)

The empty mirror is Rumi's metaphor for what the heart becomes within quietness and meditation. There is a necessary grief at the inception of ecstatic art. *I want a howling hurt!* ("Not Here," chap. 22). We Americans are familiar with this because Emily Dickinson is one of our national poets; she specializes in ecstatic grief.

As Rumi takes away the self-protecting excuses, the making of soul comes in.

> *Don't believe you're healing yourself!*
>
> (I, 3227)

Prayer is an egg. Hatch out the helplessness.

(III, 2175)

Your defects are the ways that glory gets manifested.

(I, 3210)

He celebrates the clearing and refreshment that pours through when we acknowledge the animal energies, the *nafs,* and the shadow side of personality. Singing those out loud, we wake each other up. We empty out a libation of tears. Rumi reminds us to bring what is taboo or repellent in ourselves to awareness, because that difficult attention opens the heart and keeps us intensely in the moment where the clearer passion lives.

These spectacular, in some ways comic, instances of soul-making happen in the theater of shame. Also there's some evolutionary revisioning going on, along with the sheer delight of creation in this land of fuddle and cruelty. Some mysterious opening of essence builds as we turn the refuse of mistakes over in the sun, like garbage being composted on a Damascus street (*"Mashallah,"* chap. 11). Rumi hears mistakes as a music we ride, the chant of *mashallah,* the divine presence inside desire. "Kiss the snake that guards the treasure" ("Cleansing Conflict," chap. 11). "Good and bad are mixed. If you don't have both, you don't belong with us."[4]

In a startling image he contends that love is a courtroom *where we must bring in harsh evidence* ("Cleansing Conflict"). Rumi says that he is in love with God's mercy and forgiveness and that he is also in love with God's wrath and destruction. I do not claim to live in that space, though I can say this: working with rage and jealousy and other fears, such as the fear of abandonment, impotence, or embarrassment, leads to the breakthroughs necessary for depth in relationship, which can open the soul to possible enlightenment.

Living in such dynamic mutability, we must constantly admit we don't know how the outcomes will go by saying, *Inshallah,* "If God wills." Rumi hears this as the acknowledging of an original human agreement with the divine. That agreement is most clearly felt as we understand how knowing with the linear mind is different from the way of the heart. Rational linear proof is what the mind demands. The heart's way begins when one lays one's head on a person's chest and drifts into the answer. Such knowing grows with being in harmony with the mystery of another human being, which includes remembering, listening, and the ecstatic sense of a sacred universe. As more identifications with body and personality drop away, the center of the self grows more vital.

Someone might say that center is Rumi's *companion*, Shams, the inner core, Friend, or beloved. Someone might name what walks along with, and within, him. I can't, though I hear it playing in the high-trickster humor. I hear it in the conversation Solomon has in his morning refuge, and in the "double music of existence" (Book IV, p. 319).

Rumi's bawdy stories are about opening and reading the body's letter to the creator of the universe. He says this reading is our most courageous work (Book IV, p. 318). Majnun slides down from the high camel that has been carrying him in his sleep, on its own low errands away from the direction of his longing for Layla (Book IV, p. 316). But what shall we ever say of longing and what the longing's for?

> *The clear bead at the center changes everything.*
> There are no edges to my loving now.
> ("The clear bead . . . ," chap. 5)

The shocking, off-color segments have to do with the periphery of that center, with being in a body, the fury and mire of human veins (Yeats), with love as it washes through the senses. Erect penis, wet vagina, sneeze, snore, fart, eyes-shut come cry, piss-relief sigh. Rumi puts every body noise, especially the grunting and humping, the nibbling and groans of erotic trance, in the foreground. He listens to learn what that section of human experience says of soul growth. In the *fabliau* pieces of the *Masnavi* Rumi takes us down the spine to the lower chakras. In those stories we feel the force of their pulling; then he helps us know something. The escapades always make a point about the quality of the cruder energies and their potential for transformation.

> The Caliph was sexually impotent, but his manliness was
> most powerful. The kernel of
>
> true manhood is the ability to abandon sensual indulgences.
> The intensity of the captain's
>
> libido is less than a husk compared to the Caliph's nobility
> in ending the cycle
>
> of sowing lust and reaping secrecy and vengefulness.
> (V, 4025–33)[5]

Like the captain and the caliph, we each have a different, specific work to do. The stories of the *Masnavi* help us discover what that is. Rumi explores one metaphor for this in Book IV, the world as a bathhouse (p. 274). There are furnace stokers and there are those who bathe. The fire-building energies and the emptying-out longings for purification *cooperate* to let the bathhouse flourish. There's a competitive atmosphere among the ones who heat up, the fierce furnace workers,[6] and a relaxation, a peace, in the ones who lean back and lave. But it's the action of both that lets the full range of human awareness thrive. And sometimes, members of the groups change places! The intensity-lovers and the meditators work the same shift. A "stoker" in a public bath was socially looked down on, but in Rumi's bathhouse that snobbery dissolves; stoker and bather do one work, and there are beauty and symmetry to the energy exchange. Maybe the fury that feeds intensity takes the purification deeper, or maybe the bathhouse has hidden purposes only the lover inside all love knows, the ultimate creative, morphogenetic field, deepest companion. At any rate, Rumi's bathhouse world, in the many modes and messages of the *Masnavi*, is trying to say some whole, elusive truth of human life—how lotus grows from mud, how bawdy and sublime are near of kin, and how Majnun must slide down off the camel and break his leg on the way to Layla. We leave him lying in the road. The point may be a simple one: that the life energies in passion and compassion, in lust and in the expanded state of vision, have one source. But the implications for soul growth are profound and difficult for me to say. The mystery of this "marriage of heaven and hell" we live is that *without contraries is no progression.*[7] Soul growth moves with *both* sides of the bathhouse, reason and energy, in meditation and in the flames of our wanting.

THE FORM OF THE WHOLE

I was asked once whether I thought Rumi's *Masnavi* was finished. It's a good question. The *Masnavi* doesn't have a satisfying beginning, middle, or end; it seems composed of strands and fragments, but I contend it is whole, complete as a day is, or a human life. There's no beginning or end to the flowing of heart energy.

T. S. Eliot on the long poem: "You cannot create a very large poem without introducing a more impersonal point of view, or splitting it up into various personalities." Rumi's extra large long poem (six books, sixty-four thousand verses) is a community, an ocean with layers of different temperatures that support the various life-forms of a dervish college.

For me, the best image for the form of the *Masnavi* is how an enlightened master is, and talks, with those around him or her, those held in the *nazar*, the realm of the master's *glance*. The *Masnavi* is complete, because it comes from the whole. I can't prove this, of course, or say anything more. Experiment with it. Enter the poem anywhere and swim around; listen for resonance; experience the motions. Let its filaments connect with your life. Synchronicity, I propose, is the matrix. Or say that any great artwork is a field, that the *Masnavi*, like the *Divan* of Hafez, spreads out a spontaneously exploratory, tending region of consciousness. The concept of *morphic resonance* applies. Works of literature are agents in the continuous revisioning of the language of who we are and are becoming. A rosebush lineage of old masters meets with us there in the work and prompts new energies, new grief, new ways of creating. Or it may be some other unprovable invisible reality, like love.

I had a dream recently that might be trying to show something of how these fields perform. I am walking around composing poems *about* walking around streets and gardens. I am reading the poems to a moving audience who has before them, in some form, although not pages, the growing text that I am composing. I come to a stopping place. I don't have the words. A friend in the audience gives me his text, which has my additions, though in somewhat different lineation and phrasing. I say that I'm going to use his changes. So it goes, communal, generous, and very friendly, the *making* and the stroll.

The concept of the *qutb* is that there is an infinitely complex divine field presiding over all at every moment. Maybe Rumi's *Masnavi* is a product of the working of such a field.

> In the ocean there are many bright strands
> and many dark strands like veins that are
>
> seen when a wing is lifted up. Your hidden
> self is blood in those, those veins that are
>
> lute strings that make ocean music, not the
> sad edge of surf, but the sound of no shore.[8]

Or say the *Masnavi* is the magnificent, symphonic mess we are: the gallery of scamps I have lifted my yardstick to could have included many more: Faraj, the servant who is fooled on his wedding night by the substitution of a boy for his aristocratic bride, but keeps on with his unstoppable fumbling. And the military captain of *el grand libido* who leaps from lovemaking to kill a lion roaming the camp and immediately returns, with no diminishment of tumescence, to his much-relished game, barely missing a beat. The animal energy of the strong and salad young, and not so young, is celebrated, not in D. H. Lawrence's dark-god sense, but as flutes for the divine flow streaming through.

Surely we have felt such music moving in us. The God-self flows in all mediums, but God, that's hard to know at the time! The animals embodying the animal energy in humans are prominent notations for that music in Rumi's poetry. It's a menagerie, an ark with everything from dugong to ant to parrot and porcupine, with Noah there supervising, and that's the point: we're connected *through energy* to the animals. Rumi strongly senses the human-animal bond, as did the cave-drawing masters.[9] The natural energies flow directly to our opening hearts and the clearing vision of the witness. They give the process juice and joy. They propel a widening of perception.

A lotus flower must grow out of mud: compassion and enlightened seeing flow through Rumi's stories from the moments of getting caught red-handed, *with our dangly bits in the air,* to wisdom. Sometimes he calls those animal strands the "rooster of lust," the "duck of urgency," the "peacock of wanting to be famous," and the "crow of acquiring stuff." For soul growth, one doesn't kill the animals, but *incorporates* them. You can learn much from the dog of desire, Bawa kept telling me, but don't let it drag you all over town from one piece of dung to the next thrown-out fish head to whatever piss signals others have strewn along the street. Keep your dog tied up, take it for walks at your own pace, and give it scraps from time to time. If you don't, you may find yourself on stage, where it will become more publicly obvious how you must recognize and transform the animals into the great love vision and way that Rumi's poetry, and every enlightened master from every and no tradition, draws us out onto the high plain of. Caravan fires in the middle distance. We'll be in their company by dark.

Rumi's parables of ridiculous embarrassment make fine additions to those of Jesus (we've been wanting them), the *hadith* ("traditional sayings") of Muhammad, the Zen sutras, Mayan stories, and contemporary poems, the camp-circle words that help us live with and within unconditional love and widen the concentric knowing that is our poignant mystery.

BEING GOD'S SPIES

It is rare that an enlightened being is also a great poet. Why is this? Putting aside the enormous difficulty of agreeing on what either "enlightenment" or "great art" is, it may be that someone who surrenders to living the unsayable truth most often has little interest in tending to the details, the craft of language.

My theory about why the combination of great art and enlightenment is so unusual involves the dance with the shadow and with the animal soul that I've been trying to discuss. That work helps the enlightened being grow as an *artist*. Shakespeare's treatment of the breakthroughs made in jealousy and ambition and aging petulance leads to this enlightened kindness passage at the end of *King Lear*:

> Come, let's away to prison:
> We two alone will sing like birds i' th' cage:
> When thou dost ask me blessing, I'll kneel down
> And ask of thee forgiveness: so we'll live,
> And pray, and sing, and tell old tales, and laugh
> At gilded butterflies, and hear poor rogues
> Talk of court news; and we'll talk with them too,
> Who loses and who wins, who's in, who's out;
> And take upon's the mystery of things,
> As though we were God's spies. . . .
>
> (V, iii, 8–17)

An enlightened artist takes on the mystery of *things*, and the beauty and power of the art has to do with the lively specificity of embodied energies, the song in prison. "Pray you undo this button," says Lear. Or the *fabliau* close-up: Juhi's (Nasruddin's) hand moving up the woman's thigh, so he can determine the length of her pubic hair, which is the *theological* point he's occupied with (V, 3325–50). It's true that Rumi caresses the world, as a great artist must, even as he hears the great wind of leaving it rising. Galway Kinnell says that the core of soul art is a *tenderness toward existence*. Rumi's poetry loves full sun *along with* the willow's silky shadow moving on the ground.

Willow weep for me.

A Blessing for Readers
Praise to Early-Waking Grievers

In the name of God, the Most Merciful and Most Compassionate.

This is the fourth journey toward home, toward where the great advantages are waiting for us. Reading it, mystics will feel happy as a meadow feels when it hears thunder, the good news of rain coming, as tired eyes look forward to sleep. Joy for the spirit, health for the body.

In here is what genuine devotion wants, refreshment, sweet fruit ripe enough for the pickiest picker, medicine, detailed directions on how to get to the Friend.

All praise to God. Here is the way to renew connection with your soul, and rest from difficulties. The study of this book will be painful for those who feel separate from God. It will make others grateful. In the hold of this ship is a cargo not found in the attractiveness of young women.

Here is a reward for lovers of God. A full moon and an inheritance you thought was lost is now returned to you. More hope for the hopeful, lucky finds for foragers, wonderful things thought of to do. Anticipation after depression, expanding after contraction.

The sun comes out, and that light is what we give, in this book, to our spiritual descendants. Our gratitude to God holds them close to us, and brings more besides. As the Andalusian poet Adi al-Riga says,

> I was sleeping and being comforted
> by a cool breeze, when suddenly a gray dove
> from a thicket sang and sobbed with longing,
> reminding me of my own passion.
>
> I had been away from my own soul so long,
> so late-sleeping, but that dove's crying
> woke me and made me cry. *Praise*
> *to the early-waking grievers!*

Some go first; others come long afterward. God blesses both and all in the line, and replaces what has been consumed, and provides for those who work the soil of helpfulness, and blesses Muhammad and Jesus and every other messenger and prophet.

Amen, and may the Lord of all created beings bless you.

PRELUDE

Husamuddin! *Ziya-Haqq*, God's light. You draw this
Masnavi out in the open

again, your rope around its neck leading God
knows where! Some

have expressed gratitude for this poem; this poem
itself lifts hands in

thanksgiving, glad as a vineyard in summer heat. The
caravan loads up and breaks

camp. Patience shows the way into joy. Face down, flat
on the earth. Husam, the

sun-sword of one light, many wander in moonlight,
but when the sun comes up,

the markets open. Exchange gets clear. Buyers and
sellers can tell false

coins from true. Thieves recede from the scene. Only
counterfeiters and those

who need to hide avoid sunlight. Let Book IV be part
of the light! Whoever reads it

for entertainment is himself or herself an idle hour. Whoever
hears in it a *value* to use *now*

in soul-making becomes himself or herself *that necessary*.
What was water to Moses

turned to blood for the Egyptians. May the gift of this
poem's vision not leave

the world. Husam, if some story was not finished in Book
III, begin there.

Book IV

The lover who hides from the night patrol in the orchard and sees his beloved again

Yes! The lover who hides in the orchard because of
the night patrol. He has no hope

of finding the beloved again. He has only descriptions,
remote as though they were

recalling the great Simurgh bird. He had one meeting,
lip-touched by honey, but when

the journey, the daily being inside the presence, began,
difficulties rose: the lover,

restless and fire-footed as a deer; the beloved growing
more and more elusive. As it

happens sometimes, though, the unlooked-for one appears again
in the orchard. She is *there*

with a lantern looking down in the creek for a ring she has
lost. In the delight of

her water-illumined face he feels praise coming through him
for God *and the police!*

"They brought me here! Set them free of policing!"
When word comes down

of new regulations, the police get very alive, but when
a king relaxes rules,

the police grow melancholy. The lover prays that
the night patrol be healed

of such rigid depravity, because in trying to avoid them he
has found his beloved. This is

how it goes in the time region. What's foot to one fetters
another. Venom circulates

perfectly in a snake. The ocean water that nourishes fish
brings a painful death to land

animals. Anyone's experience can multiply this common truth:
saint turns betrayer; the same act

can be both wound and shield. If you want to see the
beloved's face, borrow

the beloved's eyes. Look through them and you'll see the
face everywhere. No tiredness, no boredom.

"I shall be your eye and your hand and your loving."
Let that happen, and things

The preacher who prays for his attackers;
the soul as a porcupine and a raw hide in the tanning process

you have hated will become helpers. A certain preacher
always prays long and with

enthusiasm for thieves and muggers who attack people on
the street. "Let your mercy,

O Lord, cover their insolence." He doesn't pray for
the good, but only for the blatantly

cruel. *Why is this?* his congregation asks. "Because they
have done me generous favors.

Every time I turn back toward the things they want, I run
into them. They beat me and

leave me nearly dead in the road, and I understand, again,
that what they want is not

what I want. They keep me on the path. That's why I honor
them." Those that make you

return, for whatever reason, to God's solitude, be grateful
for them. Worry about

the others, who give delicious comforts that keep you from
prayer. Friends are enemies

sometimes and enemies friends. There is an animal called an
ushghur, a porcupine. If you

hit it with a stick, it extends its quills and gets bigger.
The soul is a porcupine, made

strong by stick-beating. So a prophet's soul is especially
afflicted, because it has to

become powerful. A hide soaked in tanning liquor becomes
leather. If the tanner did not

rub in acid, the hide would get foul-smelling and rotten.
The soul is a newly skinned hide,

bloody and gross. Work on it with manual discipline and the
bitter tanning acid of grief,

and you'll become lovely and very strong. If you can't do
this work yourself, don't

worry. You don't even have to make a decision, one way or
another. The Friend, who

knows more than you, will bring difficulties and grief, and
sickness, as medicine, as

happiness, as the essence of the moment when you're beaten,
when you hear *Checkmate*,

and can finally say with Hallaj's voice, *I trust you
to kill me.*

The night police acted out of meanness, but sometimes
that brings lover and beloved

   Jesus is asked the hardest thing to bear; the discourtesy of the lover

together. A curious man comes to Jesus and asks,
"What is the hardest thing

to bear in existence?" *Dear friend, God's anger is the most
difficult, the wrath.*

*Hell trembles within it. Everything quivers at the thought,
"How can I be safe from that?"*

By giving up your own anger at anyone or anything.
Give it up now!

The world cannot function without urine, but that stale
is not clear creek water. So

after a long absence, the lover moves to the beloved,
reaching to hold and kiss her.

"More courtesy, please!" she says. "But no one is here, only
the light wind. You and I

are alone, and I am so thirsty!" "Don't talk this
foolishness. If a wind

moves, there must be presence coming through." Wind
is no different from the portion

of air you direct with a fan, *your* purpose is there in
the air. Wind moves like breath,

sometimes speaking praise, sometimes satire. A
breath-wind lives in you,

so that you may know other winds: kindness in spring,
winter cruelty; at harvest

the wind does winnowing. Ships under sail pray for it.
Wind of toothache, push of childbirth,

victory. Wind is the motion of creation, body moved by
spirit. The lover replies,

"I may be foolish with this reaching for you, but at least
I'm not standoffish."

The sufi's wife is caught with the shoemaker

The beloved then begins a story, about a sufi who comes home
in the middle of the day, a thing

he never does, to catch his wife with the shoemaker. "It's
a small house, one room

with one door, where the wife is joined with the cobbler
in that even smaller room

where the body's work goes on. A knock comes and, though
God hides our sinning again

and again, sometimes it's the death angel. This woman has
done this with men many

times. It's a light thing to her, idle amusement, but with no
escape, she finds herself

out on a wide plain with everything obvious, no slight rise
to shield her, no low place.

She throws her hooded robe over the shoemaker and opens
the door. Like a camel standing

on the stairs, it's clear a naked man is under the *chadar*.
'One of the town ladies

is here to visit. I locked the door so some strange
man could not surprise us.'

'Is there some favor I can do our guest?' 'She wants an
alliance with our family.

She wishes that her son and our daughter be married. Her
son, though, is out of town

at present. But be certain, the young man is handsome and
industrious, a very *active*

lad!' 'Why should such a wealthy family consider a match
with us? It's like making

a double door with one of pine and one of carved ivory!'
'Exactly what I said! Evidently

they're tired of the *visible* world. They want only modesty
and purity. They want nothing,

and that's what we have! Look around: this is the bare
essence of *chastity*.' 'True.

This is a very *narrow* room, space only for one, and she in
her quietness and innocence, has

understood the nature of our condition.' I tell you this
farcical exchange,

because it's how you're talking to me. This deceptive
description of your discourtesy

as *not standoffish!* God has found names like *basir,* seeing,
or *sami,* hearing, or *alim,*

knowing, but these are for qualities, not the reality.
Bashful is not proper for an

impudent man. You might call a child *Hajji,* pilgrim, or
Ghazi, warrior, to reflect

the lineage, not what's inside. I knew your tendencies
before we met. You

think the gazelle of my soul has no shepherd, my breath
no mover. That is why

for eight years I have left you alone on your side of
the bathhouse. Imagine

The world as a bathhouse

the phenomenal world as a furnace heating water for
the public bath. Some people

carry baskets of dung to keep the furnace going. Call them
materialists, energetic,

fire-stoking citizens. One of those brags how he's collected
and carried twenty dung baskets

today, while his friend has brought six! They think
the counting up at nightfall

is where truth lies. They love the smoke smell of dried
dung. *Look how it blazes up like gold!*

If you give them musk or any fragrance of soul intelligence,
they find it unpleasant and

turn away. Others sit in the hot bathwater and get clean.
They use the world differently.

They know and love the feel of purity, and they have
dust marks on their foreheads

from bowing down. They are separated by a wall from those
who feed the fires, busy in

the boiler room belittling each other. Sometimes, though,
one of those leaves the furnace,

takes off the burnt-smelling rags, and sits in the cleansing
water. The mystery is how

the obsessions of furnace stokers keep the bathwater of the
others simmering perfectly. They

seem opposed, but they're necessary to each other's work:
the proud piling up

of fire worship, the humble disrobing and emptying out
of purification. As the sun

dries wet dung to make it ready to heat *water,* so dazzling
sparks fly from the burning

The tanner who faints in the perfumers market; lover and beloved talking

filth. Do you remember the tanner who was walking through
the perfumers market and fainted?

He was looking for the materials of his trade, took
a shortcut, and blacked out

when he smelled the jasmine and rosewater. Tanners rub
acidic excrement into hides

to soften and cure them. They get accustomed to the bitter
smell they live within.

They cannot tolerate sweetness. The perfumers try
their medicines to revive

the man. Nothing works. The skillful doctoring has no
effect. They go to

the tanners and tell them the problem. His brother
understands. He comes with some

dog dung hidden in his sleeve. He takes the unconscious man's
head in his hand, bends close

as though telling a secret, puts the dog dung next to his
brother's nose, and slowly

the man comes to. 'Ah, he knows how to enter the dream!' say
the dealers in essence. The great

Galen once advised, *Give the patient what he was used to*
before he became ill. He

is sick because of something unusual to him. The cure will
come in something familiar.

The same goes for a soul shocked into a swoon. A
sensualist will not revive with

esoteric texts. Give something more familiar. The
nourishment of revelation

must sometimes be mixed with overblown fanfare, sarcasm, and
pointless jokes. The young

man has fallen to the street again. What shall we do?
Devise your own medicine.

Egyptian alchemists tell of a way they know to hatch a bird
out of compost, and not an ordinary

bird either, but a raptor of far-seeing wisdom! It can
happen that a dung beetle

gets a sprinkle of light and grows noble." The beloved
continues talking with the lover,

"Eight years I cooked you in separation from me, but you
haven't changed! Still raw

and sour. The other grapes were dried and pressed into
raisins, but you retain

the immature qualities." The lover admits, "It's true.
I was testing whether you

were loyal to one or a lover who moves with many. Forgive
me. I knew you without

asking, but how one knows can change. Hearing's not
the same as seeing. We

are each other, you and I, a union as grand and obvious as
the sun. Please don't be

offended. I question *myself* every day to see if I've been
helpful or not. The prophets

were put through ordeals. That's how miracles came! You
are a treasure buried

in the ruins of the world. *Digging* is a way to enter your
presence. I wanted

evidence of you! Is that disrespect?" The beloved answers,
"On your side it is still night.

I'm in the light. No subtle arguing, please! Did Adam
present an elaborate defense? Did

Adam's simple confession; Lucifer's impudence;
David is told he will not build the mosque

he perch on the knowledge tree and jump from branch to branch
ramifying his case? No. He sat in

the ashes of contrition saying, *Lord, I've done terrible*
wrong. Forgive me. Stand

like the ant before Solomon, a tiny point in the vast.
Lifetimes pass before

your vision clears. The heart's eye rolls in like a wave
of harvesters. Then

these two eyes glean the stubble of what's left. Their
begging sight is

meager! As there is eye medicine made of powdered
pearls, so you must let

yourself be crushed as you say what you've done wrong.
Adam did not hedge

and make excuses with Lucifer's impudence. His pure,
direct confession was

beautiful: a pearl become powder become restored eyelight.
Wheat that has gone through

a mill rises in a perfect loaf. Abu Jahl felt he could
challenge Muhammad! And

you, the *unsure* lover, want to put *me* to the test.
Remember the man on the high

terrace with Ali. 'You say God protects you. Jump
from here and be saved, and I'll

believe.' Ali replies, 'You risk your soul with this proposal.
It's like Adam

suggesting to God that he and Eve disobeyed to plumb
the depth of grace!' Question

yourself first, then others. When you understand that you
are a single grain, you'll

begin to feel the wonder of what the warehouse holds. Trust
that God has intelligence enough

to use you appropriately. A jeweler doesn't drop rubies
down a privy hole. A farmer

stores wheat and straw separately. A disciple does not judge
the master. A dust mote brings

in a set of scales to weigh the mountain! A painting
critiques the artist.

The stalk of a carob tree starts to grow inside the far
mosque: the refuge

that is the core of praise. Keep it clear of resentment and
stubbornness. Uproot the

carob weed and let nothing grow there but full prostration
weeping for mercy." The distant

mosque began with David's resolving it should *be*. But God
gave him a revelation

that he was not to be the one who built the refuge. *What
have I done wrong?* asks David.

"Your songs were too beautiful. They ravished so many."
But when I sang the psalms,

I was lost in you. "Not completely. You were only
partially nonexistent.

Your astonishing art kept you from full surrender."
One who goes completely out

of the self, so that personal qualities mix with divine
qualities, comes *by choice*

Fana *and* **baqa***; the failure of sun*
and lamp images to show the truth of oneness

to surrender. Free will exists so free will can be given up
freely. Such a person feels

no genuine delight if he or she is not drained empty. With
all the delicious food and drink

in the world, true pleasure comes only with the extinction
of pleasure and its replacement by

soul delight. Those who have gone through *fana* into
baqa, through annihilation into

that which has always been, become all body and all
consciousness. With dissolving

begins some overwhelming joy. God told David that though his
son Solomon would build the mosque,

it would be his doing too. In the soul there is an ancient
joining of intelligence. This

truth does not apply to that part of us called the animal
soul. When one person eats

bread, his companion does not get full. *This* one grows happy
when *that* one dies, sad

if he prospers. Wolf and dog stay separate. With lions,
though, it is one thing. No

likeness can say this. Putting lions next to soul essence
makes an imperfect

comparison. But everything on this plane is a flawed
metaphor. Here's another:

at night a light comes on in each house, a lamp with six
wicks, the five senses and

the sixth, which holds the five. The fuel for these is food
and sleep. Without those they

go out, and the lamps seem to be seeking death, the way they
burn. Day comes, and lamps

go out. This is where the analogy fails. The truth of
oneness cannot be

understood with lamp and sun images. Language does not touch
the presence who lives in

each of us. The lights of our ancestors have not so much
been dowsed as *gathered into*

the sun. What happens to your irritation with a fleabite
when you're threatened by

a snake! A man jumps into a river with hornets swarming
above him. Let the water be

zikr, his remembering *There is no reality but God, there is
only God.* The hornets are his

sexual remembering, this woman, that. Or if a woman, this
man, that man. The head comes

up. They sting. Breathe water. Become the river. Hornets
will leave you alone then, even if

you're far from the river. They pay no attention. No one
looks for stars when the sun's

out. A person blended into God does not disappear. He or she
is just soaked with the qualities.

Do you need a quote from the Qur'an? *All shall be brought
into our presence.* Join those

travelers. The lamps we burn go out. Some quickly, some
last until daybreak. Some dim,

some intense, all fed with fuel. If a light goes out in
one house, that doesn't affect

the next. This is the story of the animal soul. The divine
soul shines like the sun. If

it should go down, every house would darken. Light is
the image of your teacher, a higher

consciousness that *will* find you at death if not before.
Your enemies love the dark.

A spider weaves a veil over a light. Out of himself he makes
it. Don't try to control a wild

horse by grabbing its leg. Take hold of the neck. Use
a bridle. Be sensible. Make

rules for yourself. Then ride! There is a need for self-
denial on this way. Don't be

The materials of Solomon's temple

contemptuous of old obediences. They help. When Solomon
began to build the temple made of

awakened intelligence, various materials begged to be part of
it. Stones broke away and lifted off

the mountain singing, "Take us along!" Light shone from the
mortar. The doorjambs and walls had

lively conversation. The door knocker striking made music.
Solomon's mosque beyond matter is

one that each of us must build. There's no way to say how it
will look, constructed as it is of

what we intend and compassionate action. Solomon was a king
who carried with him always the royal

rose garden of union. With friends he was like the camel
driver who serenades his camels

to keep them moving happily. As the sun and moon circulate,
spirit must travel light. So

the wealth within you, your essence, is your kingdom. The
story is told of Uthman, who when

Uthman, master of silence

he became caliph, mounted quickly the steps of Muhammad's
pulpit, whereas Abu Bakr, out of

respect for the prophet, seated himself on the second step.
There were three steps. Omar

sat on the third step. Uthman climbed to the top. When
asked why, he replied, "If I

sat on the third step, people would say I was like Omar. If
on the second step, *He's like Abu Bakr.*

But up here where the chosen one sat, no one will think to
compare *me* with that king of

the spirit!" And sometimes when he had climbed to the
preaching place, that sweet one,

Uthman, would not say anything. He stayed silent until mid-
afternoon. No one asked him for

a sermon, and no one left the mosque. The courtyard and the
dome filled with light even

a blind man could feel, the newly risen sun's warmth that opens
our wisdom and expands us

500

into freedom. In the silence many began to see with Uthman's
light. This is how a living

master opens the inner eye, so when words are heard they can
be seen *through* as a lens. Out

in the heat of the physical sun we feel body limits closing
in. In this other heat we feel

freedom and release. When a blind man gets his sight back,
he says, "I am a divine seer,

an oracle." With the excitement of the change he's a little
drunk. A drunk becoming sober

is very different from the ecstatic change that comes in
the living presence of an

enlightened one. There's no way to *say* how that is, even if
Abu ibn Sina were here. Only by

the great Names, or by meditation inside music that plays
without instruments, can

coverings be lifted. Not by sermons or mental effort. One
who tries to *do* that

will cut off his hand with his famous sword. This is all
metaphoric: there is no *covering*

or *hand*. It's like the country saying, *Yeah, if my aunt had
testicles, she'd be my uncle.*

It's what-if talking: the distance from words to living is a
journey of a hundred thousand years,

but don't be discouraged! It can happen any moment. It
takes thirty-five hundred years

to get to Saturn, but Saturnine qualities are constantly *here*
making us solemn and serious.

Influence goes the other way too. An enlightened master,
which is to say the inner

nature of each of us, is continually affecting the universe.
Philosophers say a human being is

The essence of human beings
and the source of the universe; the horse of annihilation

the universe in small, but it is more true that the essence
of a human is the whole

from which the cosmos grew. It looks as if fruit grows from a
branch, but growth comes more

truly from the gardener's hope and the work of sowing the
seed that grew inside the fruit.

The tree of the universe grows out of the fruit and its seed,
even though *in form* the tree

bears the fruit. Muhammad said, *We come after Adam and the*
prophets and we come before,

born of them, yet their ancestor. We *are* first and last.
A true pilgrim reaches

the Kaaba every second, again and again. There is a
traveling that has no *long*

or *short*. You drift off to sleep thinking you're lost at
sea, when you're really sleeping

in the hold of a ship, your head resting on the timbers of
Noah's ark. Muhammad says,

I and my friends are Noah's ark in the flooding of time.
Join us, and live inside this grace.

With your teacher you are safe, and on your way. Do not
think to go by yourself. Strong

lion that you are, without a guide you're conceited and
mistaken. Fly only with

the wings of a guide. Be carried on the waves of grace, or
on the flames of his anger.

Don't make a distinction. Such anger and generosity are one
thing. He makes you green like

garden ground. He makes you stony and sandy, so roses and
vines may grow there.

The teacher sees, and a fragrance comes to the purified
brain. Empty yourself of any

thought apart from the Friend, then sniff the air. Muhammad
caught the scent in far-off Yemen.

Mount the horse of annihilation. Climb as sugarcane ascends
to sweetness, as water turns

to vapor, as an embryo lifts into discernment. Muhammad's
horse can bring you to

emptiness. His hoof presses down on a mountain and leaps, so
step with your foot into this ship, quick,

like a lover. No tiredness, no reason. In this new
liveliness even stones talk.

What the Friend gives is a hundred times more than what
you leave behind. When

Sheba (the body's wisdom) brings gifts to Solomon (divine, luminous wisdom)

the Queen of Sheba thought to honor Solomon, she loaded forty
mules with gold bricks, but

286

when her caravan reached the wide plain leading to Solomon's
palace, they noticed that

the top layer of the plateau was pure gold! For forty days
they journeyed on gold. What

foolishness to take gold bars to Solomon when the very dirt
there is gold! You that think to

offer your intelligence to God, reconsider. Intelligence on
the way is less than road dust.

The embarrassing commonness of what they bring slows them
down. They argue. They

discuss turning back, but they continue, carrying out the
orders of their queen. Solomon

laughs when he sees them unloading. "When have I asked you
for a sop for my soup? I do not

want gifts from you. I want you ready for the gifts I give.
You worship a planet that creates

gold. Worship instead the one who creates universes. You
worship the sun, which is only

a cook. Think of a solar eclipse. What if you get attacked
at midnight? Who will help you

then? Astronomical matters fade. Another intimacy happens.
A sun at midnight with no east, no

night or day. The clearest intelligences faint when they see
the solar system flickering, tiny

in the immense lightness. Drops fall in vapor; vapor
explodes into a galaxy; a ray

strikes a bit of darkness; new suns appear. One slight
alchemical gesture and Saturnine

qualities form inside Saturn. The physical eye needs
sunlight to see. Use your other

eye. Vision is luminous. Sight is igneous, and sun-fire
very dark." Sheikh Maghribi,

Sheikh Maghribi walks through the night desert with his students

whose name means "The place of sunset," declares, "For sixty
years I have never known

the quality of night. I have not seen darkness by day or
night or because of any disease."

His companions know this is true. "We follow him in the
desert at night, through steep

ditches and thorns. He lights up the landscape like a full
moon. He doesn't look back,

but he calls, *Watch out for the ravine! Go left! There are
drop-offs in there.* At daylight

we come to kiss his bare feet, which are white and smooth
as a bride's. No trace of mud,

no scratch, or any bruise from the terrain." Such a sunset is
sunrise, a light that protects

from scorpions and thieves. The text says, *Light goes
before*, tearing danger to pieces. That

light will increase at the resurrection, but we should beg
for it now in the clouds and mist

of these bodies. So keep your gold, embarrassed gift
bringers. Bring me your selves.

Lay yours on mine. As you give sexual trembling to a woman,
give that intimate gold-shimmering

light to me. A lover's gold is the pallor that comes from
looking at the Friend. The color

of minerals derives from the sun and the sun's regard from
this other. You make a shield

against me, when I already have you surrounded. A bird
lights on the roof and notices

the bait. Wings outspread, but already caught! It seems to
be walking around free, while

each look is another knot tied around its leg. The bait
says, "You may turn your eyes,

but I am constantly removing resistance. When finally you
draw close, you will know how

The druggist and the clay eater

I have been giving attention to you." A clay eater goes to a
druggist to buy a pound of

fine sugarloaf. The druggist is a keen observer, interested
in how his customers behave.

He tells this man that he doesn't have the regular metal
balance weight. "Would you mind

if I used a pound of clay?" "Fine. I'm in a hurry. Any
balance weight will do." Thinking,

Yes, let's have clay! This is like the go-between, who finds
a bride for a young man. "Only

one thing, she's the confectioner's daughter." "All the
better. She'll be sweet!"

The druggist puts the clay on the scale and turns away to cut
sugar from the loaf. The

clay eater cannot restrain himself. He steals pinches of
the clay. The druggist sees and

prolongs his cutting. "Steal away. You're taking from
yourself. You'll pay for

a pound, but when you get home, you'll discover how you've
cheated yourself, being so

secretive and impulsive, wanting a taste of clay instead of
waiting for sugar." When

the bird of desiring looks at what the physical world offers
and moves that way, it's

really pecking at its own side. Any passionate ache over
distances devours you, whether

for money or longing for a spirit home, both are building a
prison. Solomon resumes talking to

Solomon's message back to Sheba

the envoys of Sheba: "Go back and tell her what you have seen,
how the rare substance she

thinks we value can be scraped up anywhere as soil. Tell her
the elaborate throne she loves

looks more like a bandage over a hurt place. We admire
Ibrahim, who *left* his kingdom so

quickly. With us, one genuine kneeling down in total
humility would buy hundreds

of governments. Our currency is an eagerness to accept the
gift of soul change. Nothing

else. Sheba's sumptuous life is just a hole in the ground
with children playing in it,

pretending to be kings and prime ministers. We perform
reverse alchemy, transmuting

A dervish tells his dream in the night-talking

gold mines into abandoned sites!" A certain dervish
tells a dream in the night-talking.

"I saw the sheikhs who are connected to Khidr. I asked them
where I might get some daily food

without being bothered about earning it, so I could continue
my devotions uninterrupted.

'Come to the mountains and eat the wild fruit. Our
benedictions have made its

bitterness sweet. That way your days will be free.' I did as
they said, and from the fruit

came a gift of speech that made my words exciting and
spiritually transporting, valuable

to many. 'This is dangerous,' I thought. 'Lord of the
world, give me another, more

hidden, gift.' I escaped. The beautiful speech left,
and a joy came that I have

never known. I burst open like a pomegranate. 'If heaven is
nothing but this feeling,

I have no further wish.' I had two coins left from my former
eloquence, sewn into the sleeve

of my robe. A poor man came toward me carrying firewood. He
looked exhausted. I thought,

'Since I have no need of money—I have this joy, a little
fruit to eat, and hardly any

appetite anymore—I'll give these coins to him. Maybe
for two or three days he'll be

happy having enough to eat.' But that man was one of those
who know the inner thoughts.

He heard what I was thinking. 'You condescend to the masters
who have given you

what you need.' He glared and threw down his bundle, his
ecstatic state so radiant

that I trembled and almost fell down. 'Lord,' the wood
carrier prayed, 'bless those

whose comings and goings are auspicious, and let your grace
alchemize this wood into

gold sticks.' The woodpile glowed between us like strange
treasure. 'But Lord,'

he continued, 'your saints flee from celebrity. Make it
as it was before.' It became

firewood again. He picked it up and started walking toward
town. I wanted to follow, but

it was as though my limbs were tied. I could barely move."
This is how it is with admission

to the presence. If a way ever opens, go and lay down
your head and offer that.

Your being drawn is the gift being given. Don't live
like a fool who gains favor

with the king and then forgets or wastes it. More blessings
come, in the form, say,

of food, and he says, "Ah, what a fine cut of meat." Not so.
The connection itself is more

than any pleasure. That generosity springs from grace.
Solomon's courtship of Sheba

continues, conversation against the shore depositing pearls
and peacefulness. "Even if

you never thought to ask for soul growth, still come. This
is a time when the Friendship

door is open, like the moment Ibrahim decided not to return to
his Khorasan kingdom. The music

of waves disintegrates on the edge and returns soul to its
harmony. Ibrahim had guards who

were musicians. They played the flute and rebeck on his roof
at night. They were not really

guards. Just men need no protection. He loved music because
he heard in it a mysterious conversation.

Voices singing, strings, the low menace of the drum, clear
flute and trumpet. Philosophers

How music keeps remembering fresh;
the man listening in the walnut tree

have said that we love music because it resembles the sphere-
sounds of union. We've been

part of a harmony before, so these moments of treble and bass
keep our remembering fresh. But

how does this happen within these dense bodies full of
forgetfulness and doubt and

grieving? It's like water passing through us. It becomes
acidic and bitter, but still as

urine it retains watery qualities. It will put out a fire!
So there is this music

flowing through our bodies that can dowse restlessness.
Hearing the sound, we gather

strength. Love kindles with melody. Music feeds a lover
composure, and provides

form for the imagination. Music breathes on personal fire
and makes it keener. The waterhole

is deep. A thirsty man climbs a walnut tree growing next to
the pool and drops walnuts one

by one into the beautiful place. He listens carefully to the
sound as they hit and watches

the bubbles. A more rational man gives advice, "You'll
regret doing this. You're so far

from the water that by the time you get down to gather
walnuts, the water

will have carried them away." He replies, "I'm not here for
walnuts. I want the music

they make when they hit." A certain kind of thirst wants
to circle the watertank, as

pilgrims the Kaaba. The *sound* of water, all they desire.
When we're speaking this *Masnavi,*

the radiance of God is our subject. Husam is that light
and water. This book is a tree

The tree of the Masnavi; a flute player farting

with roots and branches fed by what accepts bad and good
alike. Plant

a little tree. Give it water and freedom. Untie the knots
in its roots. With this

expanding I want only to hear the voice of the mystery.
Husam's. Lover is

not separate from beloved. In the union beyond description
and metaphor the lord of being

becomes human. *Huuu-mankind.* A true person knows the
soul-growing capacity inside

his life. We so rarely question what a human being *is*. We
recite texts like *You did not*

throw when you threw, but still we think of ourselves as being
bodies. We are Sheba

resisting Solomon.
                        Do these words stick
                                      in your throat?
I'll be quiet.
                        Find your own.
                        A flute player farted once
while he was playing the flute.
                        He held the instrument behind him.
"You think you can do better? Play on."
                                      Muslims, sometimes
those with good manners humor
                                      those with bad manners. When
you see someone irritated
                        with someone else's ill-temper, realize

294

the complainant is identically moody. This is not true,
though, of the correction

sheikhs give. They have emptied themselves and God speaks
through them. Listen to

Solomon, Sheba! Or you'll find your own servants turning
against you. The chamberlain

will smash the door! Every part of you and your body finds a
way to be obedient to God, even

if you won't! Leave attachments and come to me. Without me,
you are a picture on a bathhouse

wall, beauty for others to appreciate. There are those who
go around saying, "I am this.

I am that." You are *not* these images you see. You are the
unique one: raptor, prey,

and snare. Throne, floor, roof. Adam and all his progeny.
A jar floating in the river

has river in it. The city lives in the room. Think of the world
as the jar and your immense

heart as the river. This world is a chamber in the
wonderfully subtle, urban

complexity of love. My message to you is that we are
oceans covered with straw,

a sun momentarily blotted with ash, two or three days trying
to imagine that they're eternity.

Ibrahim hears footsteps on the roof

Ibrahim, the king, one night is meditating in his throne
room; he hears footsteps

on the roof. "Who could this be?" A group of marvelous
beings put their heads

over the roof edge. "We're looking for camels." "Whoever
heard of camels on a roof?" "Yes,

and whoever heard of trying to be in union while acting as
head of state?" That's all

it took for Ibrahim. He's gone, vanished. His beard
and robe are there, but he

is on an ecstatic dervish retreat on Mt. Qaf. Everyone
still brags of what he did.

This world is proud of those who suddenly change.
The story of

Solomon's invitation to Sheba

Solomon's invitation to Sheba is a love poem
for the moment when spirit

enters the body. There's a grand nobility in it, and
whatever else we've forgotten,

we can always remember the fragrance of this story. So rise
and recall how it is with love!

Pour for others what's been poured you. Move out of your
houses into the wind.

You've been given, like Solomon, the knack of understanding
and singing every birdsong.

When a bird that knows transcendence flies close, sing the
rising note. For a bird with

broken wings, make patient contemplative sounds that help it
heal. To a great transformation

bird resurrected from its compost heap whisper a song of Mt.
Qaf. It feeds on those.

Warn the pigeon when the falcon floats over. To the falcon,
speak lordly deliberation. Urge

the bat into half-light. Teach the partridge peacefulness,
the rooster how to recognize dawn.

Talk truth to the hoopoe and eagle. Solomon whistled one
note to the people of Sheba's

kingdom and caught them all! Or maybe there was someone
there totally deaf. No,

I'm saying it wrong. Solomon's love note opens *new ears*
on the side of a head with

no ears, sprouts language in the voiceless. Sheba *remembers*
something when she finally comes

to Solomon. She leaves her kingdom and her wealth the same
way lovers leave their reputations.

Her servants mean nothing to her, less than an onion. Her
palaces, so many piles of dung.

Sheba's throne; the body's sad song

She hears the inner meaning of LA! No! And comes to Solomon
with nothing, except her throne.

As the writer's pen becomes a friend, as the tool the workman
uses day after day grows

profoundly familiar, so her filigreed throne is her one
attachment. I would explain

more about this, but it would take too long. It's a large
throne and difficult to transport,

because it cannot be taken apart, being as cunningly put
together as the human body.

Solomon sees that her heart is open and that this throne
will soon be less important

to her. "Let her bring it," he says, "It will become a lesson
to her like the old

shoes and jacket of Ayaz. She can look at her throne and see
how far she's come." In

the same way the process of generation stays constantly
before us: the smooth skin

and the semen and the growing embryo are there to remind
us what's beyond and within.

When you see a pearl on the bottom, you reach through the
foam and broken sticks on

the surface. The sun comes up; you forget about locating
the constellation of Scorpio.

When you see the splendor of union, the attractions of
duality seem poignant and lovely,

but much less interesting. There are times we enjoy the
taste of clay. We say,

Nothing could be better! But that denial of soul proves the
heart's core intention is still

clear and rational, as when you knock at a door and hear
the master's voice inside

saying, "The master is not home." That *is not* keeps you
close. The taste of the body

keeps claiming, *There is no state of grace, no divine
sweetness,* while from inside its

sad song comes the affirmation. Solomon's wise advisor Asaf
and the demon Ifrit were arguing

about Sheba's throne. They conjure it up for Solomon to see.
"That's it!" says Solomon.

"The marvelous tree that so beguiles its devotees. The stone
lion next to a real one, a bone

thrown to occupy the dog. Everyone gets this to chew on!"
I will tell you now

Halima loses the baby Muhammad; the stone images talk

what happened to Halima,
                              the baby Muhammad's mother, after
she weaned him.
                              Maybe this story will clarify other matters.

She holds Muhammad as tenderly as if he were a bouquet of
roses and basil. So carefully,

she brings him to his grandfather. But first she goes to the
Kaaba. As she enters

the open area called the *hatim* between the well and the Kaaba
itself, she hears a voice in the air,

"Hatim, today the sun is visiting you. The king of destiny
puts his baggage down inside

you." Halima is there alone with the baby Muhammad. She
is so confused by

the invisible voice that she puts her child on the ground
and runs about looking.

"Where is the source of this? Lord, show yourself."
Trembling like a willow, she

finds no one. When she comes back to where she put
Muhammad, he's not there!

She runs to nearby houses. "Who has taken my pearl?" "We
have seen no child." She weeps

so deeply that others weep with her. An old man with a staff
comes by. "Halima, what's wrong?"

"I was carrying Muhammad to see his grandfather when I heard
voices. I set the child down

to discover where they came from. The sound was so lovely.
No one was there, yet

the voices kept on. I came back from that bewildering joy,
and Muhammad was gone!"

"Do not grieve. I know a woman who can help." He takes
her to the clairvoyant Uzza.

"Halima has come because her child Muhammad is lost."
When he says that name,

the magical images around the woman fall prostrate and start
speaking. "Old man,

get out of here! This searching for Muhammad has deposed us.
Now we're nothing but rubble.

During the interval between Jesus and Muhammad, we had power
and value. That's over now.

Real water has come, so sand will no longer be used for
ablutions. You don't know

what you've said, old man! The advent of Muhammad will
change the ocean and sky, dragon

power and the earth itself." As the stone images talk,
the man drops his staff

and runs. Halima calls after, "Old man, at first the wind
made a speech to me. Now

stones are telling you the real nature of things. Once
before, the green man carried away

this child. Who can I complain to, crazy with these
mysteries? I can only say,

My child is lost. If I say more, they'll lock me up."
He comes back and comforts her.

"Your child is not lost. Rather, the whole world will be lost
in your child. The images

fell to pieces at the sound of his name. This begins a new
era, like nothing that has

happened before." Finally, Muhammad's grandfather, Abdul
Muttalib, heard Halima's

grieving, from a mile away! He goes to the Kaaba and prays,
"You who know the secrets

of night and the mysteries of the day, I am not worthy to be
told anything by you, but

Muhammad is different. Even as a child your signs are
visible on him. Tell me

where he is." From within, a voice, "He is safe. We make
his outward appearance in the world, but

his inner nature must stay hidden. From water and clay we
make gold. From gold we

fashion an anklet or a seal or a shoulder strap or sometimes a
chain for a lion's neck. Or

1000

an orb for the top of a throne, or a crown. We love the
earth because it lets us shape it!

Now we've made a spirit king, we'll also make the frenzy of
longing for his presence. This

is what our work is, to the great confusion of those who have
no inclination toward spirit.

We give value to a piece of ground for the same reason we
give food to the poor. The

ground has external dullness and internal luminosity. The
two seem opposed like a jewel

embedded in common rock. The outside says, 'This is all
I am.' The inside, 'Look

further. Look everywhere.' The outside, 'There's nothing
inside.' Inside, 'Wait. I'll

show you what's true.' So we make laughter. Physically,
the world is grief, but

within there are many kinds of laughing. Our work reveals
this, as the prosecution must

show what the thief has done. Parts of earth have stolen
bits of God. We make them

confess. Muhammad is a sun that never sets. Outer form,
darkness. Spirit, roses within

roses." Some sufis look disgusted all the time to fend off
those who would dowse the inner

light. Like hedgehogs they hide behind prickles and
austerities, like an orchard

in a thorn thicket. Grandfather Abdul kept asking about
Muhammad. Finally,

"He is in such-and-such a village sitting under a certain
tree." The grandfather set out

with the princes of Qurash and all the ancestors of Muhammad,
though these are not the true

Essence does not come from a lineage

ancestors. Essence is not from any lineage. Muhammad does
not descend from anything in

this universe. Such light did not come into existence at a
particular moment. That robe

is not woven with warp and woof. Sunlight is a wonderful
garment, embroidered as it is

with moving shadow, but it's nothing like this other. A
voice keeps calling to Sheba!

Come, see this other kingdom. Many of your sisters are
already here enjoying it.

Don't be surly and stubborn like a dog guarding a carcass!
You have no idea what gifts

will be given! From Solomon's side, you look like someone
who's hired a few drummers

and is parading around saying, "I am the queen of fancy
bathing rooms." Do you remember

the story in Book II about the dog who attacked the cloak of
a blind beggar? The blind man

addressed the dog, who was snarling into a mouthful of cloth.
"So here you are, on a back street

doing this ridiculous thing, when your friends are after real
prey in the wilderness. You tear

a blind man's rags, while they, with dignity and courage,
chase the mountain antelope."

So we should rise and disappear in a search for the beloved,
as a dead bird slips into the hand

The dead bird's truth

of the hunting king. That dead bird says, "I used to move on
the wings of my impulses. Now

wherever I go, I go because the king goes there. Don't think
of me as dead when I'm so alive

in my soul! Jesus did this. I'm in the hand that made
Jesus. I am Jesus. Lazarus

rose once, then died again, but this rising does not fall
back. It builds a bridge

across the ocean." The dead bird speaks truth. Moses and
Joseph left Egypt in different ways.

One with a powerful walkingstick, one with a cup hidden in a
sack of grain and the keys to

the granary. Many stories and objects can help us be free.
And there are cynics who sneer

at all this, their shallow laughter like a poisonous grass
they fatten on, but not you, not

today. Today the door of generosity opens; each of us goes
through that differently.

The herb garden of soul growth

Soul growth is an herb garden, where every spice for the soup
has a separate bed. Capers

in one spot, garlic another, saffron, rosemary, mint. Each
gets tended with those that are

similar. Those of you in the saffron section, be saffron.
Don't combine with other growings.

You'll be needed as saffron when we fix the rice. Don't
associate with turnips. They're not

like you. They have different habits. The visible world is
obviously spacious enough for

all kinds. Think how the unseen must be! A wide desert
plateau here is a single hair on

that ocean. Underground water is fresher than this creek we
drink. Spirit hides how it moves.

Listeners are drifting off. I'll stop. Talking to someone
sleepy is like
                           drawing pictures
                                      on water with your finger.

Sheba! *Decide* to leave and go to Solomon! Choose freely
before death brings you

by the ear like a thief to a judge. You've been stealing
old shoes, when you

could be holding a priceless ruby in your hand. Your sisters
have come here rejoicing,

but you linger where nothing satisfies. There is a kingdom
within, a rose garden where

we rest, as outwardly we're singing to the camels to keep
them happily moving along.

The garden goes wherever we go. Sun, full moon, new moon—
they move without wings as we do

in spirit. We eat without sustenance. We are luck itself
and lucky, bare as beggars,

Solomon's far mosque

living inside the self, which is true majesty. Solomon was
told to build the house of his

inner life, the *far mosque*. Each prophet builds an edifice
of revelation and awareness,

but Solomon's is of another order. I do not mean to
disparage other prophets, though

even praise I *say* of them has to be disparagement. Words
resemble the bricks and beams of

the physical world, while this building is magnificently
without form! Solomon went

every morning to worship there. He would bow and listen to
discourse and music and a great harmony.

Make such a place for your early mornings, seeker of truth,
if you're really looking for

truth. Build the place with love that has no greed or fear in
it. Those motives drag you around

earning and digging, from market to crops and back to market.
Intention colors action. When

children get greedy for fantasy, they pretend their pants are
horses. They hold on and ride

about. Then we get older and see what we've been doing, but
no one ever outgrows

the bright soul-making that happens in Solomon's sacred
mosque. It keeps changing

and renewing itself. Solomon is not dead! He is the one
inside us bowing to wisdom.

Solomon helps make these refuges. Demons are also at work
who trick and prevent us

from having such a place, though sometimes, it is possible
to let those forces work at

building the secret chamber. Solomon does that. Like two
weavers, the hands perform, one

set making coarse burlap, another Solomon's silk. Which
reminds me of the poet who

The poet, the king, and his two advisors named Hasan

brings a poem to the king in hopes of wealth and the robes
of honor. The king is impressed

and generous in his response. He awards the poet a thousand
dinars of red gold! But

the king's advisor, Hasan, says, "That is not enough. In such
a fine poet intelligence

itself becomes visible, and in a king like you the oceanic
abundance of existence should be

revealed. Give more!" They argue and talk philosophy in
the king's chamber, until

the entire matter is threshed and sorted like piles of corn
on the threshing floor, with

a healthy tithing set to one side for the poet, *ten* thousand
dinars, *and* the robes of honor!

"Who did this?" asks the poet. "Who put my case so
powerfully?" "It was Hasan,

which means *good,* and he certainly is." The poet writes
another poem for Hasan

and then returns home, while without words the robes are
praising the king's generosity.

After several years the poet falls on difficult times. No
food, no seed grain, no means

of growing food. He thinks, "When poverty gets acute, it's
best to go where one has found relief

The world exists within a refuge

before." A saint once said that the meaning of the Name is
that worshipers can take sanctuary

there, as in times of sudden danger when people call out, *My God!* Would they keep doing this,

if it didn't help? Only a fool keeps going where nothing happens. The world lives within

a safeguarding: fish inside waves, birds held in the sky, the elephant, the wolf, the lion

as he hunts, the dragon, the ant, the waiting snake, even the ground, the air, the water,

every spark floating up from fire subsists in that refuge; nothing is alone for

a single moment. All giving comes from there, no matter who you think you put your hand

toward. So the poet goes back for a second time with a new poem honoring the king. Kings

Why humans enjoy being praised

love praise. The first human wanting is for food. Then, when food is no longer a worry,

a person wants the praise of eloquent poets, song that drifts like fragrance over his or her

life. Don't condescend to this desire! The creator wants glorification! It's built in

to the nature of humanity to enjoy praise. Especially devotees of God! A strong

leather bag fills with wind and shines in the fullness. A weaker, damaged bag tears

and flaps dully in the same wind. Friend, I have not made this analogy up. Muhammad

said something similar when asked why he got so happy when honored. The poet came again

saying, "Givers die, but acts of generosity live on." This is
another topic. Let it go.

The poet waits at the king's door. The king reads the poem,
marveling. "A thousand dinars to

this poet." The king's new advisor, also named Hasan, says,
"We cannot afford that much. A poet

will be satisfied with a fortieth of that." But others around
the king say, "Last time

he received ten thousand!" "I will explain it to him," says
the new Hasan. "I can handle

these matters." He tells the poet to come back later.
"Funding will be settled in

December." In December he says, "Spring, perhaps by spring."
Expectation lengthens, with the poet

becoming desperately poor. "Soon he'll be grateful for a
handful of road dirt." Finally

the poet, "Please, if there's to be nothing for me, don't
lead me on. This anticipation

is killing me. It's like being tied tighter and tighter."
Courtiers take him aside. "Accept

this from us and go. This new man is bitter and querulous.
It's best not to have dealings

with him." "What's his name?" "Hasan." "I can't believe it!
Two such opposites, one giving,

the other so stingy." He goes home with his pittance. This
is the mystery: same

generous king, same eloquent poet, different intermediary
ministers with the same name!

Mean-spirited advisors can cause shattering damage to ancient
human alliances, like that

of king and poet. Many times Pharaoh listens to Moses'
incomparable words that

could draw milk from a stone. He begins to feel the great
love they come from. But

then Haman, his cynical advisor, says, "You now *believe*
in men dressed in rags!" One

snide question destroys for Pharaoh the elegance of Moses'
discourse. Haman is your mind

and the way it protects your sensual comforts, saying about
wisdom and the light of spirit,

"Be sensible. There's no evidence for these claims. Mystics
are often insane." There's another

inner advisor, one like Asaf is with Solomon. Listen to
that voice, light pouring

into light, ambergris on jasmine. Perfect your ability to
distinguish the two

advisors. There is a demon who sees Solomon and imitates
his actions and appearance

so well that he can sit on the throne and govern
the country. But people feel

an inner difference. "This one is asleep. The other Solomon
was awake." Discernment

is not fooled. The universal intelligence will not bow
to a false Solomon. It's as

though a hand comes up out of the ground to hold you
back and say, "Not this one,"

so that you can't physically touch the earth. Let your
clarity make every determination.

You connect with Solomon when that happens. And remember
the daily practice: every morning

Solomon goes to the place he built and finds a new plant
growing. He asks, "Are you

a medicine?" The plant tells him how it can be helpful to
some conditions and detrimental

to others. "What are you called?" The plant reveals its
name. Solomon gives this

information to his physicians. This is how knowledge of
medicine and of astronomy

comes to us, from the universal intellect into individual
minds. Every tool and craft

and art comes first from pure intelligence, then gets
modified by the personal. Be

apprenticed to Solomon. Master what he teaches and practice
it. Have you heard how

the idea of grave digging originated? Cain has just killed
Abel and is wondering where he

can hide the body. He sees a raven flying with a dead raven
in its beak. It lands and begins

scraping with its talons, quickly clawing out a place, then
puts the dead bird in and covers it.

Cain cries out, "This crow is smarter than I am!" It is said
of universal intelligence, *That*

seeing does not turn away. Clever, particular minds look
everywhere. The one does

not wander. Crow-mind acts as sexton for the spiritually
dead. Whoever is taught by

the crow stays near a graveyard. Live instead in the
orchard. Led by the soul-bird

of your deep love, fly to the far mosque. Every second
a new plant sprouts in the soil

of the soul's distant greenhouse. Investigate like Solomon
how plant varieties interpret

qualities inside the earth. Reeds, sugarcane, roses—
through inner consciousness plants

How different levels of discourse get drawn out of a teacher

rise and reveal the secrets of the ground. Sometimes someone
draws a discourse out of me

and like a garden I grow roses. With someone else, I say
shallow things. There is a true

and a false pull, and all degrees between. The cord is not
visible. We are blind camels

being drawn somewhere. If we could see what's going on, the
world would change completely.

Eyes would recognize consequences! If a cow knew what the
bran she ate from the butcher's

hand *meant,* she would not eat it. Such blindness is within
all our frantic back-and-forth.

Run, something tells the scared donkey loose and lost in the
wilderness. Run.

We're no better than the donkey. We rush around enthusiastic
with some new project, because

we can't yet see what's wrong with it. If we saw, we'd quit
the project, but if we did

that, we'd never feel the nature of its wrongness, so it's
good we're blinded for a while; that

helps us *learn!* And don't get caught in repentance.
Distraction and regret

are addictions. The deeper state is Friendship, a work
those are not part of.

Polarities need to be lived through—impotence, power—
then new plants grow like the ones

The man meditating in an orchard; Solomon and the carob tree; paradise is full of foolishness

Solomon finds in the dawn. A man sits in an orchard, fruit
trees full and the vines plump.

He has his head on his knee, eyes closed. His friend says,
"Why stay sunk in mystical

meditation when the world is like this? Such visible grace."
He replies, "This outer

is an elaboration of this inner. I prefer the origin."
Natural beauty is a tree

limb reflected in the water of a creek, quivering, there, not
there. The growing that moves

in the soul is more real than tree limbs and their reflection.
We laugh and feel happy or sad

over all *this*. Try instead to get a scent of the true
orchard. Taste the vineyard

within the vineyard. One morning Solomon asked a bright
green plant, "What is

your name, and do you have a purpose?" "I am a carob tree.
Wherever I grow, the building

becomes a ruin. I am a reminder of what comes to everyone."
Consider this. You have a choice

about what you want, and you can argue twenty different
points of view in intellectual

matters, but with the mysteries of spirit and love, it's best
to be bewildered! In

an ocean with no edge, what good are swimming skills? Better
be like the baby reaching

for its mother. Drown in the breath of the one who teaches
you. Don't bring more competing

books! Let love carry you in its wandering boat. Follow
what feels simple and most

foolish. On this matter Muhammad said, "Paradise is full of
foolishness." The intellect

must have awards to strut about with. Be foolish and let
your heart grow larger. Be a lost

and wandering lover like those Egyptian women who cut their
hands instead of vegetables

because Joseph was so handsome. The Friend is real.
Sacrifice your intellect for

that. When mind is gone, every tip of every hair becomes
new intelligence. Orchards

spring up spontaneously. You'll hear discourses coming from
the fields. Be led by

the guide of your spirit. Move only where that one moves.
If you follow something

else, you're wounding yourself and others. Avoid half-baked
pretenders with no real experience.

Muhammad as Muzzamil, "The one who wraps himself"

Muhammad used to hide from charlatans. That's why God called
him *Muzzamil*, "The one

who wraps himself." "You so fond of hiding, don't cover your
face. The world is a reeling drunken

body, and you are the intelligent head. Don't hide the
candle of your clarity. Stand up

and burn through the night, my prince. Without your light a
great lion is held captive

by a rabbit! Be captain of the ship in this ocean of
spiritual purity, Mustapha,

my chosen one. Look how the caravan of civilization has been ambushed. Fools are everywhere

in charge. Do not practice solitude like Jesus. Be *in* the assembly, and take command.

As the bearded griffin, the Humay, lives on Mt. Qaf because he's native to it, you should live

most naturally out in public and be a communal teacher of souls. The full moon slides

silently across the sky, not swerving when dogs bark down here. Be that aloof with

critics. You are the guide out of the grief time just past, into now. If anyone asks what

resurrection is, say *I am the resurrectioning wind.* Don't listen to cynics. Sometimes

silence is the only answer." This is a subject that must be harvested, but it might take

eternity to get it in! A proverb says, "Failure to reply is a reply." A story:

The servant who neglects his service to the king; three kinds of creatures

there is a king who has a servant who neglects to do some service for the king.

Instead, he does what he wants and feels pleased with the cleverness. The king

reduces the man's allotment of food to see if that will make him more conscious. He

gives him the chance to walk around and observe his life. When a tethered donkey becomes

genuinely asinine, tie the front feet together. In the *hadith* of Muhammad it's

explained how there are three kinds of creatures: one made of
clear reason and generosity,

always prostrate in worship. That one is called the *angel*.
Another has no transcendent

knowledge, lives only to eat and sleep and never considers
the future. It's called the *animal*.

1500

The third descends from Adam and is called *human*, half angel,
half donkey. Half turned

toward sensuality, half toward clarity and grace. All these
have human shapes, but one

is as pure as Gabriel, one undisciplined and angry; the other
wrestles between the two.

The animal kind is a most subtle craftsman, who knows how to
weave gold, how to find pearls on

the ocean bottom, and how to construct the elaborate
artifices of geometry and

astronomy, philosophy and medicine. These arts and sciences
are the roof and walls of

the stable where the animal lives protected for a few days,
though their practitioners

call them "mysteries." The real way opens only with love.
When that waking comes, we finally

understand our dreams. It's like we've been trying to read
the book upside down! We

turn it over, and the meaning becomes instantly clear. We
understand that we have

the capacity to transform any nourishment. Any guidance
serves as a drawing energy.

Majnun rides his she-camel toward Layla, dismounts, and breaks his leg

This is how it is with Majnun and his camel. He's drawn
by love toward Layla, but his

camel wants to go back the way they have come, toward
her foal. As Majnun drifts off

in a love reverie, the reins go slack, and the she-camel
turns in the direction she

wants. When clarity comes back, Majnun recognizes
the landscape and turns the camel

around. In this way a three-day trip can take years! "We
are both lovers," he tells his

camel, "but we can't be traveling companions. You love what
you love, and I am pulled by

a longing for God." Union is two steps away, but it might
take sixty years if you insist

on riding Majnun's camel. "How long must this go on! I am
sick of this back-and-forth!"

Majnun cries out and slides down off the animal. He lands
on a stone and breaks his leg. He

bandages it with a splint and says, "Now I trust totally
in God. I am a ball waiting to be

struck. I can do nothing on my own." This is how it looks
when you dismount from

trying and allow the source that's pulling you complete
control. We must leave

Majnun sitting there on the ground.
                            Farewell, friend! Back
now to the servant who is writing
                            letters to the king to
                    protest how his food allotment
                            has been reduced. He thinks

316

he is writing in a calm and reasonable style, but the king
can hear the conceit and bitterness

Opening the letter of the body's life

inside the words. This body, your life, is a letter
to the king of the universe.

Go to a private place and open it and read to see if
the words are right. If they

aren't, start another! And don't think it's easy to open
the body and read the secret

message. This is the most courageous work, not something
for children playing with knucklebones

in the dirt. This is like Majnun flinging himself off
the high camel. Open to

the title page. Is what it says there the same as what you
have said it says? If

you're carrying a heavy sack, empty out the stones! Bring
only what should be given

The pilgrim with a turban stuffed with rags

a king. A certain man on pilgrimage wants to look very
grand as he approaches

those gathered between the inner wall and the Kaaba, so he
stuffs his turban with rags

to make the outside cloth seem more expensive. There are
all sorts of cloth and bits

of fur inside the turban, even a shred from a dervish robe.
He sets out before dawn,

but a thief who steals clothes is waiting in the dark. He
snatches the turban and runs. "Wait,"

cries the man. "Unwrap the cloth and feel inside. If you
still want it, it's yours!"

The thief unties the turban as he runs, and rag pieces fall
on the road. He stands holding

a single tatter. "You've cheated me." "Yes, but at the same
time I warned you of the fraud."

This is how the world speaks to us. It delights in spring
blossoms, even as they fall.

"Come taste me," say the senses, and the next sentence is,
"Leave. This is nothing much."

The young prince of the morning, the pride of everyone with
his glistening body, fumbles along

at evening, laughed at, unable to remember his name. Smell
the aroma of beautiful food, then

go to the latrine and sniff. "What *happened* to you?"
Your dung will answer,

"My beauty was a lure, a trick to get inside you."
Every matter particle does the same

enchantment. Try to see the beginning and end at once. Would
you willingly wear manacles

just because they're made of gold? Admire the genius of
an artist, but also watch what

happens to him or her in old age, how the expert craftsman's
craft diminishes. Listen

   The double music of existence; Bu Masaylim's false claims

to the song of the flower and the song of the thorn
blending. "Buy this!"

"Keep away!" "I'm ready now!" "Beloved, we are gathered
here today . . ." If you can't hear

this double music, it's difficult to recognize what's real.
With people you can look at

their teachers. Who do they follow? Each foal has a mare
that feeds it. What nourishes

318

humans comes from higher. Donkeys drink from underneath.
Magicians can be confusing, but

when Moses arrives and throws down the rod that becomes
a dragon, how do the trick bowls

look then? When something that alive comes, illusory matters
fade. They quit bragging!

A body's death, even, is beautiful to those who see with
the soul's eye. Every genuine

form of money has a counterfeit counterpart. Bu Masaylim, who
always added wrong

elements to any situation, said, "I am the guide of souls,
beyond religion." Reply

to such claims, "Don't act like you know things to get money
and power." Follow a true

sheikh's candle. The full moon shows the traveler where to
go. When it's night, take

a lantern, so you can tell a falcon from a crow. Crows
sometimes learn to mimic the

language of falcons, as a human being can make the hoopoe's
call, but without Solomon's

secret within the sound. Distinguish a natural cry from an
artificial. Shameless people

memorize the words of gnostics and dervishes. This is the
way every great civilization

falls apart, by ignoring the difference between sandalwood
and pine. Discernment! Everyone has

discernment, but greed obscures the subtlety. Physical
blindness brings God's mercy.

Blindness from wantings, nothing. Christ's crucifixion is
one thing. The self-crucifixion

of jealousy, something else. Fish, don't keep staring at
the hook. Remember where appetites

lead. Notice every set of eyes—the ox, the one-eyed man
leading his donkey, the true

human being—there are so many powers and ways of seeing!
No end to this. Back to

The complaining servant again; the fake ecstatic who returns from Iraq; the garden of HU

the servant writing his letter asking for more bread! But
before he writes, he goes

to the kitchen steward and complains, "This is beneath
the dignity of a king, to

reduce by a small amount my mid-morning meal. *Why* should he
consider such minutiae?" "He

has his reasons, which are not ungenerous, and since it is by
royal command, the food must

be withheld." A small portion then is kept back each day
from the servant's plate, and it so

infuriates him that he writes the letter, which outwardly is
courteous and rational, but inwardly

venomous. The king can hear the anger inside the servant's
praise. Do you remember the account

of the man who returned from Iraq in a torn and threadbare
cloak? His friends ask how

it went. "There was the pain of not seeing you for a long
while, but in other ways

the journey was blessed. The caliph there honored me with
ten robes of honor." He begins

then a formal declaration of praise to the Iraqi king. "Wait
a minute!" interrupt

his friends. "What you are wearing tells us you're lying!
Your words say praise, but

your appearance whines and complains." "I gave those new
clothes to the poor." "Well,

bless you for that, but still there is a murky smoke of
sadness coming from you. Where

are the signs of joy and of pleasure in God? If a torrent of
love for spirit has gone

by, where is the streambed? Why are you sour?" When true
praise and generosity

come, there is no loneliness. A hundred beings arrive and
live in the chest! When

seeds are sown in that ground, sprouts *will* come up. It's
impossible not to! In

the garden of *HU*, the breath of God makes a spaciousness, and
there are clear streams

and room to sit in companionship, flowers of all colors,
with the beloved's presence

felt everywhere, like an oyster shell around a pearl. Fake
enthusiasm has none of this;

there are those who know the difference immediately. When
someone claims to have tasted

rosewater but smells of onions, everything he says is nonsense.
The heart is a great house

that has an opening in the wall that neighbors can see
through. The owner

of the house, though, does not know he is being spied on.
Everyone can see in! Everyone

knows what's going on in your heart. Think how doctors
determine your health by

examining your urine, your pulse, your complexion. How much
deeper do spirit doctors go!

They have seen you before your birth and all the
circumstances that formed

Bestami's precognition of Bu'l-Hasan

you. Remember how Bestami announced the spiritual state of
Bu'l-Hasan. One day he

and his students were walking on the plain in the region of
Rayy. Suddenly Bestami inhaled

a sweet scent from Kharaqan. He wept in ecstasy from the
sweetness. He closed his eyes

and took in the wine of the breeze. When water beads appear
on the *outside* of a pot of

ice water, it's not because water has escaped from inside.
Rather it's condensed from

the outside air because of the coldness of the jar, so the
breeze from Kharaqan became tears

on Bestami's face, and his inside turned to wine. He swayed
as though drunk. A student

begged him, "What are these unseen signs that make your face
rosy, then pale? You

are the desire of those of us who desire God. Every moment
messages come from

elsewhere. You inhale like Jacob holding the shirt of
Joseph. Share

what you're knowing! Say one word. Let your falcon show
what it has caught." This

happened once to Muhammad. He felt a spirit coming from the
unseen and the rapture

of *that* dissolving in *this* came over him, but that's an
endless story! Bestami

replied, "A spirit king, a friend, is on his way here. His
face will be God's rose."

"What will his name be?" "Bu'l-Hasan." Bestami described
his features, the way his

chin and eyebrows would be, his height, his hair, and exactly
how his face would look.

The soul qualities and the form his devotions would take.
Body features and animal

energies last for an hour. Don't love those with your most
vital love. In your house

there is lamplight and sunlight. The ceramic oil holder is
your body, the source of

one light. Your real being is magnificent, immense, cruising
the vastness, and the origin

of that other light inside your house. There's the *shape* of
the rose you hold beneath

your nose, and there's a fragrance ascending to the palace
of your brain. Learn to enjoy

the qualities of God-light. Joseph's shirt was carefully
packed away in Egypt

by his brother, Judah, so that the sweet aroma could cover
Canaan. Bestami's students

wrote down the predictions, and everything happened
accordingly. Bu'l-Hasan's

generosities, even his way of sometimes holding back, all
had been minutely described on

the well-guarded tablets. Well guarded from what? Erroneous
alterations. Inspired

predictions that come like Bestami's are not the same as
astrology or geomancy or

dream interpretation. Sufis call it *heart-knowing* to
disguise it from those

who shouldn't hear. It *is* from the heart. That's where God
comes through. No mistakes

can be made or said when your consciousness is in your love
and your love is in

God. In that light there are no distractions. Consider
poverty, for example, where,

if you're in that state, having nothing becomes your food.
Paradise grows from things thrown

out. Healing comes to the broken and the helpless.
Aggression only gets

aggressiveness back. Sufis know that grace comes when
something is taken away.

A prayer bead becomes a pearl, and the dervish becomes
the ocean that hides the pearl

in gratitude. As this material world recedes, the presence
flows in. What one like that

fears losing is the jasmine scent of feeling near to God. When
that happens he wonders

what he has done, like the servant, baffled by having his
food reduced. Remember him?

The king read only the interior meanness of the letter and
wrote no reply. "How can this be?"

asks the servant. "Maybe the letter carrier concealed it
out of envy. I will write

another and send it by a different courier." He does,
and the king keeps silent

again. Five times this happens! Finally the king's
chamberlain suggests, "Perhaps

it would be fitting to give him some reply. He is, after
all, your servant." "Yes,

it would be easy to answer this man, but he doesn't
really want a connection with me.

He wants sweetmeats and a portion from the kettle; that's
all. He doesn't want contact

with my intelligence, and he certainly doesn't want union.
He's a fool, and I forgive

that, but we mustn't associate with him." Imagine that the
sky and the earth are an apple

that has grown from the tree of divine power. There is a
kind of worm that lives

happily inside the apple, totally ignorant of the tree,
the orchard, and the orchard

keeper. Another splits the apple open with its movements.
Prophetic fire reaches out

timidly at first, from the flint to fragments of cotton, but
eventually it becomes a sulfurous

How human beings can move into a deeper place, beyond animal energies

dragon flying into starlight. This is how human beings move
from their attachments to

food and sleep to some unsayable state beyond the angels.
In the spirit you are a prince

for whom Baghdad and Samarcand are half a step away. Animal
energy lights your eyes

and quickens your step. Your hair grows and shines with
that energy, but move into

the deeper energy that derives from. There Muhammad
will welcome you, and

Gabriel will back away saying, "If I came closer, your
glory would consume me."

Another infinite subject.
The servant is still complaining
about being ignored, as

wind once was blowing around Solomon's throne. "Why are you
so malicious today?" asks

Solomon. "Don't be angry with me when you yourself are acting
perversely. Be honest

Solomon's crooked crown and what it tells him; Bu'l Hasan in the snow at Bestami's tomb

with me and I'll be honest with you!" Solomon's crown tilts
to one side on his head. He

puts it straight, but it slides crooked again. Eight times
this happens. "Why are you doing

this?" The headpiece replies, "I have to. When your power
loses compassion, I have to

show what that looks like." Immediately Solomon recognizes
the truth. He had been

busy judging others, while some personal desire of his was
disrupting the community. He

kneels and asks forgiveness. The crown centers itself on
his crown. If something

goes wrong, accuse yourself first. Don't be like Pharaoh
chopping off the heads

of innocent babies, when the enemy he is looking for, Moses,
was in his own house.

Even the wisdom of a Solomon or a Plato can wobble and go
blind. *Listen*

when your crown reminds you of what makes you cold toward
the outside world, as you pamper

the greedy energy *inside*. After Bestami died, it happened as
he said that Bu'l-Hasan

became the sheikh for his community. Every day Bu'l-Hasan
would go to Bestami's tomb

to receive instruction. He has been told to do this in a
dream by Bestami himself. Every

dawn he goes and stands facing the tomb until mid-morning.
Either the spirit of Bestami

comes and talks to him or in silence the questions he has
are answered. One day

a deep snow has fallen overnight. The graves are
indistinguishable. Bu'l-Hasan

feels lost. Then he hears his sheikh's voice. "The world is
made of snow. It falls and melts

and falls again. Don't be concerned with the snow. Come
toward the sound of my voice.

Move always in this direction." From that day Bu'l-Hasan
begins to experience the enlightened

state that he has only heard and read about before. That
servant is *still* nervously

writing his complaining letters! There's a part of us that's
like an itch. Call it

The animal soul, the intelligent soul, and two kinds of knowing

the animal soul, a foolishness that, when we're in it, makes
hundreds of others around us

itchy. And there is an intelligent soul with another desire,
more like sweet basil or the feel

of a breeze. Listen and be thankful even for scolding that
comes from the intelligent soul.

It flows out close to where you flowed out. But that
itchiness wants to put food

in our mouths that will make us sick, feverish with the
aftertaste of kissing a

donkey's rump. It's like blackening your robe against a
kettle without being anywhere

near a table of companionship. The truth of being human
is an empty table made of

soul intelligence. Gradually reduce what you give your animal
soul, the bread

that after all overflows from sunlight. The animal soul
itself spilled out and sprouted

from the other. Taste more often what nourishes your clear
light, and you'll have less use

for the smoky oven. You'll bury that baking equipment in the
ground! There are two kinds

of knowing: one acquired, as a child in school memorizes
facts and concepts from books

and from what the teacher says, collecting information from
the traditional sciences as well as

the new sciences. With such intelligence you rise in the
world. You get ranked

ahead or behind others with regard to your competence in
retaining information. You

stroll with this intelligence in and out of fields of
knowledge, getting always more

marks on your tablets. There is another kind of tablet, one
already completed inside you.

A spring overflowing its springbox. A freshness in the
center of your chest. This

intelligence does not turn yellow or stagnate. It's fluid,
and it doesn't move from outside

to inside through the conduits of plumbing-learning. This
second knowing is a fountainhead

from within you moving out. Drink from there! Someone comes
to Bu'l-Hasan for advice.

Bu'l-Hasan's talks with his enemy

"Ask someone else," he says. "I'm your enemy. I'll answer
according to my own advantage.

Don't put a wolf in charge of your sheep! Sit with your
friends and ask them. In

the past you have behaved with hatred toward me, and I have
responded. Look for help

from someone who loves you more than I do." "I know this is
true, Bu'l-Hasan.

You have long thought of me as an enemy, but you have a
beautiful clarity, which I know

will not allow you to deceive me." There is a bright reason
that restrains the ego's desire

for revenge, as a gentle old police inspector at the heart of
a city keeps the whole place sane

and watchful. Like a cat waiting in front of a mousehole, but
"cat" is wrong.

The kind strength that oversees our thieving energies is a
lion. He roars,

and smaller animals scatter. But what if the city is *all*
sneak thieves who will even grab

the clothes off the wash line? Then it doesn't matter who
the police inspector is.

Muhammad makes a young man from Hudhayl commander

Muhammad appoints a young man from Hudhayl as commander
of his force. Pay

attention to the inner one who commands you! There *is*
a rational soul leading

your donkey through the mountain wilderness. When the donkey
pulls away and takes off

on its own, that clear one chases, calling, "This
place is full of wolves

who would love to gnaw your bones and suck the sweet   2000
marrow." This sovereign

self in you is not a donkey, but more like a stallion, and
Muhammad is the stable keeper

speaking quietly, *Ta'alaw,* in Arabic, *Come, come. I am
your trainer.* You stumble

along. I urge you to canter, to be lively and gentle and
right for a king to ride.

Everyone shies from discipline. Easy. *K-k, kk-k.* Listen
for that *come, come.* Some hear

with these ears and some with a secret hearing the invitation
into peace. When you become God's slave,

you will say it yourself to everyone, *Ta'alaw, Come back,
come.* So Muhammad selects

a young man to be leader, and many object. This youth
is the human spirit, envied

and gossiped about, not seen for what it is. One of
the marvels of the world is

The soul in prison; words as chaperone

the sight of a soul sitting in prison with the key in
its hand! Covered with dust,

with a cleansing waterfall an inch away! A young man
who rolls from side to side,

though the bed is comfortable and a pillow holds his head.
He has a living master, yet

he wants more, and there is more. If a prisoner hadn't
lived outside, he would not

detest the dungeon. Desiring knows there's satisfaction
beyond this. Straying maps

the path. A secret freedom opens through a crevice you
can barely see. Your love

of many things proves they're one. Every separate stiff
trunk and stem in the garden

connects with nimble root hairs underground. The awareness
a wine drinker wants cannot

be tasted in wine, but that failure brings his deep thirst
closer. So the heart keeps ignoring

the waterfall and the key, but there is one guiding through
all the desiring restlessness.

The old captains are blind to the young man's qualities.
They keep arguing their tired

arguments: how spiritual maturity arrives like leaflessness,
the lightness of winter trees

that comes with age. Such predictable phrases breeze
out of the old soldiers

who presume to advise Muhammad! Don't use words in the
presence of the Friend. When

you sit down with your beloved, tell the chaperone, the
word-woman who brought you

together, to leave. Silence is better. Speak only if asked,
and quietly, as you hear

Husam draws the words out

these words being drawn from me by Husam. Husam shortens my
sermons on righteousness and

lengthens the sections that mention the Friend. Husam, you
have the inner vision. Why

do you want words? Maybe it's like the line from the poet
Abu Nuwas, who said in Arabic,

As you pour me wine, talk to me about it! When the cup rises
to the lip, the ear says *I want*

some. "Blushing is not enough? Look how red you are." *No. I
want more than heat,* said the ear.

I want the taste! Muhammad listens to the conventional
eloquence as long as

he can. "You bring camel dung and ask me to eat it?"
Muhammad is tasting continually

the wine of the agreement he made with God before the
creation of the universe,

the wine of the question *Am I not your Lord?* and of the
answer *Yes!* The seven

sleepers sipped that and slept three hundred and nine years.
The Egyptian women drank

one cup and were lost in Joseph's beauty. Pharaoh's
magicians inhaled this fragrance,

and the gallows looked like lovers coming toward them.
Jafar lost his hands and feet

in battle, yet flew because he tasted this *Yes. Yes.*
Bestami, totally lost

in this one night, proclaims to his students, "There is
no God but me! I am God."

The ecstasy passes, and his students confront him with what
he said. "If I say that

again, kill me. God is beyond the body, and look at me,
still in this body." The next

night Bestami soars again into ecstasy. Dessert is served.
Dawn rises. His candle flutters

helplessly in sunlight. His reason creeps to a corner like
a minor official in the presence

of the sultan. When the creator of life enters a human
being, the *he* or *she*

dissolves: a Turk who knows no Arabic begins speaking Arabic;
the Logos consumes fancy turns of phrase.

"Within this robe is nothing but God. Why look elsewhere?"
Bestami speaks even more powerful

heresy than before. His students draw their knives and
stab, but they strike only

themselves. "Bestami" is not there. The ones who aim
for the throat cut

their own. Those who point at his chest pierce
themselves. A selfless one

The dangers of sitting on the ecstatic roof, why wine is forbidden

becomes a mirror. Whatever you see there is *you*. Language
must stop here. We have poured

love wine and come to the edge of the roof. Sit down and
do not say your secret.

This is the place the soul is most afraid of. On this
height, this ecstatic

turret, it is possible to lose the delight by raving in
careless discourtesy. As when

some of Muhammad's state penetrated the arguing soldier, and
he lost control. He couldn't quit

babbling. This is how restrictions on alcohol came to
be. Wine makes one beside

oneself, and in that state a person with deep gentleness
at the core becomes humble

and quiet, but someone with repressed rage will get mean,
and since with most people this is

the case, wine is forbidden to all. Such matters are decided
by the general, rather than

the specific, which might be exceptional, like the young man
from Hudhayl who had mature

intelligence despite his youth. There *is* a universal
intellect that sees through

appearance. Without proof or explanation that pure light
cuts the skin of objectivity

and goes to the center. To one who looks at the external
there's little difference

between the genuine and a good copy. How could he
know what's in the date

basket? Gold gets blackened with smoke, so the
thief won't notice.

Copper is gilded to seem valuable to the undiscerning.
But there are ways of

distinguishing gold from gilded copper. Clip shavings with
scissors and put them

in the solution where everything becomes clear. Look inside
and find where a person

loves from. That's the reality, not what they say.
Hypocrites give attention to

form, the right and wrong ways of professing belief. Grow
instead in universal light.

The one not in need of anyone

When that revealed itself out of nonexistence, God gave it
a robe and a thousand different names,

the least of those sweet-breathing names being *the one
who is not in need of anyone.*

When that comes, daylight looks dark, and when your foolish-
ness, which doesn't recognize

such beauty, becomes visible to you, night dark will seem
glowing beside it. Let your eyes

get used to light. Don't miss your own splendor!
Don't stay in the batlike

mind that loves complexity and doubt, the unlit niches.
Bats seek those to live

in, because there a bat's accomplishments seem greater than
they are. He can impress

as he confuses you with cave ramifications. Little by little
accustom yourself to your own light,

Trusting the knowing-light within; the story of the three fish

those times on the roof. An intelligent man, or woman, is a
lamp that guides itself. Let

him or her lead. Trust the knowing they browse. A half-
intelligent person is one who lets

the intelligent person be guide. He holds on like the blind
to the coat of a helper. Through

another, he acts and sees and learns. There is a third kind
with no intellect at all, who

takes no advice, strolls out into the wilderness, runs a
little to one side, stops, limps

through the night with no candle, no stub of a candle, no
notion what to ask for.

The first has perfect intellect. The second knows enough
to surrender to the first. One

breathes with Jesus. The other dies, so Jesus can breathe
through him. The third

flops and flounders in all directions, with no direction,
lurches and leaps, trying

everything, with no way or way out. For you really stubborn
people I'll tell a story.

You may have read it in the *Kalilah*, but that's only its
external form. This is the heart-core.

There was a lake with three big fish in it. Fishermen came
to the edge with nets. All three

fish saw them. The most intelligent decided at once to
leave, to start out on

the long, difficult trip to the ocean. He thought, "I won't
consult with these other two. They

might weaken my resolve. They love this lake so!
They call it *home*. That feeling

will keep them here." When you're traveling, ask a traveler
for advice, not someone whose

lameness keeps him in one place. Muhammad said, "Love of
one's country is part of

the faith," but don't take that literally. Your real
"country" is where you're

heading, not where you are. Don't misread that *hadith*.
According to tradition, in the ritual

ablutions there's a separate prayer for each body part.
When you snuff water up your nose to

cleanse it, beg for the scent of spirit. The proper prayer
is *Lord, wash me! My hand has*

washed this part, but my hand cannot wash my spirit. A
certain man used to say the wrong

prayer for the wrong hole, the nose prayer when he splashed
his behind. Can the odor

of heaven come from our rumps? Don't be humble with fools,
and don't take pride into

the presence of a master. It's right to love your home
place, but first ask, *Where*

is that, really? The wise fish saw the men and their nets
and said, "I'm leaving."

Ali was told a secret doctrine by Muhammad and told not to
tell it, so he

whispered down the mouth of a well. Sometimes there's no one
to talk to. You must just set out

on your own. The intelligent fish made its whole body a
moving footprint, and, like

a deer the dogs chase, suffered greatly on its way, but finally
made it to the edgeless

safety of the sea. The half-intelligent fish thought, "My
guide is gone. I ought to have

left with him, but I didn't. I've lost my chance to escape.
I wish I'd gone with him!" Don't

regret what's happened. It's in the past. Let it go.
Don't even *remember* it!

The bird's threefold advice

A man caught a bird in a trap. The bird says, "Sir, you have
eaten many cows and sheep in

your life, and you are still hungry. This little bit of meat
on my bones won't satisfy

you either, but if you let me go, I'll give you three pieces
of wisdom. One I'll say

standing on your hand. One on your roof, and one I'll speak
from the limb of that tree." The man

was interested. He freed the bird and let it stand on his
hand. *Number one: do not believe*

an absurdity no matter who says it. The bird flew and lit
on the man's roof. *Number two:*

*do not grieve over what is past. Never regret what has
happened.* "And by the way,

in my body there's a huge pearl weighing as much as ten
copper coins. It was meant to be

the inheritance for you and your children, but now you've
lost it. You might have owned

the largest pearl in existence, but evidently it was not
meant to be." The man started wailing

like a woman in childbirth. The bird, "Didn't I just say
'Don't grieve for what's in

the past,' and *'Don't believe an absurdity'?* My entire body
doesn't weigh as much as

ten copper coins. How could I have a pearl that heavy inside
me?!" The man came to his senses.

"All right. Tell me number three." "Yes. You've made such
good use of the other two." *Don't*

*give advice to someone who's groggy and falling asleep.
Don't throw seeds on the sand. Some*

torn places cannot be patched. Back to the second fish, the
half-intelligent one. He mourns

the absence of his guide for a while, then thinks, "Perhaps if I pretend to be already dead . . .

I'll belly up on the surface and float like weeds float, giving myself entirely to

the water. To die before I actually die, as Muhammad said to." He did that. He bobbed

up and down within arm's reach of the fishermen. "Look at this! The best and biggest fish

is dead!" One of them lifted him by the tail, spat on him, and threw him on the bank. He

rolled over and over, slid secretly near the water, then back in, outside the circle of

their nets. Meanwhile the third fish, the dumb one, was jumping about in great agitation,

trying to escape with agility and cleverness. The net closed around his thrashing, and as he lay

in the terrible frying-pan bed, he thought, "If I get out of this, I'll never live in the limits

of a lake again. Next time, the ocean! I'll make the infinite my home." Such a stated

intention must not always be taken seriously! There are those who cannot do what they say

The quality of reason

they're going to. They lack the quality called spiritual reason. Seized by a net

of painful circumstances, they cry out and *imagine* how they might have acted, but if

the situation goes away, they forget and go back to the lake of comfortable pleasure,

a moth with singed wings returning to the candle. Reason, or spirit clarity, exists as a *pir*, a

teacher, a strength like Moses, a grasp, a remembering
power. Once, before the assembled court

Pharaoh and Moses begin their exchange

Pharaoh challenged Moses. Hear their conversation as a
confrontation of clarity with

sensual imagination. Pharaoh and the imagination are
world-incendiaries. They

consume. Moses and reason are spirit-kindlers. They
enlighten. Who are you? asks Pharaoh.

Moses: Reason, a messenger from God. Pharaoh: Don't give
me some ecstatic nonsense. I want

to know your name and lineage. Moses: Out of the dust pit,
born of slaves, and shall

return there, nothing born of nothing, but with the gift of
love and spirit-knowing.

That's who I really am. The rest you can have to rule and
rot in the frightening grave with.

Pharaoh: You will not then acknowledge publicly my role in
your nurturing? Moses: There is

only one Lord. You could not even fashion one hair of my
eyebrow. How can you claim

some part in forming my soul! You murdered thousands of my
countrymen's children trying to

kill me and failed. Here is the truth of our natures: I am
despised and threadbare, but

sovereign in my poverty. You are blood-thirsty and impotent.
Pharaoh: Granted this may be

true, but why are you embarrassing me in front of my people?
Moses: Think of me as a gardener

Gardening work

preparing soil for roses. There was a man breaking up the
ground, getting ready to plant, when

another man came by, "Why are you ruining this land?" "Don't
interfere. Nothing can grow here

until the earth is turned over and crumbled. There can be no
roses and no orchard without

first this devastation. You must lance an ulcer to heal it.
You must tear down parts of

an old building to restore it." So it is with a sensual life
that has no spirit. A person must

face the dragon of his or her appetites with another dragon, the
life energy of the soul. When

that's not strong, everyone seems to be full of fear
and wanting, as one thinks

the room is spinning when one's whirling around. If your love
has contracted into anger, the

atmosphere itself feels threatening, but when you're
expansive and clear, no matter

what the weather, you're in an open windy field with friends.
Many people travel as far as Syria

and Iraq and meet only hypocrites. Others go all the way to
India and see only people buying and selling.

Others travel to Turkestan and China to discover those
countries are full of cheats

and sneak thieves. You always see the qualities that live
in you. A cow may walk

through the amazing city of Baghdad and notice only
a watermelon rind and a tuft of hay

that fell off a wagon. Don't repeatedly keep doing what your
lowest self wants. That's like

deciding to be a strip of meat nailed to dry on a board
in the sun. Your spirit needs

Let spirit follow the changes it knows about

to follow the changes happening in the place it knows about.
There the scene is each

moment new and new again, a clairvoyant river of picturing
more beautiful than any

river on earth. Purify your eyes there where the sufis wash,
and the present will fill

with radiant forms. It's a cleaning of the spirit senses.
If you were blindfolded

and a lovely woman came by, you could only know her beauty
by hearing her speak.

What if she didn't say anything! Vision is how we measure
the world. But there is

another way of looking that lets us recognize true human
beings. Wash your eyes and

let yourself see! Imagine if the world were populated with
light-forms, and you

had your eyes shut. Who would you know? You might ask your
ears to describe the beauty.

They would say, "If we *hear* anything, we'll let you know, but
we can only interpret spoken

words and sound, not *visible* or unspoken things." Then, you
might call your nose, "Hey nose,

what's going on?" "Jasmine, rosewater, musk, dung, that's
it." Muinuddin,

Rumi talks directly to Muinuddin, a local official

there are marvels you're not aware of. Don't judge me with
your eyes. Look at me through

my eyes. See into the region beyond phenomena, and all these questions you ask will dissolve

into love within love. Peace be with you, sir, in your position of leadership. Don't

judge God's beloved ones with the subject-object senses. See unity from within union. God

put divine light in human eyes. That sweet-tongued spirit king Hakim Sanai used to

say that every hair on a mystic's body becomes an eye. He didn't mean ordinary sight. Some

seeing does not depend on that mechanism. You saw in the womb and you see in dream without

opening your eyelids. As birds ride air, as *Adam* means "earth" and came out of it to glorify

the ground, as Egypt's illness grew Moses to heal it, as a brittle gourd cup holds wine, so

eyes receive the invisible, and the mixing of their filmy substance with that is

love's great mystery. And it isn't just eyes that have this light. Rocks,

mountains, and water, everything has it. The pulpit post moaned when Muhammad drew

his hand away, and the bits of gravel in *your* hand might start singing *zikr,* as

they sang to the skeptic Abu Jahl. Remember? Unfold your bright, intelligent wings. Read

Sura 99, beginning *When the earth began to quake.* That trembling could only come if

the ground had seen and known secrets and could tell us its medicinal values. Listen:

Moses and Pharaoh

Moses is talking still to Pharaoh: My being here with you
is clear evidence that your illness

and your country's condition desperately need the cure a
prophet brings. You had dream visions

warning you that I was coming to heal your blindness, but you
said, "It must be the rich meat

I eat." Nevertheless, you went out to the frontier to keep me
from entering: You went

to the mountain passes of sex and birth. You tried to *close*
those roads that lead from

the human to the divine! In spite of all the effort, here I
stand *saying* the medicine you

cannot hear. You're not aware of how I'm bandaging your
wound. If you could wake up, you

would see that every stumbling unconscious action gives birth
to a response, an indication, a

hint from God. You could be so different, unsotted,
observant, subtle, pure. As

a dark granular iron surface can be polished to a mirror
full of transparent hilarious

beings, so you could shine with usefulness, as the rusty saw
blade, scoured and polished,

reveals a resplendent world of lights darting new energy.
The agent that polishes

is reason. What does the work is prayer. Pray! And let the
unseen streak its glints

through you. Not praying, letting pleasure prompt your
action, is stirring the

gunk on the bottom of your pool. You've done that often
enough! Let it clear now

and the moon and stars will circle in the space. Human
beings are like creek water.

When it's muddy, you can't see the riverbed where the jewels
are. Let the water be as it was

at the origin spring. Or say the human spirit is air: dust
swirls up and the sun looks

murky. All that can blow away. God has given you dreams
to show your inner state. Remember

the man with excrement on his face who looked in the mirror
and said. "You look terrible!"

The mirror replied, "Friend, this ugliness belongs to you."
Once in a dream you saw

your clothing burning up. Another time your eyes and mouth
were sewn shut, or a wild

animal had your head in its mouth, or you were hanging
upside down in a latrine, or

drowned in blood-smeared water, and worse things than these,
which I won't mention, because

in your present state the saying of them would make you
angry. Just know that I

know everything, even the ways you try *not* to see what dreams
tell. But you can change!

The repentance door is always open, the western gate, the
sunset entrance to paradise.

There are eight ways in. One of them is repentance. Others
are sometimes open, sometimes

shut, but the evening opening is always possible. Quickly,
bring *all* your baggage through here!

Moses proposes a bargain with Pharaoh: Accept one thing I say
and practice it; then take

four gifts from me in return. Pharaoh: What is the *one
thing?* Moses: That you

acknowledge publicly that there is no God but God, the
creator of the universe, of ocean

and mountain and desert, star and human being and bird
and all invisible entities, that

that one is infinite, sovereign, and without likeness.
Pharaoh: What will I get

for doing this? Tell me the four things, or better, bring
them for me to see! Maybe the sight of

them will unlock my stubborn no-faith. The river of honey
may sweeten my hatred. The river of

milk may nourish the prison of my mind. The wine river may
let the fragrance of obedience

come into me, which I have never felt. Or of the four
paradisal rivers, the one

of pure water may give refreshment to my thornbrake, turn it
green, and transform me into

one who looks for the Friend. As it is, I'm caught in
boiling heat, then cold,

cruel, poisonous to everyone. Will your gifts release me
from how I live?

Moses: The first gift is continuous health. The second,
longevity. And death will not

surprise you. You will get to choose your time to leave the
world. You will move into the

next as a nursing child moves toward the breast, not to avoid
more pain, but eager to

taste the secret that hides in the body's house, the treasure
that's buried under the ruin.

You'll take up the pickax expectantly. You'll be like the
worm, addicted to eating grape

leaves, who suddenly wakes up; something wakes him, call it
grace, whatever, something wakes

him and he's no longer a worm; he's the entire vineyard,
the orchard too, the fruit, the

trunks, a growing wisdom and joy that doesn't need to devour.
You'll be a living explanation of

I was a hidden treasure, and I wanted to be known. But if
you don't do the tearing-down work,

if you stay in the house hypnotized by the pictures hanging
there, the pickax will have no

force in your hand. It might as well be a pomander, an
apple-shaped ornament full of

potpourri to scent the bedroom. Grow up! Use the worker's
tool to find your real value. Remember

how Sanai said in his *Ilahinama:* "You are a child in a
gallery of imaginations. Destroy

that utterly." Pharaoh interrupts again: Enough! I want to
hear the third present that

you will give me if I do as you say. Moses: A double empire,
one temporal, one spiritual, and

both impervious to attack. Pharaoh: The fourth? Moses: You
will remain youthful, your hair dark,

your face rosy. In other words, you'll get what you want.
Your wishes are not profound, but

they are yours. As I might bribe a child to go to school with
walnuts and pistachios, or

promises of a pet bird, so I promise you that your muscular
strength will not diminish nor

will your sexual potency. Some people want that more than
anything! They look forward

Muhammad's foreknowledge of the time of his own death

to that, while Muhammad longs for paradise. Muhammad was
aware that when the month of Safar

ended, he would leave his body and enter the unseen, so he
proposed a reward for the first

to bring him news that a new moon had risen and the new month
of Rabi begun. Ukkasha

is the one who brings that information. *You mighty lion,*
paradise is yours, at once!

This is how a true human being feels the freedom of leaving
the body. Children, like

Pharaoh, love to stay. He breaks in on Moses' discourse
again: I understand what

you are offering, but I need time to consider and confer
with advisors. He went

Asiya's advice to Pharoah

to Asiya, his Israelite wife. She screams at him, "How
could you not say *yes*

immediately? Don't you hear the blessings underneath what
Moses spoke to you! The sun

is being offered as a crown for your baldness! It's true that
sometimes hesitation allows

profit to build, but this! What he's offering is beyond
amazement. When

will you find another market like this? Where,
with one rose you

can buy hundreds of rose gardens? Where, for one
seed you get a whole

wilderness? For one weak breath, the divine wind! You've
been fearful of being absorbed

by the ground or drawn up into the air. Now, let your
water bead drop into the ocean where

it came from. It will no longer have the form it had, but
it's still water. The essence is

the same. This giving up is not a repenting. It's a deep
honoring of yourself. When

the ocean comes to you as a lover, marry, at once, for God's
sake! Don't postpone it.

Existence has no better gift. No amount of searching will
find this that has been offered

you. A perfect falcon, for no reason, has landed on your
shoulder and become yours."

Pharaoh is not convinced. I'll ask Haman and see what he
says. Asiya replies that

The old woman and the noble falcon

Haman, in this matter, is like the old woman who's given
the king's white falcon to keep.

Haman will not understand the nature of the exchange. When
you give a noble falcon to a fussy

old woman who knows nothing of falconry, she will clip its
talons short, *for its own good.*

"Young man, where has your mother been that your toenails have
gotten this long?" Those

talons are how the falcon hunts and tears its food. The old
woman fixes him *tutmaj,* dumpling

stew. He won't touch it. "Too good to eat my *tutmaj*, huh?"
She ladles some broth and

holds it to his beak. "If you don't want pastry, at least try
the soup. One sip."

The inner nature of the white falcon is strong and
determined. Her anger builds,

and suddenly she pours the ladle of hot soup over his head.
Tears come from those beautiful

falcon eyes. He remembers his former life, the king's love
whistle, the great circling

over the ocean, the distances that can condense so quickly
to a point. Falcon tears

are food for a true human being, perfume for Gabriel. Your
soul is the king's falcon

who says, *This old woman's rage does not touch my glory
or my discipline.* I must be

quiet now and let the deliberations of Pharaoh and Haman take
their appointed course. Those

who are connected in their natures must go toward each other.
Abu Bakr and Muhammad were profoundly

together in spirit. Pharaoh and Haman live in a place of
power and pride and must always move

Ali and the woman whose baby crawled out on the roof

toward each other there. A woman comes to Ali. My baby
has crawled out on the roof near

the water drain, where I cannot go. He won't listen to me. I
talk, but he doesn't understand

language. I make gestures. I show him my breast, but he
turns away. What can I do?

Take another baby his age up to the roof. The woman does, and
the child sees his friend and

crawls away from the edge. The prophets are human for this
reason, that we may see them

and delight in their friendly presence, and crawl away from
the downspout. Muhammad calls himself

a man like you. Likeness is a great drawing force. Those of
mean dispositions learn hatred

from each other, and they try to draw others in. Anyone
whose haystack has burned

does not enjoy seeing someone else's candle lit. Beg for an
inner occupation that will ally you

The many wines

with others doing inner work. Find the wine most suitable
for you. God has given us

a dark wine so potent that, drinking it, we leave the two
worlds. God has put into hashish

a power to deliver the taster from self-consciousness. God
has made sleep so that it erases

every thought. God made Majnun love Layla so much that just
her dog would cause confusion

in him. Don't think all ecstasies are the same. Jesus was
lost in his love for God. His donkey

was drunk with barley. Drink from the presence of the
saints, not those other jars.

Every object, every being, is a jar full of delight. Be a
connoisseur and taste

with caution. Any wine will get you high. Judge like a
king. Choose the purest,

the ones unadulterated with fear or some urgency about
"what's needed." Drink

the wine that moves you as a camel moves when it's been
untied, and is just ambling

about. When the tendency of two friends is toward spirit,
toward the heart, they go,

like wind and flame, upward together. Stop the mouth of a
jar and put it in the river.

It won't go under because it's trying to breathe with its
companion, air. So someone

who loves the prophets moves, holding a draught of sky
inside. That emptiness keeps

pulling you into the presence of those who love wisdom. But
it's not always easy. We feel

drawn to Moses and drawn to Pharaoh at the same time. Be
glad when you end up with a friend

who mixes with the inner atmosphere of your heart. Pharaoh
found Haman and repeated the

offer Moses made. "This man insults your royal dignity! How
could such a reversal happen? It's

like the sky has become earth and the earth sky! A
rose garden has turned into a tomb!"

This is how a false advisor sees Moses, as a threat! Haman
and Pharaoh live in the pride

The danger of getting public attention

of competing egos. If your fortunes rise in that world,
watch out! You may be like

the blind man playing backgammon backward. With people you
consider friends, enemies,

and all your good luck, a lot of running around to get hit
on the head in different ways.

Whatever comes here, goes away. East and West themselves
dissolve. How could either culture

give what you need? Don't feel honored. Feel cautious,
careful, and alert. Public attention

is a poisoned wine that delights for a moment, then your
head drops over. Eminence burns

like oil fire, hard to control. Your truth comes when you're
flat on the ground, so keep

your head down. Get off the ladder! You are not in some
copartnership with God! That's not

how it is. I cannot explain. Understanding begins in the
mirror of devotional work. If I

told all of what I know, many could not stand it, so I'll
refrain. I shout twice

at the edge of a village, then leave. Whoever is supposed to
hear will hear. Back to

the Egyptian story: Haman destroyed Pharaoh's chance to
change with his mocking of Moses.

Protect kings from such advisors. Moses: I have been
generous, but it was not

Muhammad and the Arab chieftains

your destiny to be able to accept what I give. Muhammad
and the Arab chieftains were once

in a similar circumstance. They came to him and requested
that he divide the power

equally. "No," replied Muhammad. "Your authority is
different than mine." A flash flood

rose, and Muhammad used it to show them. Each chieftain
threw his wooden staff into

the water, and Muhammad threw his as well. Their lances were
carried away, but Muhammad's

stood up on the flood, and the water receded. Some kingship
is weak and artificial, while

prophetic sway grows naturally strong. Pay attention to that.
It is a taste of light.

Without it the mountain dragon comes down and this world
becomes hell. Hell

can be anywhere: there at the top of the cloud, a
birdcage! Or in your tooth,

a pain comes like fire, or from the same mouth roots, sweet
paradise water. Don't bite

anybody with those teeth! Who knows what might be there now?
We do not know how God's light

moves through form, making the trees salaam, the river
decide, and the sun and moon

keep their perfect appointments. Someone was saying
yesterday, "This world

The materialist and the gnostic argue

began in time, but eternity will inherit it." A materialist
questioned, "But how

do you *know* that the universe began in time? What can rain
know of the cloud? You are

a tiny worm living in a dung pile. How can you talk about the
birth and death of the sun?

This is something you were told by your father. You
memorized it and now you

claim it's true. Say what you really know, or be quiet."
The man answered, "One day I saw

two people arguing. A crowd gathered. One was saying, 'The
sky is a building that will one day

dissolve, because it was created.' The other, 'How do you
know that? Maybe it made itself.'

And the first, 'Do you deny the creator, who alternates night
and day and gives us food?'

'Without clear evidence I cannot accept what some ignoramus
passes along to another ignoramus.

Give better proof.' 'The real proof lives hidden in my soul
like the tiny arc of a new moon.

Just because I see it and you don't, don't deny it's there.'
There was much debate, and

the people listening got confused as to the beginning and
end of this intricate cosmos.

The first man finally said, 'Friend, I have a way to solve
this, to prove that I have

within me the origin of the sky, as lovers have the certainty
of their love, although they

can't *say* it. My words cannot reveal the truth, but look at
the haggardness of my face. My

tears prove the beloved's beauty.' 'This is not acceptable
evidence.' 'We're like two coins,

each claiming the other is counterfeit. Fire is the test for
what is genuine, fire or water. Let us

fall in the ocean, and become signs for others to judge by.'
They did, and the God-man came

through the death test. The other, not." There are no
minarets built in praise of

what doubters say, no passionate talk about their lives.
The coin faces of officials

keep changing, but not the flame-tongued book of the sun. Be
plain as day and a friend to what

lasts. Cynics say the same thing over and over, "I only know
what I see." Every external form is

a text to study, embodying a truth, the way medicine contains
healing. Does a painter paint

for the sake of the picture and not for the eyes of those who
will look at it? Think how

children look at images and remember things, and you yourself
recall someone you haven't seen

for years. A potter makes a jar, remembering water, a bowl,
anticipating food. A calligrapher

loops and curves the elegant lines, but not so that the words
are illegible. What takes shape

does so to reveal something that does not yet have form.
Corollaries exfoliate to the third,

fourth, and tenth degree according to your insight. You act,
and some essential move is implied,

as in chess. Proceed so that eventually it can be said,
Checkmate. Each rung for the sake

of the next. The desire to eat produces semen, and semen
comes so that light will

appear in a new person's eyes. Someone who doesn't know that
the invisible moves within the human form

is like a plant stuck in dense ground. He or she answers the
wind with a leaning head, *I'm coming!*

but the rooted foot says, *I'm staying here*. Or if a dull
person moves, it's done blindly

like dice with eyes glazed, no fire for seeing into the next
ten years. Human beings can do that.

The wall in front and the wall behind fall away, and the
tablet may be read. Everyone

Use of the longings we're given

can see how they have polished the mirror of the self, which
is done with the longings

we're given. Not everyone wants to be king! There are
different roles and many choices

within each. Troubles come. One person packs up and leaves.
Another stays and deepens in a love

for being human. In battle, one runs fearing for his life.
Another, just as scared, turns

and fights more fiercely. God spoke to Moses, *You are the
one I have chosen, and I*

love you. Moses replies, *I feel the great generosity, but
say what it is in me that*

causes your love. God explains, *You've seen a little child
with its mother. It*

*doesn't know anyone else exists. The mother praises or
scolds, a little slap*

*perhaps, but the child still reaches to be held by her.
Disappointment, elation, there's*

*only one direction the child turns. That's how you are with
me.* We worship you.

Imadu'l-Mulk and how it is with Friendship

We ask for help only from you. Remember the story of
the king who is so enraged

with his close friend that he's about to *kill* him!
A privileged mediator,

Imadu'l-Mulk, steps in and saves the man, but then the king's
close friend, who

has just been saved, turns away and will not thank the
intercessor. A teacher comes

and asks, "Why do you act so strangely toward this man who
saved you from being beheaded?"

He answers, "I was in the state Muhammad describes as, *No
other has been this way*

with God, this near. If the king wishes to cut my head off,
he may furnish a new one,

or not." Pitch-black night in the king's presence is worth
a hundred festival days without

357

him. Inside presence there's no religion, no grace, no unfaithfulness, no punishment,

and no language can say anything about it, except that it is *hidden, hidden.* The names

were received by Adam, but when he was given his body and his head made of watery clay

and fiery wind, the qualities inside the names became *that:* a human life being lived.

The names were then just breath and alphabet; from one point of view, revelation, but

from ten others, a covering, a distance from how it is to be in Friendship.

Abraham takes offense at Gabriel's question

Gabriel asks Abraham if he can be of help to him in any way. Abraham says, "After being

inside the presence, what is *help?* Why call for intermediaries? What

message is needed? Do I need a guide? To what?" What might seem a normal courtesy

in this case is an insult to Abraham. Language itself causes pain to such a

Friend of God. This may be difficult to understand. Companions in the cave

feel words as *thorns.* They hurt. Such companions hear separation and hidden

purposes in the wording. As bills of sale, as graffiti drawings have concealed reasons, so   3000

every form puts a limit on mystery. Moses asks God the most basic

Moses questions God about death

question, "You create us; then you
kill us. *Why?*"

God says, I understand the purpose within your question;
therefore I'll answer.

You want to know the *meaning* of phenomenal duration, so
you can teach others

and help their souls unfold. Anyone who asks this question
has some of the answer.

Sow seed corn, Moses, and you will experience the purpose of
taking a form. Moses

plants and tends the crop; when the ears have ripened to
the shape of their beauty,

he brings out to the field his blade and sharpening stone.
The unseen voice comes,

Why did you work to bring the corn to perfection only now
to chop it down? "Lord,

it is the winnowing time when we separate the corn grains
we use for food from the straw

we use for bedding and fodder. They must be stored in
different cribs in the barn."

Where did you learn this threshing-floor work? "You
gave me discernment." *Do you*

not feel that I should have a similar discernment in
the planting and harvesting

of forms that I do? So creation has a purpose. God
has said, *I was*

a hidden treasure, and I desired to be known. That desire
is part of manifestation.

The churn work of being incarnate

Like a deep truth inside a lie, like the taste of butter
in buttermilk, that's how

spirit is held in form. For a long time butter stays
invisibly present in

the churn mixture. Then a prophet comes with a dasher, or
it might be someone

who has heard the words of a saint and is connected to that
one as an infant is when

it hears its mother. The baby doesn't understand language,
but it knows the voice sound,

and gradually learns what talking means. We're all
born dumb. Only God

did not have to be taught to speak a tongue, though Adam
learned without a nurse or

a mother, and it is said Jesus came articulate into
the world, but the rest of us

need a lot of attention, much shaking by a sheikh, much
turning and paddling. Slowly the inner

butter emerges. Don't throw away buttermilk too soon!
Do the work, and you'll

begin to hear even inside the maundering drunk talk of
the tavern, the presence

of the host who served this wine to us. The life-energy in a
body *contains* eternity.

The play of the banner lion

You've seen a lion that plays and jumps about on a banner.
If there were no invisible

wind, how would it play? Flags know an east wind from
a west. This body

is a dancing banner lion thought and spirit cause to move.
Refreshing easterly,

saddening from the west. The inner directions are real, as
are the inward sun and moon

in your dreams. Dreams are like death, but with a
difference! Don't believe

what you are told. Learn by experiencing. Asleep you see
what you do not see awake.

You run to dream interpreters wanting to know where that
sight *came from.* This talk

of derivation wastes your time. The true watchers and
seekers are those who

remember, who return in sleep like elephants to Hindustan.
If you're not an elephant,

let the alchemists of soul, who are all around us, do
their work. Every night

they tend us in different ways. New plants spring up in
awareness. Ibrahim dreams

the truth and frees himself. Muhammad says the sign
of this happening comes

when one loses interest in illusion, and also in paradise!
Here is a story of

The young prince and the old woman of Kabul

a young prince who suddenly sees that the ambitious world is
a big game of king

of the mountain, a boy scrambling up a pile of sand to call
out, "I am king"; then another

throws him off to make his momentary claim, then another
and so on. World complications

can sometimes become very simple very quickly, and age
has no bearing on this

realization. And neither are words necessary to *see* into
mystery. Just *be* and it *is*.

A king dreams his young son has died. He falls into such
grief in the dream that

the world darkens, and his body grows inert. Suddenly
he wakes into a joy

he's never felt. His son is alive! He thinks
to himself, "Such sorrow

causes such joy." It is a kind of a joke on human beings
that we are pulled between

these two states as though with ropes on the sides of
a collar. Dream interpreters

say laughter in dream foretells weeping and regret;
tears, some new delight.

Now the king has another thought, "What occurs in dream
can actually happen

any second!" If my son dies, I will need a keepsake.
When a candle goes out,

you need another lit candle. My son must give us offspring.
He's of marriageable

age. I'll find him a bride. This is flawless reasoning,
dear reader. Open any medical

text and look at the table of contents: tumors, rashes,
fevers, there are a thousand

ways to die! Every step takes you into a scorpion pit.
He found a wife for the prince,

not from royal blood or from wealth, but from a poor, honest
worker's family, with

the greater riches of an open heart. A beautiful young
woman clear as morning

sun. The women in the court object vigorously, but the
king has decided. He knows

the value of inner wealth as opposed to the other: a long
curving file of moving camels,

as against bits of hair and dung. If you own the caravan,
why bother with refuse

left behind? In a quirk of destiny, as the marriage
approaches, the old woman

of Kabul falls in love with the handsome, generous-spirited
prince. She enchants him

with Babylonian magic, so that he leaves his bride at the
wedding, and for a year he

kisses the sole of her Kabulian shoe. Everyone weeps
for him, while he laughs

in his ignorance. His father the king prays constantly,
Lord, Lord! and because of

that surrendered calling, a master comes from the road
to save the prince. "Go to

Instructions to the prince from a master

the graveyard before dawn," says the master. "Find the
bleached-white tomb beside

the wall. Dig there in the direction your prayer rug points.
You'll discover how God works."

This story is long, and you're tired. I'll get to the point.
The prince does as the master

says and *wakes.* He runs to his father carrying a *sword*
and a *shroud,* the signs

his digging brought, showing that he recognizes his mistake
and that he is ready for

whatever the consequences are. The king orders that the
entire city be decorated

to celebrate the new marriage. Such an extravagant feast is
prepared that sherbets

are set out for the street dogs. The prince is so astonished
by how the old woman

enthralled him, and by the return of his wisdom, that he
falls down in a swoon for three

days. Little by little with rosewater remedies he wakes
again. A year passes in

this new life; then the king begins to joke with his son,
"Do you remember that old

friend of yours, how it was in her bed?" "Don't mention it!"
screams the son. "That

was delusion. I have found my real bride now." This prince
is the soul of humanity, your

essence. The old woman of Kabul is the color and perfume
of the sense world. Release

from the spell comes when you say, *I take refuge with
the lord of daybreak.* The woman

has great power. She can tie knots in your chest that only
God's breathing loosens. Don't

take her appeal lightly. The prince was in her net for one
year; you might stay there *sixty*.

You say you grow restless when you don't drink the dark
world-drink, but if you could

see a living one for one moment, you would draw out that
thorn from your foot and walk

with no limp. Let the lamp of the Friend's face show you
where to go. Selflessness is

Thirsty, we dream of an oasis, while sleeping next to a stream

your true self, sword and shroud. Whereas this is how
most people live: sleeping

on the bank of a fresh-water stream, lips dry with thirst. In
your dream you're running

toward a mirage. As you run, you're proud of being the one
who sees the oasis; you brag

to your friends, "I have the heart-vision. Follow me to
the water!" This love of spying

far-off satisfactions, this traveling, keeps you from tasting
the real water of where

you are, and *who*. Nearer than the big vein on your neck,
with waves lapping against

you: *here, here*. The *way* is who and where you already are,
sleeping in your very being: that

which sleeps and wakes and sleeps, and dreams the sweet water
is the taste of God. Maybe

another traveler will come to help you see the stream,
like the man who laughs

during a long drought when everyone else is weeping. The
crops have dried up. The vineyard

leaves are black. People were gasping and dying like fish
thrown up on shore. But one man

The man who laughs during a drought

is always smiling. A group comes and asks, "Have you no
compassion for this suffering?"

He answers, "To your eyes this is a drought. To me, it's a
form of God's joy. Everywhere

in this desert I see green corn growing waist-high, a sea-
wilderness of young ears

greener than leeks. I reach to touch them. How could I not!
You and your friends are like

Pharaoh drowning in the Red Sea of your body's blood. Become
friends with Moses and see

this other riverwater." When you think your father is guilty
of an injustice, his face

looks cruel. Joseph, to the envious brothers, seemed
dangerous. When you make

peace with your father, he will look peaceful and friendly.
The whole world is a form

for truth. When someone does not feel grateful to that,
the forms appear to be *as he feels.*

They mirror his anger, his greed, his fear. Make peace
with the universe. Take joy

in it. It will turn to gold. Resurrection will be *now.* Every
moment a new beauty.

And never any boredom. Instead, the pouring noise of many
springs in your ears. The tree

limbs will move like people dancing who suddenly know the
mystical life. The leaves

snap their fingers like they're hearing music. They are!
A sliver of mirror shines out

from under a felt covering. Think how it will be when the
whole thing is open to the air

and sunlight! There are mysteries I'm not telling you.
There's so much doubt everywhere,

so many opinions that say, "What you announce may be true in
the future, but not now."

But this form of universal truth that I see says, *This is not
a prediction. This is here*

Uzayr and his two sons

in this instant, cash in the hand! Which reminds me
of the sons of Uzayr, who are

out looking for their father. They have grown old, and their
father has miraculously grown

366

young! They meet him and ask, "Pardon us, sir, but have you seen Uzayr? We hear that

he's supposed to be coming along this road today." "Yes," says Uzayr, "he's right behind me."

One of his sons replies, "That's good news." The other falls on the ground. He has recognized

his father. "What do you mean *news*? We're already inside the sweetness of his presence."

To the mind there is such a thing as *news*, whereas to inner knowing, it's all in the middle

of its happening. To doubters, this is a pain. To believers, it's gospel.

The rules of faithfulness, beyond sweet and bitter, and union with the Friend

To the lover and visionary, it's life as it's being lived. The rules of faithfulness are

just the door and the doorkeeper. They keep the presence from being interrupted. Being

faithful is like the outside of a fruit peeling. It's dry and bitter because it's facing

away from the center. Being faithful is like the inside of the peeling, wet and sweet.

But the place for peelings is the fire. The real inside is beyond sweet and bitter. It's

the source of deliciousness. This cannot be said: I'm drowning in it! Turn back,

and let me cleave a road though water like Moses. This much I will say and leave

the rest hidden: your intellect is in fragments, like bits of gold scattered over many matters.

You must scrape them together so the royal stamp can be
pressed into you. Cohere,

and you'll be as lovely as Samarcand with its central market,
or Damascus. Grain by grain, collect

the parts. You'll be more magnificent than a flat coin.
You'll be a cup with carvings

of the king around the outside. The Friend will become
bread and springwater for

you, a lamp and a helper, your favorite dessert and a glass
of wine. Union with that

What talking is for

one is grace. Gather the pieces, so I can show you what is.
That's what talking is for,

to help us be one. Many-ness is having sixty different
emotions. Unity is peace

and silence. I know I ought to stop now, but the excitement
of this keeps opening my mouth

like a sneeze or a yawn does. Muhammad says, *I ask
forgiveness seventy times*

a day, and I do the same. Forgive my talking so much, but the
way God makes mysteries

manifest quickens and keeps the flow of words continual.
A sleeper sleeps while his bed

clothes drink in riverwater. The sleeper dreams of running
around looking for water

and pointing in the dream to mirages, "Water! There!" It's
that *there* that keeps him asleep.

The here and now of God; the guide

In the future, in the distance are illusions. Taste
the here and now of God.

This present thirst is the real intelligence, not some
back-and-forth mercurial

argument. Discursiveness dies and gets put in the grave.
This contemplative joy does not.

Scholarly knowing is a vertigo, an exhausted famousness.
Listening is better.

Being a teacher is a form of desire, a lightning flash. Can
you ride to the town of Wahksh,

far up the Oxus, on a streak of lightning? Lightning is not
guidance. Lightning

simply tells the clouds to weep. The streak lightning of our
minds comes so we'll weep,

longing for our real lives. A child's intellect says,
"I should go to school," but

that intellect cannot teach itself. A sick person's mind
says, "Go to the doctor,"

but that doesn't cure the patient. A few devils were sneaking
close to heaven trying to

hear the secrets, when a voice came, "Get out of here. Go to
the world. Listen to

the prophets." Enter the house through the door. It's not a
long way. You are empty

reeds, but you can be sugarcane again, if you'll listen
to the guide. When a handful

of dirt was taken from the hoofprint of Gabriel's horse and
thrown inside the golden calf,

it lowed! That's what the guide can do. The guide
makes you *live*. The guide

will take your falcon's hood off. Love is the falconer,
your king. Be trained by

that. Never say, or think, "I am better than . . ." That's
what Satan thought about

Adam. Sleep in a spirit tree's peaceful shade and never
stick your head out from that green.

How to live with one who guides

Be silent in submission under the shade tree of a teacher.
Otherwise, your abilities

grow deformed with pride; even your good qualities
may disappear. Don't resist

the master of mystery who gives you your knowing. Have
patience doing the simple cobbling

or you may be demoted to rag stitcher. Those who sew patches
on old clothes *with patience,*

though, become tailors who work with new cloth. Stay with
the Friend; be like the old

philosopher on his deathbed, who realizes that his mind
has been no help to him. "I've

been foolishly galloping around trying to avoid the holy
ones." Strenuous intellectual

swimming goes nowhere. Lift yourself into the ark with
Muhammad and Jesus and the true

human beings, who seem contemptuously "low" to the
"mountains" of intellect.

A single flood wave covers that prominence. Try to have the
philosopher's insight before

your last day. Sharpen seeing with dust-medicine from a
dervish's foot. It may burn as

it heals. The camel's eye stays filled with light because he
loves to eat desert thorns. One day

The camel and the mule talking

a camel and a mule are put in the same stall. "Why is it?"
asks the mule. "I've always

wanted to know. Why do *I* come stumbling down the mountain
frightened, with my pack

saddle crooked and the driver beating me, while you
glide over the same grade

in pure felicity? Have you been given a special
dispensation? Why

don't you ever fall on your face like me?" The camel:
"Every smooth descent is

a gift. But also there are differences between us.
Unlike yours, my head stays

high, so that from the top and all the way down, I see
the foot of the mountain

and every hollow and rise, fold on fold. A true human
being does this in life. He

or she sees to the death day and knows what will happen
twenty years from now, and in

the interval, not only for him- or herself but for everyone.
Intelligent light lives

in the loving knowledge of such a saint. Why?
Because that's where it feels

at home. Joseph dreamed the sun and moon were bowing down
to worship him. Ten years

went by and that came to pass. The saying, 'He sees by
God's light,' is not an idle

idiom. It *means* something. There is light that can
shatter this earth-and-sky.

It cannot be seen with eyes. This vision sees only the
next step, what's directly

in front. Another difference between us is that my nature
is more pure than yours."

The mule responds, "You're right. Everything you say is
true." He begins to cry,

kneeling before the camel. "Will you let me serve you
in some way?" "Since

you make this confession in my presence, you will be
spared consequences. Your

braying complaint was not from your deep self. Like
Adam's, that lapse was

temporary, but now these tears have taken you inside the
text, *Come in among my workers.*

You found a secret way in. You were fire; now light.
You were a hard, unripe grape;

now juicy, now a sweet raisin. A star point becomes
the sun. Live the joy

of this knowing." Husam, stir honey in the milk of this
story, so it won't go sour.

Combine it with the agreement we made before we were. Roar
the lion's knowledge. Write

with gold ink so whoever reads this will feel the ocean's
light around them and grow

The Egyptian and the Israelite

in the spirit. An Egyptian comes to the house of his friend,
the Israelite. "I need

your help. Moses has turned the Nile to blood for us,
while for you it is still

pure water. We Egyptians are dying of thirst. Please,
fill a cup for yourself and then

give it to me." The Israelite says, "My friend, I would love
to serve you this way."

He fills a cup, drinks half, then tilts it toward his friend,
the Egyptian. "Drink

the rest." Instantly the water becomes blackened blood. He
turns the cup back to himself;

it's clear water again. This so enrages the Egyptian he has
to sit down to let his anger

leave. "My brother, how can this difficulty be loosened for
me?" "Only one who honors God

can drink this water. Moses has caused this to show you
what you really consume.

You have a dark hatred in you for those who serve God. Ask
forgiveness. Open the eye

of your heart. Listen to guidance from the Friend.
Rejoice in that and

you'll be able to drink this cup with me. You have
been drinking that which

The obligations that come from reading this poem

slowly wastes your soul." Reader! Did you think you could
read these *Masnavi* words

for free? You must give something back! This mystery does
not come easily; it's more like

a lover with a veil, or a difficult text. Some claim
the *Shahnama* and the *Kalilah*

are like the Qur'an. Let a holy collyrium open their eyes.
When the nose is congested,

one can't tell dung from musk. Sometimes you read books
because you're bored or you

want relief from worry or from the desires you feel.
Urine, springwater, anything

will do to dowse a fire. But try to find the clear water
that takes you to an orchard

with a stream running through. We do not see the faces of
saints as they really are.

Muhammad is amazed how people can *not* recognize the light
of his face. A revelation

comes, "Your face is hidden, as a moon is clouded over, so
that those who should not see

won't. They have eyes like figures on a bathhouse wall, but
they don't see." When

you do an act of worship, God gives something in return,
as a waterdrop turns to

pearl, as stone to gold. A piece of ground receives
the wisdom spark. Be careful

with it. Power in the world is like those painted faces
in the bath that seem to

recognize you, but really they don't. Back to the Egyptian,
who begs, "Pray for me.

I am not fit to pray or to sit at your table, but maybe
inside your presence this dead

stick will bloom." His Israelite friend falls to his knees,
"You that give the desire

to pray and the response, you are first and last. We are
the nothing in between. 3500

How can we say anything?" He keeps on until he falls over
in ecstatic trance. He comes to.

He hears the answer, *Human beings shall have nothing but
what human beings make,*

The Egyptian opens to the source of thirst

and he hears the heart-roar from the Egyptian, *All praise
to God! I have been given*

*a new fire! Tell me how to say this faith! This Friendship
that has taken my hand*

like a palm bough in a flood carries me downstream into
the ocean. I am gathering

pearls *by the bushel basket.* His friend hands him the cup
to drink from. *No.*

I don't need that. The source of rivers has opened
a spring in my chest. This

heart, which was dry, hot, and thirsty, now is a source of
grace: I will give you

every good thing without intermediary, fullness without
food, sovereignty without

soldiers, wild roses without springtime, instruction without
book or teacher. I will heal

you without medicine and make the grave a wide playing
field. Come into my eyes,

Kaf, Ha, Ya, Ayn, Sad! *I came for water and have become*
a spirit Nile. I flow,

but am still. Muhammad saw the world as luminous motion,
all in conversation. The clod

with the stone, hill with cove. I am inside his hearing and
delighted laughter that says,

Did there not come? There's a way of seeing things
the reverse of how they are.

From the top of the pear tree of phenomena what looks like
a thornbrake of scorpions,

when you come down, you find is a crowd of rosy children
with their nurses. There is

Climbing up and down the pear tree

a woman who wants to make love with her lover in the presence
of her husband. She says,

"Lucky you, I'm going to climb the pear tree and gather
fruit." In the branches

she screams down pointing at her husband, "Who is that
you're on top of?"

"You've lost your mind," says the husband. "I'm standing
here by myself." "I see what

you're doing, you humping bastard!" "Come down," he says.
"You're going daft.

I'll pick the fruit." She climbs down; he climbs up.
Immediately she and her lover

begin what they enjoy. "Hey whore! What's going on?"
"Don't be silly," she calls

from underneath the lover. "I'm here by myself. It must
be the tree making another

illusion. I saw things just as weird when I was up there."
A joke is a teaching. Don't

be distracted by its lightness or the vulgarity. Jokes are
profound. Come down

from the pear tree that's making you dizzy, pear tree
of ego and mind, pear

tree of the personal predicament that skews your sight.
Look back at the trunk

and branches. When you separate from it, the tree
changes. Your humility

in descending, lets you see truly. This coming down is
not easy. Muhammad

longs for it, praying, "Show me each part in its wholeness,
from under and above, as You

see." With yourself out of its tangle, the tree receives
the creation word *BE*, and

becomes Moses' burning tree, a green-fire truth, *I AM
THAT I AM*, rooted in ground,

yet spreading to sky. This tree is the body, Moses'
wooden walkingstick. *Let*

it drop from your hand, he is told. Then, *Lift it up.*
His letting go and taking up again

frees Israel, eventually, though Moses doubts it ever will.
God tells him, *Just deliver*

the message. Don't consider how it may turn out. Pharaoh
kneels before Moses

asking mercy, but not meaning it. "Lord," says Moses,
"this rascal fools with

your rascal." *Shake your stick and make his land grow*
crops, then shake it and call

the locusts back. We have no interest in any outcome.
Unlike this worried hypocrite

walking to market at dawn without washing his face or having
done devotions. Looking

for bites of food, he becomes himself a morsel. There is
an unconsciousness that eats

and gets eaten like a lamb being fattened for slaughter.
Butchers enjoy the mindless

The appetites and soul intelligence

chewing of lambs. Likewise the appetites work for
a shadow king. Do the

soul work instead. Feed daily on wisdom. Expand your heart.
Rest the appetites. They

are bandits on the road. They stop your spirit and steal
valuables. The most vital

thing about you is your soul intelligence. The rest
is a mask for that. Don't

lose touch with it. Sensual wantings sometimes block
and blur that intelligence as

surely as wine or hashish can. Arrogance too is drunken,
making you

think things true that aren't. There's no end to this
talking! God says

to Moses, *Move your lips with language, and let my seeds*
break open in the ground.

He does; rare grains and hyacinths and luscious greenery
come up. The Israelites

are suffering a prolonged famine. Then for several days
they have enough to eat;

they no longer fear that the abundance will be withheld again.
With bellies full,

they become insolent. This is how the animal soul is.
Satisfy it, and it recalls

how comfortable it was with Pharaoh in Egypt. It needs
to remember instead its own

death and how it feels to be led by Moses through
the wilderness. Iron

must be red-hot before it can be shaped. Hunger makes
the body move toward God.

Even Pharaoh came and bowed to Moses during the famine.
When the crops grew back, he

forgot devotion. Some things are certain. If you take
the load off your donkey, he *will*

The two cities

kick you. We live in a glorious spirit city. We go to sleep
and dream another city full

of good and evil. As we begin to believe in the dream city,
we forget where we really are. We

don't say, "I'm just passing through. I don't live here."
Soul intelligence has great

difficulty remembering its home. Dense clouds cover
the stars. Civilizations

build and crumble in place. The dust of that destruction
work burns our eyes. We

need to live with a greater longing that purifies love and
opens the eye of mystery

that sees beginning and end at once. That soul intelligence
has come to us through

many states, forgetting each in turn, through the inorganic,
from mineral to vegetable.

The animal then forgets that it's been a plant, except
for the longing in spring

that walks out in the green, as the secret of suckling turns
a babe to its mother, as

every eager apprentice looks for a master. Particulars
derive from the universal,

as the motion of a shadow on the ground comes from
the branch of roses above.

Human soul intelligence has been led along, one universe to
another, getting wiser, but

without clear memories of its former ways of knowing. We
will migrate from this

too, out of self-absorption into a hundred thousand new
amazements. It will feel

like waking up, but remember, we will be held responsible
for what we've done in our

sleep here. Don't think, *I'll die and be set free!* The deception and
coldness we're

part of with our brothers, those torn coats of Joseph, become
wolves *inside,* shredding us.

A light slap payback turns to fierce retaliation.
Harmless circumcision

here, full castration there! God says to Moses finally
about the Egyptians who won't

listen, *Let the donkeys go to pasture. You've done all
you can. Let their sleep*

*deepen and cover the gifts you've offered. Their grief
will come, for though*

they have not known me, I've been secretly near each.
God is there, as

The nearness of soul intelligence

your soul intelligence is always overseeing your body,
even though you may not

be aware of it. If you start acting against your
body's health, that

intelligence will scold you. If it hadn't been so
lovingly close by, so

constantly monitoring, how could it rebuke? You
and your soul intelligence

are like the precision parts of an astrolabe. *Together*
you calculate how near this

existence is to the sun! Soul intelligence is marvelously
intimate, but it's not

in front or behind you, not to the left or right. Now
try to say how near the

creator of this intelligence is! No searching will find
a way to that! The movement

of your finger is not separate from your finger. You go
to sleep, and there's no

intelligent motion. Then you wake, and your fingers fill
with meanings. Now consider

the jewel-lights in your eyes. How do *they* work?
The visible universe

has many weathers and variations. But friend, the universe
of the creation word *BE*

The human connection with the universe of the creation word BE

is beyond pointing to. More intelligent than intellect,
more spiritual than spirit. No

being is unconnected to its reality, and that connection
cannot be said. *There,* there's

no separation and no return. There are guides to show
you. Use them.

But they will not satisfy your longing. Keep wanting
the creation word with all

your pulsing energy. A throbbing vein takes you further
than any thinking. Muhammad says,

Don't theorize about essence! Speculations are just more
layers of covering. Human beings

love coverings! They imagine the designs on the curtains
are what's being concealed. Everyone

gets naturally drawn toward some illusion, a form. We think
God is like *that!* Best not

think. Observe the wonders as they occur around you. Don't
claim them. Feel the artistry

moving through; be silent. Or say, "I cannot praise You as
You should be praised. Such

Alexander talks with Qaf Mountain

words are infinitely beyond my understanding." As Alexander
the Great approaches Qaf

Mountain, he sees it's made of emerald and that it has
become a ring around the world.

Amazed at the immensity of creation, he asks, "If you are
a mountain, what are these

others?" Mt. Qaf replies, "They are my veins. When God wills
an earthquake, I throb through

one of them. When God says *Enough!* I rest, or it appears I
rest. Actually, I'm

always in motion." Like the quickening energy of a medicinal
ointment, like intellect

An ant sees a pen writing

with speech in rapid exchange, so Qaf Mountain power flows
through existence. A tiny ant

sees a pen moving on paper and tries to tell the mystery to
another ant. "It was wonderful

how that pen point made pictures of basil leaves and beds of
roses and lilies." Another ant

suggests, "The real artist, though, is the finger. The pen
is only an instrument."

A third ant, "But consider. There's an arm above whose
strength controls the fingers . . ."

The argument goes on, up and up, until the chief ant says,
"Do not regard any accomplishment

as proceeding from material form. All living shapes become
unconscious in sleep and death.

Form is just the clothes of spirit." But even the wise ant
neglects to say what flows

inside *that.* He never mentions God, without which
intelligence and love

and spirit are inert. So Alexander the Great loves listening
to the wisdom of Mt. Qaf. He

wants to hear everything! "Explain to me about the
attributes of God." "Those

qualities are too vast to put in language." "Say then
something that can be said

about the wonder of those." "Look at the snow mountains.
You can travel through

them for three hundred years, and still there will be snow
mountains in the distance,

and snow falling to replenish the cold. The Himalayan
snow storehouse keeps the world cool

and safe from destructive wantings. As God's coolness is
greater than God's fire, snow-

mountain grace is more powerful than desire's tropical heat,
and prior to it." Remember

this. It is unqualified and unconditional, though the
before and *after* are really

one. Punishment and clemency, the same. Did you know that
already? Don't say *yes*

or *no*. And don't blame a religion for your being in between
answers. A bird can fly

in the air only after it's born of bird lust into a bird
body. Be helpless and

dumbfounded, unable to say *yes* or *no*. Then a stretcher will
come from grace to gather us

up. We are too dull-eyed to see the beauty. If we say, *Yes,
we can*, we'll be lying. If

we say *No, we don't see it*, that *no* will behead us and shut
our window into spirit. So

let us not be sure of anything, beside ourselves, and only
that, so miraculous beings

come running to help. Crazed, lying in a zero circle, mute,
we will be saying finally,

with tremendous eloquence, *Lead us.* When we've totally
surrendered to that beauty,

Muhammad asks Gabriel to show himself; Gabriel's feather

we'll become a mighty kindness. Muhammad in the presence
of Gabriel asks, "Friend,

let me see you as you really are. Let me look as an
interested observer looks

at his interest." "You could not endure it. Eyesight is too
weak to take in this

reality." "But show yourself anyway, so I can understand
what may not be known with

these senses." Body senses are wavering and blurry, but
there is a clear fire inside,

a flame like Abraham that is alpha and omega. Human beings
seem to derive from this planet,

but essentially we are the origin of the world. A tiny
gnat's outward form flies

about in pain and wanting, while the gnat's inward nature
includes the entire galactic

whirling of the universe. Muhammad persists in his request,
and Gabriel reveals a single

feather that reaches from east to west, a glimpse that would
have reduced a mountain range

to powder. Muhammad stares, senseless. Gabriel comes
and holds him in his arms.

Awe serves for strangers. This close-hugging love is for
friends. Kings have formidable

guards around them with swords drawn, a public show
of power that keeps order

and prevents mischief and other disasters. But when the king
comes to the private banquet

with his friends, there's harp music and the flute. No
kettledrums. No keeping

accounts, no judging behavior, no helmets, no armor. You
know how it is, silk

and music and beautiful women bringing cups, but who
can say it! Conclude

this part my Friend, and lead us the way we should go.
Muhammad's body is buried

now in the ground of Medina, but there is another part that
lives in truth, a sun

with no east or west. *Declining, change, sickness:* these
words do not refer to spirit.

If I were to *say* that, space and time would tremble and
shatter to pieces. The fox-body

thinks of ways to rob the sleeping lion-soul, but it never
sleeps! Though it pretends to

The ocean's foam

very well. The ocean splashes on shore because it loves
foam! That's how spirit

loves the body. Muhammad's moon hands light around
generously. You say the moon

has no hands? Still it gives itself. What if Muhammad had
shown *his* inner nature to Gabriel?

As Muhammad is passing the boundary into paradise, he invites
Gabriel to follow him. Gabriel

says, "I cannot be your companion past the Lote Tree."
Muhammad, "But I have not

gone as far as I must." Gabriel, "If I go beyond here, I'll
be consumed." This

conversation of one spirit with another is wonder on
wonder! How could they lose

their senses? Are there limits on what they can know? Other
unconsciousnesses pale

by comparison. This is about giving up your soul!
How long will *you*

hold on to that? "Gabriel," you are not the moth or the
candle. This is turn-and-turn-again

The donkey-head absurdity of this poetry

talking: antelope stalking lion. Cork the word-sweating
waterskin. This poetry is absurd

to those still solid in their earth senses. Be courteous
when visiting those

houses. Honor their traditions; give them whatever they
want, a traveler from

Rayy talking with citizens of Merv. Moses mild in
Pharaoh's court. Don't

put the water kettle in boiling oil. Speak quietly and say
nothing that is not true.

It's afternoon. We need to be quiet for a while. Speaking
would be such an orchard

to walk in, if we could do it without letters and sounds!
These stories and images

and conversations through which we show the life
of spirit, Husam and I,

they're like a donkey's head we carry from the skinning pit
to the kitchen. Let further

changes come! I give word shape to this poetry. Husam
supplies the essence. No,

that's wrong. Both come from Husam. *Ziya-Haqq*, the sun
that's one with earth and sky, one

with his intention and heart. Husam, when my spirit
completely recognizes yours, they

recall our being one. When my spirit partially recognizes
yours, that partialness blocks

the truth. Many turn away when that occurs. Read
Sura 98 again, beginning *Lam yakun.*

Be reminded of stubbornness and duality. Before Muhammad
appeared in form,

Recognizing Muhammad

there were scriptural references. People imagined
how he would be and called

on his presence in battle and sickness. They had thoughts
and language about Muhammad.

What good was that? Not everyone recognizes Muhammad.
Many have a conception

of him they can stand to live with. They don't know
that if the shadow of

Muhammad's true form falls across a wall, the wall will
bleed! And it will

no longer have two sides! What a blessing to be one thing.
When others saw Muhammad,

their awe evaporated, as counterfeit coins turn black
in the flame. There are false

coins who claim they want to be tested, all bravado. And
there are touchstones that

do not reveal impostors. There are mirrors that hide your
flaws. Avoid hypocritical

praise, and keep away from flattering mirrors, if
you possibly can.

(They break for afternoon rest and silence.)

A Note on These Translations and the Currency of Rumi in the United States

A culture will suffer from shallow inflations if it's not energetically engaged in translation. Every living region needs to incorporate new ways of being into its field of action. Soul growth needs variety and permeable boundaries of custom, law, religious doctrine, and worldview.

The literatures of Greece and Rome since the Renaissance and of Germany, France, Spain, and Russia since the nineteenth century have had obvious influences on American culture. But it has been mostly in the last forty years that the inner tonalities of South America and eastern Europe, Scandinavia, India, eighteenth-century Japan, and thirteenth- and fourteenth-century Persia, along with many indigenous songs and stories, have enriched the American arts, our thought, and the growing inner core we call soul.

I don't know why Rumi is so popular in the West now, but I feel it has to do with soul. Robert Bly guesses that since the ecstatic material was expunged early on from the Christian canon, Rumi is filling that need.

I can only hope that American culture is beginning to assimilate Rumi's great opening heart, his playfulness, his tremendous grief, and the courage he has to live in pure absence.

With his quintessential American eye, Mark Twain in the late 1860s described the *sema*, the moving meditation spontaneously originated by Rumi. He saw the ceremony in Istanbul:

> We visited the dancing dervishes. There were twenty-one of them. They wore long, light-colored, loose robes that hung to their heels. Each in his turn went up to the priest (they were all within a large circular railing) and bowed profoundly and then went spinning away

deliriously and took his appointed place in the circle and continued to spin. When all had spun themselves to their places, they were about five or six feet apart—and so situated, the entire circle of spinning pagans spun itself three separate times around the room. It took twenty-five minutes to do it. They spun on the left foot, and kept themselves going by passing the right rapidly before it and digging it against the waxed floor. Some of them made incredible "time." Most of them spun around forty times in a minute, and one artist averaged about sixty-one times a minute and kept it up during the whole twenty-five. They made no noise of any kind, and most of them tilted their heads back and closed their eyes, entranced with a sort of devotional ecstasy. There was a rude kind of music part of the time, but the musicians were not visible. None but the spinners were allowed within the circle. A man had to spin or stay outside.

His is a clear and sympathetic vision, if somewhat like that of a skating coach with a stopwatch, of Rumi's emblem of what surrender and discipline look like moving together, until we get to Twain's punch line, "It was as barbarous an exhibition as we have witnessed yet."[1]

Mark Twain has the no-nonsense attitude that an ecstatic poet meets head-on in this country, and yet I feel the two men, Rumi and Twain, would have gotten along. They both have an ecstatic sense of the present and a fine clarity too. I can see them together at the railing.

As I've said in other volumes, these are not scholarly translations, though to produce them I collaborate with scholars who know the original language, Farsi. I do not work from the Persian. Some people would not call these translations, but rather "translations," or versions, or imitations. I hope the work is faithful to the spirit of the original impulse in Rumi and that they bring across some of his power and fragrance.

Some of the *ghazals* are reworkings of Nevit Ergin's translations of the *Divan*. He translates from the Turkish of Golpinarli. Others are from texts given me by John Moyne, who works from the Persian. Others have been done from Arberry's translations, the quatrains from the Arberry listed below and a few from unpublished manuscripts of John Moyne. The Jami poem is also from John Moyne.

For the *Masnavi* sections I have consulted Nicholson and M. G. Gupta's more recent work. Here is a complete list of the texts used:

The Mathnawi of Jalaluddin Rumi. Translated by Reynold Nicholson. 8 vols. London: Luzac, 1925–40.

Maulana Rum's Masnawi. Translated by M. G. Gupta. 6 vols. Agra, India: MG Publishers, 1995.

Mystical Poems of Rumi. Translated by A. J. Arberry. Persian Heritage Series, no. 3. Chicago: University of Chicago Press, 1968.

Mystical Poems of Rumi. Translated by A. J. Arberry. Persian Heritage Series, no. 23. Boulder, CO: Westview Press, 1979.

The Rubaiyat of Jalal al-Din Rumi: Select Translations into English Verse. Translated by A. J. Arberry. London: Emery Walker, 1949.

Discourses of Rumi. Translated by A. J. Arberry. New York: Samuel Weiser, 1961.

Divan-i Kebir: Mevlana Celaleddin Rumi. Translated by Nevit Ergin. 16 vols. Los Angeles: Echo Publications, vols. 1–14, 1992–2001; vols. 15–24, forthcoming. These are available from Maypop Books, 196 Westview Drive, Athens, GA 30606. 800–682–8637. *maypopbooks.com*

Notes

INTRODUCTION

1. Seventeen of Rumi's letters are translated in my *This Longing* (Putney, VT: Threshold, 1988; Boston: Shambhala, 2000), pp. 81–107.

2. You might say that Rumi's poetry moves in a *liminal* place, an area between worlds. *Liminal* derives from the Latin *limen*, which means "doorsill," the wooden crosspiece at the base of a door, the threshold. The word *dervish* also, perhaps, derives from the word for "door" in Sanskrit, *dvara*, though I am told this is more likely a poetic etymology, that *dervish* comes from an Avestan stem meaning "poor." I will stay then with the *metaphor* of poem as doorway, as in Jim Morrison and The.

3. Brooks Haxton, trans., *Fragments: The Collected Wisdom of Heraclitus* (New York: Viking, 2001), p. 45.

4. Elmer O'Brien, trans., *The Essential Plotinus* (Indianapolis: Hackett, 1964), p. 83.

5. From a conversation cited in Miguel Serrano, *C. G. Jung and Hermann Hesse: A Record of Two Friendships,* trans. Frank MacShane (New York: Schocken, 1968), p. 56.

6. *Night & Sleep,* with Robert Bly (Cambridge, MA: Yellow Moon, 1981); *Open Secret* (Putney, VT: Threshold, 1984); *Unseen Rain* (Threshold, 1986); *We Are Three* (Athens, GA: Maypop, 1987); *These Branching Moments* (Providence, RI: Copper Beech, 1988); *This Longing* (Threshold, 1988); *Delicious Laughter* (Maypop, 1990); *Like This* (Maypop, 1990); *Feeling the Shoulder of the Lion* (Threshold, 1991); *One-Handed Basket Weaving* (Maypop, 1991); *Birdsong* (Maypop, 1993); *The Hand of Poetry: Five Mystic Poets of Persia* (New Lebanon, NY: Omega Press, 1993); *The Essential Rumi* (San Francisco: HarperSanFrancisco, 1995); *The Illuminated Rumi* (New York: Broadway, 1997); *The Glance* (New York: Viking, 1999); *The Soul of Rumi* (San Francisco: HarperSanFrancisco, 2001).

CHAPTER 1. THE GREEN SHAWL

Introductory note: the Fariduddin Attar quote is from *The Hand of Poetry: Five Mystic Poets of Persia* (New Lebanon, NY: Omega Press, 1993), "The Newborn," p. 58.

"Entrance Door": Mahmud was a king whose name means "Praise to the end!" For his servant Ayaz, just the presence of the king was more important than any form. In the story, no matter what value the court and the courtiers put on the pearl, Ayaz was willing to crush it when the king asked him to. See "Ayaz and the King's Pearl," in *The Essential Rumi* (San Francisco: HarperSanFrancisco, 1995).

CHAPTER 2. INITIATION

"Work in the Invisible": *Qutb* means "axis," "pole," or "center." The *qutb* is a spiritual being, or function, that can reside in a human or several humans, or in a moment. It is the mystery of how the divine gets delegated into the manifest world and obviously cannot be defined. The *abdals* are helpers of the *qutb*. It is said there are always 128 present on earth.

"Pain": Al-Hallaj Mansour was a Sufi mystic martyred in Baghdad in 922 for saying *Ana'l-Haqq*, "I am the truth" or "I am God." In Sufism a *sheikh* is one who guides soul growth.

CHAPTER 3. BAQA

Introductory note: Hayden Carruth quotation is from *Reluctantly: Autobiographical Essays* (Port Townsend, WA: Copper Canyon Press, 1998), p. 57.

The Opener: Ya Fattah, "The Opener," is one of the names of God.

CHAPTER 4. THIS SPEECH

"Hometown Streets": a *matzoob* is someone so ecstatic with being conscious and *here*, that he or she may appear insane. To others, *matzoobs* are the purest sanity.

"Omar and the Old Poet": Omar is 'Umar ibnul-Khattab, d. 644, father-in-law of Muhammad and second caliph of Islam.

CHAPTER 5. ONE ALTAR

Introductory note: I feel uneasy with "sacred texts" as a category. Certainly since I looked, in college, into the great opening eyes of Thomas Wolfe's praise-prose and Shakespeare's cauldron-glory and e e cummings's sexy love poems, the literary and the sacred have been too tangled to separate. Passages from Ruskin or Agee or Dickinson or Keats or Chaucer or Cormac McCarthy are just as numinous as anything else. I don't want to offend Muslims or Christians or Jews, or the Indian subcontinent or China, but I guess I will: the Bible, the Qur'an, the Torah, the Zen sutras, the Vedas, the *Upanishads*, the *Tao Teh Ching*, indigenous stories and aboriginal dream-time drawings in sand have no *exclusive* claim on scripting beauty and truth, or revelation. John 8, Agee listening to foxes, Yeats casting out remorse, Harrogate killing a shoat, and Samuel hearing his name called, they're all chapter and verse.

If the stance reflected above and in the introductory note seems *off* to you, dogmatic in some new (or old) pan-religious way, please forgive me and don't let it keep you from receiving Rumi's poetry. Church is a blind spot for me. My son Cole and his family, my sister Betsy, my ex-wife Kittsu, and my friend Jim Kilgo are devout Christians. Bawa Muhaiyaddeen supervised the building of a mosque for the prayers behind the Fellowship at 5830 Overbrook Avenue in Philadelphia's City Line district. I contribute to its upkeep. I love the old shaped-note hymns. I sing them in the night. *The growing of the corn . . .* I'll stay open.

Kabir Helminski's book of traditional Mevlevi prayers is *The Mevlevi Wird: The Prayers Recited Daily by Mevlevi Dervishes*, available from the Threshold Society, P.O. Box 1821, Soquel, CA 95073.

"Let the Way Itself Arrive": Saladin Zarkub, the goldsmith in Konya, became Rumi's friend after Shams's death. Rumi's son, Sultan Velad, married Saladin's daughter.

"Four Words for What We Want": *Angur, inab, uzum,* and *istafil* each mean "grapes."

"Spiritual Windowshoppers": there were no window displays in the thirteenth century, of course. Rumi says, "those who go to the market and handle merchandise without buying it." I recently bought the last Waterman fountain pen and the last bottle of Mont Blanc ink. The Office Max manager would not let me try the pen out, that is, fill it with ink, until I'd actually completed the sale.

6. A SMALL DOG TRYING TO GET YOU TO PLAY

"The Core": Husamuddin is Husam Chelebi, Rumi's scribe. He was a student of Shams and is often associated with images of sunlight; "Shams" means "the sun." Quzuh is an Arabian pre-Islamic sky god, the angelic being in charge of clouds and mist and associated through a Persian idiom with the rainbow. I thank Junnaiyd Moore for identifying this obscure being. For Khidr, see note on chap. 27 below.

"Pebble *Zikr*": *zikr*, "remembrance," is the vocal or silent repetition of the phrase *La'illaha il'Allah* ("There is no reality but God; there is only God").

8. THE KING'S FALCON ON A KITCHEN SHELF

"The City of Saba": the Sheba and Solomon stories are about the magnificent dance that body-knowing (Sheba) and divine, luminous wisdom (Solomon) do together. Sheba's chief city, Saba, is an image of how a place can get when it has nothing of Solomon's presence in it. It makes me think of Elvis's Graceland mansion in Memphis: the air of rotten glitz, the unnatural old-gold pallor, the drugged hype of his jumpsuits. The middle-aged Elvis gives a clear image of how creativity looks cut off from soul.

9. WITNESS

"*Inshallah*": *In sha Allah*, "If God wills."

"To the Extent They Can Die": there was a Platonic academy in Iconium (Konya), so there was probably a strong tradition available to Rumi for studying Plato's *Dialogues* and Plotinus's *Enneads* as well as the Muslim philosophers, Ibn Rushd, known as Averroës (1126–98), Ibn Tufayl (d. 1185), Suhrawardi (1154–91), and Ibn Arabi (1165–1240).

11. TURNING THE REFUSE OF DAMASCUS

"*Mashallah*": *Ma sha Allah*, "What God wills," implying something ongoing, not completed. *Inshallah* refers to something that hasn't happened yet. *Alhamdulillah* gives praise for what God has already done.

13. AT THE OUTERMOST EXTENSION OF EMPIRE

Introductory note: Diogenes, the sunbathing philosopher. A few stories have come down about Alexander's conversations with Diogenes. Diogenes is naked in his tub out in the sun. Alexander comes and asks if there is any service he can render Diogenes. "Yes. You're blocking my sun. Please stand to the side." Alexander is so struck with the reply, he says, "If I were not Alexander, I should wish to be Diogenes."

Another time Alexander comes and asks, "Is it true that you live in that tub, or is it one of the pranks philosophers do so that people will admire them?" Diogenes answers with a question, "It is true you want to conquer Persia and so unite the Greeks under your leadership, or do you do all this to get the admiration of people?" Alexander liked the answer and touched the tub saying, "One tub full of wisdom." Diogenes quickly replies, "I would prefer one drop of luck to a tub full of wisdom."

CHAPTER 15. LIVING AS EVIDENCE

"Border Stations": Majnun and Layla are lovers in classical Persian literature. Majnun figures prominently in Rumi's poetry as the lover who loses his reason in the overwhelming experience of his love for Layla.

CHAPTER 16. GARNET RED

"Evening Sky Garnet Red": the *qibla* is the point on a prayer rug that directs the intention.

CHAPTER 17. EXTRAVAGANCE

"Come Horseback": Nevit Ergin tells me there's a note in Golpinarli about the Islamic tradition of Circis (St. George). Circis was a prophet who was martyred seventy times by his people, and resurrected each time.

CHAPTER 19. DAWN

"Drawn by Soup": there is a legend that when the Mongol armies led by Bugra Khan got close to Konya, Rumi went out alone to meet them. The general was so impressed that he spared the city. "There may be more beings like this there. We mustn't harm them."

CHAPTER 20. THE BANQUET

"YHU": *Yhu* is a combination of letters I saw once in a dream. I took it to be a melding of the English second-person singular and plural, *you*, with the Arabic expression of joy, *hu*.

CHAPTER 21. POETRY

"*Glory* to *Mutabilis*": *Glory*, *Mutabilis*, and *Penelope* are varieties of roses. *Mutabilis* is Latin for "changing."

CHAPTER 22. PILGRIM NOTES

"Cry Out Your Grief": *Hu* is the breathing out of the divine presence from the human.

"Two Sacks": this incident reminds me of Nasruddin, a Middle Eastern trickster figure. He was riding a donkey once with a sack over his shoulder. "Why don't you tie the sack across the back of the donkey?" "Oh, I couldn't," Nasruddin replies. "He's carrying me. I couldn't ask him to carry the sack as well."

CHAPTER 24. THE JOKE OF MATERIALISM.

"Book Beauty": Zuleikha is the wife of Potiphar the Egyptian. She is so lost in her love for the handsome Joseph that she sees everything as a message from him. For Rumi she is a type of the lover, like Majnun.

"Under the Hill": Nasruddin: See note above on chap. 22.

CHAPTER 25. FANA

Introductory note: anyone interested in the pack of poetry lines I made for my granddaughter Briny may contact Maypop Books, 196 Westview Drive, Athens, GA 30606. 1-800-682-8637. *maypopbooks.com*

"Blessing the Marriage": Rumi's poem for the marriage of his son, Sultan Velad, to the daughter of his friend, Saladin Zarkub. Her name was Nizam al-din Kattat. The poem is still used in wedding ceremonies.

CHAPTER 26. HUMAN GRIEF

"A Delicate Girl": Junnaiyd (d. 910) and Bestami (d. 874) were early Sufi masters.

CHAPTER 27. INNER SUN

Introductory note: the Hasidic story is told in Gershom Scholem's classic, *Major Trends in Jewish Mysticism* (New York: Schocken, 1946, 1995), pp. 349–50.

"A Deep Nobility": Khidr is the guide of souls. He exists on the edge between the seen and the unseen. The detail here of his being one "who doesn't flinch when it's time to die" connects him again with the story of *Sir Gawain and the Green Knight* (see note in *The Essential Rumi*, pp. 287–88).

CHAPTER 29. WHEN FRIENDS MEET

Introductory note: the Rumi quotations are from other volumes. "How can I be separated and yet in union?" (*The Glance* [New York: Viking, 1999], p. 62). "Fall in love in such a way that it frees you from any connecting" (*The Glance*, p. 2). "When living itself becomes the Friend, lovers disappear" (*The Essential Rumi*, p. 171).

"Like Light over This Plain": Hamza was Rumi's flute player.

"Wake and Walk Out": Hakim Sanai (d. 1131), a court poet of Ghazna, was the first to use the *masnavi* form, rhyming couplets expressing mystical and didactic themes.

CHAPTER 30. THE REEDBED OF SILENCE

Introductory note: the Jung quotation is from C. G. Jung, *Word and Image*, Bollingen Series 97 (Princeton, NJ: Princeton University Press, 1979), p. 189.

CHAPTER 32. EYE OF WATER

Abd al-Qadir Gilani was born in the Gilan region south of the Caspian Sea in 1077. At the age of eighteen he left his native region and went to Baghdad, the center of religious learning in Islam. He studied under two teachers, al-Mukharrimi and Abu'l-Khair Hammad ad-Dabbas, before leaving the city to wander the desert wilderness for twenty-five years. He was over fifty by the time he returned to Baghdad in 1127 and began his public teaching. He died in 1166. His tomb is a place of pilgrimage in Baghdad. Several of his works have been translated by Muhtar Holland: *The Sublime Revelation, Utterances, Revelations of the Unseen, The Removal of Cares, Sufficient Provision for Seekers on the Path of Truth,* and *Fifteen Letters* (Houston and Fort Lauderdale: Al-Baz Publishing). Tosun Bayrak has done Gilani's *The Secret of Secrets* (Cambridge, England: Islamic Text Society, 1992).

CHAPTER 33. MUSIC

"The Camel Driver's Song": the poet Jami (1414–92) was born in Jam, near Herat. Among his works is the collection of poems *The Seven Thrones*, which includes the allegory "Salaman and Absal," which Edward Fitzgerald translated in the nineteenth century, and a version of the story of Joseph and Zuleikha.

CHAPTER 34. GRATITUDE FOR TEACHERS

Introductory note: the quote from Virgil is Aeneas getting a glimpse of the other world in Book VI of the Aeneid, 1.541. Osho Rajneesh's tapes and videos are available from Osho Viha Meditation Center, P.O. Box 352, Mill Valley, CA 94942; oshoavi@aol.com. A collection of Joe Miller's talks, Great Song, edited by Richard Power, is available from Maypop Books, 196 Westview Drive, Athens, GA 30606. 800-682-8637.

"To Trust the Ocean": Rumi often mentions Ibrahim (d. 783), a prince of Balkh. He represents to the Sufis someone who in one visionary moment gives up the external kingdom for the inner majesty. There are striking similarities between his life and Gautama the Buddha's. The story goes that Ibrahim was riding hard after a deer, when the deer turned and addressed him, "You were not created for this chase." Ibrahim heard these words in his soul, cried out, dismounted, and changed his life. As Rumi says of Ibrahim's transformation in Discourse #44, "God lives between a human being and the object of his desire. It is all a mystical journey to the Friend."

"Strange Gathering": the figures in this poem, from both Christian and Muslim romantic and heroic traditions, are having a free-form party. It is important that the poem ends with those two who are so completely and insistently free of form, al-Hallaj Mansour and Shams of Tabriz.

CHAPTER 35. FORGIVENESS

Introductory note: James Kilgo's short piece "Mountain Spirits," in Inheritance of Horses (Athens: University of Georgia Press, 1994), is an American classic.

"Now I lay me down to stay . . ." I play a variation here on a prayer I was taught, and said, as a child:

Now I lay me down to sleep.
Pray the Lord my soul to keep,

(And if I die before I wake,
Pray the Lord my soul to take.)

My mother left that part out in our family, the gruesome possibility.

Bless Mama and Daddy and Herby
And Betsy and Grandma and Aunt Pearl, etc.

It went on indefinitely.

CHAPTER 38. THE MYSTERY OF RENUNCIATION
"Not a Food Sack, a Reed Flute": Ibn Rushd, or Averroës as he is known in the West, was born in Cordova, Spain, in 1126. He is best known for his commentaries on Aristotle and for his combining of medicine and theology into a philosophy of spiritual health. He had a profound influence on Christian thinkers in the Middle Ages, especially Thomas Aquinas.

CHAPTER 39. WARRIOR LIGHT
Introductory note: the quote is from a quatrain in *The Essential Rumi* (p. 278):

This moment this love comes to rest in me,
many beings in one being.

In one wheat grain a thousand sheaf stacks.
Inside the needle's eye a turning night of stars.

The "mystics agree" quotation is from Bawa Muhaiyaddeen, *Questions of Life: Answers of Wisdom*, vol. 2, *Sessions with a Sufi Mystic* (Philadelphia: Fellowship Press, 2000), p. 86.

INTRODUCTION TO BOOK IV
1. In earlier volumes I have followed Nicholson with the Arabic spelling *Mathnawi*. Persian scholars tell me *Masnavi* is how it's said by those who read the original.

2. Of the eleven or so passages that Reynold Nicholson in his 1929 translation put into Latin so that only the priestly, or the prudish, could read them, two appear in Book IV: the sufi who returns home early to find his wife with the shoemaker and the pear tree story.

3. Geoffrey Chaucer, *The Canterbury Tales*, trans. Nevill Coghill (Baltimore: Penguin, 1952), p. 120.

4. *Essential Rumi*, p. 205.

5. *Essential Rumi*, p. 61.

6. From the Latin *fornix*, "arched oven," comes "fornication"; bathhouses haven't changed much since Ephesus.

7. William Blake, *Complete Writings*, ed. Geoffrey Keynes (New York: Oxford University Press, 1959), p. 149.

8. *Open Secret* (Putney, VT: Threshold, 1984), p. 65 (#2693).

9. For more regarding the powerful energetic connection between humans and animals, see Rupert Sheldrake's *Dogs That Know When Their Owners Are Coming Home* (New York: Three Rivers Press, 1999).

BOOK IV

P. 270: The Simurgh bird is a symbol of the divine. It lives on Mt. Qaf.

P. 284: Abu Ibn Sina, or Avicenna (d. 1037), was a Persian physician and philosopher.

P. 283: "The great Names" refers to the *Asma'ul-Husna*, or the Ninety-Nine Beautiful Names of God that were revealed to Muhammad in the Qur'an.

P. 290: Ibrahim: see note above on chap. 34.

P. 290: night-talking: sometimes dervishes stay up and talk, telling dreams and other experiences, doing *zikr* (the chant of remembering God), and asking questions of the teacher.

P. 290: Khidr: see note above on chap. 27.

P. 297: Rumi loves the stories of Sultan Mahmud and his favorite officer, Ayaz, who visits his old work jacket and boots every day as a way of remembering his gratitude for Mahmud's generosity. He also appears in "Entrance Door" in chap. 1 and "Being Slow to Blame" in chap. 37.

P. 316: Majnun and Layla: see note above on chap. 15.

P. 323: Bu'l-Hasan al-Khurqani (d. 1034) was a student of Bestami, even though he lived many years after. His practice was to go to Bestami's grave and sit until he felt his teacher's presence. Then he would say the question he came with, and as soon as it was said, the answer was also apparent.

P. 336: the *Kalilah* is a collection of fables of Indian origin that came over into Arabic in the late eighth century. Most of Rumi's animal stories originate there.

P. 373: the *Shahnama* is the epic poem of classical Persian literature written by Firdausi (941–1020).

P. 375: *Kaf, Ha, Ya, Ayn, Sad.* These five letters stand at the beginning of Sura 19 of the Qur'an. Islamic kabbalists have interpreted them as *Kaf*, the "all-sufficing," *Ha*, the "guide of the faithful," *Ya*, the "hand which bestows grace," *Ayn*, the "omniscient," and *Sad*, "he who keeps his promise."

P. 380: an astrolabe is an ancient astronomical device for locating oneself in time and space with relation to the sun and the stars. On movable brass plates it shows how the sky looks at a specific place and time. One adjusts the components to conform with variables. For Rumi it's a metaphor for longing. Shams means "the sun." Anywhere sunlight comes into the poetry, it's that longing for the Friend.

P. 385: Lote Tree. In Islamic legend Muhammad and Gabriel travel until they reach the absolute limit of created intellect, which is named *sidrat al-muntaha*, "the Lote Tree of the Farthest Boundary." The Lote Tree carries the knowledge of God's growing creation from the beginning of its sequence in time. Whatever is created is part of it and contained in it. It is the "tree of the farthermost boundary," because beyond it, where Muhammad can go and Gabriel cannot, begins a new life.

A NOTE ON THESE TRANSLATIONS
1. Mark Twain, *Innocents Abroad* (New York: Signet, 1966), pp. 269–70.

References

When the reference for an ode (*ghazal*) has two numbers, it refers to Nevit Ergin's volumes, or "meters," as he calls them, the first number being the volume number and the second (with the pound sign) the number of the poem within that volume. If a poem has only one number beside it (with a pound sign), it refers to the numbering for odes and quatrains in Furuzanfar's edition of *Kulliyat-e Shams*, 8 vols. (Teheran: Amir Kabir Press, 1957–66). The *Masnavi* references (a Roman numeral, I–VI, followed by the line numbers) are to Reynold Nicholson's edition (London: Luzac, 1925–40). The shorter poems, quatrains, are reworked from A. J. Arberry's translation, *The Rubaiyat of Jalal al-din Rumi* (London: Emery Walker, 1949). Page numbers for those are not given.

1. A GREEN SHAWL
"Entrance Door," 8a, #92; "What Was Told, *That,* III, 4129–36; "Mary's Hiding," III, 3700–3720; "The Husk and Core of Masculinity," V, 4025–34.

2. INITIATION
"Work in the Invisible," III, 3077–3109; "A Necessary Autumn Inside Each," I, 1878–1912; "Pain," II, 2817–43; "A Surprise of Roses," III, 4345–74; "More Range," 8a, #43; "Choose a Suffering," 8a, #98; "Climb to the Execution Place," 7a, #116; "Watch a One-Year-Old," 8b, #174.

3. BAQA
"Walkingstick Dragon," 8a, #109; "*The Opener,*" 8a, #99; "Soul Light and Sun the Same," 3, #31; "The Pattern Improves," 7a, #94; "Begin," 8a, #158; "Back to Being," #853; "Three Travelers Tell Their Dreams," VI, 2395–2456, 2484–2500.

4. THIS SPEECH

"Looking into the Creek," III, 1824–34; "Forth," 8a, #50; "Hometown Streets," 3, #59; "A Trace," #100; "Creator of Absence and Presence," from Discourse #53; "A Ship Gliding over Nothing," #2756; "Omar and the Old Poet," I, 2072–2101, 2104–9, 2163–2222.

5. ONE ALTAR

"One Song," III, 2122–27; "The Indian Tree," II, 3641–80; "Your Face," 8a, #72; "Let the Way Itself Arrive," 8a, #16; "A Cross-Eyed Student," I, 324–36; "Dear Soul," VI, 969–71; "Four Words for What We Want," II, 3681–92; "Four Interrupted Prayers," II, 3027–45; "Spiritual Window-shoppers," VI, 831–45; "The clear bead at the center . . .," #511.

6. A SMALL DOG TRYING TO GET YOU TO PLAY

"Pictures of the Soul," 3, #149; "Soul and the Old Woman," VI, 148–50, 160, 142–47; "The Core" VI, 84–128; "Duck Wisdom," III, 398–401, 411, 417–38; "Pebble *Zikr*," I, 2154–60; "Feet Becoming Head," 8a, #29.

7. THIRST

"What We Hear in a Friend's Voice," II, 3573–3601; "Talking and God's Love of Variety," VI, 10–16, 29–43, 61–66; "Amazed Mouth," 7b, #147; "No longer a stranger, you listen . . .," #1618.

8. THE KING'S FALCON ON A KITCHEN SHELF

"The City of Saba," III, 2656–67, 2675–80, 2726–32; "The Thief," VI, 357–65; "The King's Falcon," II, 323–41, 1131–46, 1156–77; "The Ground's Generosity," II, 1797–1808; "Sick of Scripture," 3, #97; "Medicine," III, 2669–2709.

9. WITNESS

"The Creek and the Stars," VI, 3166–83, 2816–25, 2833–59, 2867–70; "Night Thieves," VI, 2816–25, 2833–59, 2867–70; "*Inshallah*," VI, 3685–98; "*Thinking* and the Heart's Mystical Way," V, 557–73; "Paradox," VI, 3567–81; "Empty Boat," #622; "Whereabouts Unknown," 8a, #155; "The Level of Words," II, 1716–19; "To the Extent They Can Die," 8a, #87.

10. SOUL JOY

"Moving Water," VI, 3487–3510; "Uncle of the Jar," 8a, #124; "When Words Are Tinged with Lying," II, 2733–38; "The Source of Joy," #423; "A Story They Know," #1649; "Roses Underfoot," 8b, #136; "I open and fill with love and . . . ," #606; "Any cup I hold fills with wine . . . ," #618.

11. TURNING THE REFUSE OF DAMASCUS

"Mashallah," 8a, #58; "Cleansing Conflict," I, 4000–4026; "Shadow and Light Source Both," #2155, partial; "Wealth Without Working," III, 1450–64, 1479–1509; "Love for Certain Work," III, 1616–19; "The Hoopoe's Talent," I, 1202–33; "When school and mosque and minaret . . . ," #611; "Not until a person dissolves, can . . . ," #604; "While you are still yourself . . . ," #605.

12. GRIEF SONG, PRAISE SONG

"On the Day I Die," #911; "Time to Sacrifice Taurus," #1092; "The Sheikh Who Lost Two Sons," III, 1799–1823; "What's Inside the Ground," 8b, #135; "A Brightening Floor," 8a, #32; "The Death of Saladin," 8b, #180.

13. AT THE OUTERMOST EXTENSION OF EMPIRE

"Qualities," #1590; "Wooden Cages," #1615; "Prayer Is an Egg," III, 2149–75.

14. MUTAKALLIM

"Evidence," 8a, #89; "Two Donkeys," 3, #55; "The Indian Parrot," I, 1814–33, 1845–48.

15. LIVING AS EVIDENCE

"I Pass by the Door," 8a, #163; "Border Stations," 8a, #104; "Wind That Mixes in Your Fire," 8a, #117; "The Different Moon Shapes," #359; "Husam," V, 4204–38.

16. GARNET RED

"Evening Sky Garnet Red," 8b, #211; "The Sweet Blade of Your Anger," 8a, #76; "Fourteen Questions," 8a, #54; "Asylum," 8b, #209; "The Silent Articulation of a Face," no ref.; "A Small Green Island," V, 2855–65; "Both Wings Broken," 8a, #56.

17. EXTRAVAGANCE

"There You Are," 8a, #216; "Come Horseback," 8a, #57; "Wilder Than We Ever," 8a, #82.

18. NIGHT

"What Hurts the Soul?," I, 3689–92; "Some Kiss We Want," #1888.

19. DAWN

"The Generations I Praise," 8a, #55; "Hunt Music," 8a, #62; "Knowledge Beyond Love," 8b, #224; "Soul, Heart, and Body One Morning," 3, #58; "Drawn by Soup," 8b, #214; "She Is the Creator," II, 2432–37.

20. THE BANQUET

"This Is Enough," 5, #54; "The Music We Are," #782; "Joseph," #707; "YHU," 8a, #707; "The Moment," I, 1142–48.

21. POETRY

"Cup," 8b, #215; "Glory to Mutabilis," 8b, #146; "All We Sell," VI, 1983, 1990–2006, 1522–28; "Poetry and Cooking Tripe," from Discourse #16; "Is This a Place Where Stories Are Acted Out?," no ref.; "A Song of Being Empty," no ref.; "A Salve Made with Dirt," #1586; "What I Say Makes Me Drunk," 8a, #83.

22. PILGRIM NOTES

"Not Here," 8b, #175; "Cry Out Your Grief," 8b, #168; "Broom Work," 8b, #188; "A Clean Sandy Spot," 8b, #192; "Two Sacks," II, 3176–3207; "Any Chance Meeting," #19; "The One Thing You Must Do," from Discourse #4.

23. APPLE ORCHARDS IN MIST

"You Are Not Your Eyes," no ref.; "Prayer to Be Changed," V, 780–803, 806, 823–33; "A Small Market Between Towns," VI, 4276, 4281–82, 4298–4300; "Lovers in Law School," III, 3842–59; "Cup and Ocean," I, 1109–16.

24. THE JOKE OF MATERIALISM

"Mounted Man," 3, #86; "This Disaster," 8b, #25; "Sneezing Out Animals," no ref.; "Not Intrigued with Evening," no ref.; "How Attraction

Happens," II, 2036–58; "Book Beauty," VI, 1268–92; "Under the Hill," II, 3088–3110, 3116–29.

25. FANA

"In the Waves and Underneath," V, 2887–2911; "Infidel Fish," 8b, #151; "A Star with No Name," III, 1284–88; "Rush Naked," III, 3884–89, 3901–9, 3912–14; "Die Before You Die," VI, 4044–53; "Refuge," #122; "Love with No Object," III, 2248–80; "The Road Home," VI, 806–18; "Come Out and Give Something," V, 2694–2743; "Two Human-Sized Wedding Candles," 8a, #90; "Blessing the Marriage," #2667; "One Swaying Being," 8a, #31.

26. HUMAN GRIEF

"I've broken through to longing . . . ," #603; "The center leads to love . . . ," #1990; "This Battered Saucepan," 7a. #120; "A Delicate Girl," 8b, #123; "The Threat of Death," III, 1133–47; "Twenty Small Graves," III, 3399–3416; "Sour, Doughy, Numb, and Raw," 8a, #25; "I could not have known . . . ," #602.

27. INNER SUN

"The Breast My Heart Nurses," 8b, #221; "No More *the Presence*," 8a, #115; "Out in the Open Air," II, 1077–1128; "The Eye of the Heart," VI, 3511–12, 3516–17; "A Deep Nobility," III, 704–20.

28. SACRIFICE

"Remember Egypt," 3, #141; "Astrological Bickerings," 8a, #133; "Extract the Thorn," I, 1951–71.

29. WHEN FRIENDS MEET

"The Most Alive Moment," 8b, #162; "The Soul's Friend," III, 212–35; "Inside Shams's Universe," 8a, #22; "Like Light over This Plain," 2, #79; "Wake and Walk Out," 4, #16; "Form *Is* Ecstatic," 8a, #27.

30. THE REEDBED OF SILENCE

"Back into the Reedbed!," 8a, #105; "A Vague Trace," 8b, #156; "The Taste," V, 2279–88.

31. THE USES OF COMMUNITY

"Love Dervishes," 8a, #39; "The Communal Heart," V, 4206–28; "Bowls of Food," 8b, #164; "Blade," 8a, #109.

32. EYE OF WATER

"Cooked Heads," 8b, #126; "Float, Trust, Enjoy," VI, 1450–66; "Light Breeze," III, 1610–15; "Sitting Together," #2114; "Seeing with the Eye of Water We Float On," III, 1251–74; "Solomon's Sight," I, 1030–40.

33. MUSIC

"We No Longer See the One Who Teaches Us," 8a, #61; "Music Loosens Deafness," 8a, #86; "Jami's The Camel Driver's Song," no ref.

34. GRATITUDE FOR TEACHERS

"The Three Stooges," V, 1314–29; "Listen to the Dogs," III, 286–330; "The Bow to Adam," II, 3325–35; "To Trust the Ocean," II, 3303–25, 3333–35; "Strange Gathering," 8b, #227; "Auction," 8a, #51; "Scatterbrain Sweetness," #259; "Every Section of Road," III, 535–60; "A Cap to Wear in Both Worlds," #1620.

35. FORGIVENESS

"The Spring," V, 3257–85; "The Way That Moves as You Move," V, 1105–51, 1162, 1226–41; "We Prescribe a Friend," 6, #9; "What You've Been Given," III, 3635–57; "Grace Got Confused," 8b, #190.

36. SOUL ART

"One Human Gesture," VI, 2180–89; "The Mangy Calf," #1447; "Beggars," I, 2744–72; "If You Want to Live Your Soul," 8b, #225.

37. MORE PILGRIM NOTES

"Habits That Blind the Psyche," V, 3482–92; "Dolls That Pull the Stuffing Out of Each Other," V, 1197–1225; "Being Slow to Blame," V, 2134–49; "Cuisine and Sex," 8a, #83; "The soul fell into the soup . . . ," #610; "Be clear and smiling for those who . . . ," #601; "No Discussion," 14, #51; "One Who Can Quit Seeing Himself," 14, #44.

38. THE MYSTERY OF RENUNCIATION

"A Way of Leaving the World," V, 700–718; "One-Handed Basket Weaving," III, 1634–42, 1672–90, 1704–20; "Not a Food Sack, a Reed Flute," no ref.; "The Flower's Eye," 3, #117; "Sheikh Sarrazi Comes in from the Wilderness," V, 2667–69, 2677–99, 2706–8, 2715–17; "I Throw It All Away," 8b, #181.

39. WARRIOR LIGHT

"Warrior Light," VI, 3029–41, 3044, 3053–54; "Inside Solitude," III, 4258–66; "The Bear's True Dance," III, 69–84, 94.

40. CHOOSING AND TOTAL SUBMISSION

"Choosing and Total Submission," V, 3077–84, 3093–3100; "These Decisions," VI, 403–20; "Fringe," VI, 570–81.

Index of Titles and First Lines

Contents of Book IV

Acknowledgments

Robert Bly set in motion the translation work responsible for making the great Persian and Indian poets available in English. We are grateful to him, his sweet joy and his ire.

Nevit Ergin with superb dedication has opened up the *absence* of Rumi's *Divan*. His strong heart-donkey has pulled *all* of that brilliant text out of Golpinarli's Turkish into English for the first time.

John Moyne, generous companion of twenty-five years, continues his clear attention to Rumi's poetry.

Bawa Muhaiyaddeen lived in the station of Rumi and Shams. He told me to do the Rumi work. He showed me a glimpse of where the poems come from, and I am grateful to him beyond saying.

Osho, in his wildly original enlightenment, has some part here in the dance of Solomon and Sheba.

Jane Windsor

COLEMAN BARKS is a renowned poet who was prominently
featured in both of Bill Moyers's PBS television series on
poetry, "The Language of Life" and "Fooling with Words." He
taught English and poetry at the University of Georgia for
many years, and he now focuses on writing, readings, and per-
formances. He lives in Athens, GA.